WILLS AND TRUSTS

Books LLC®, Reference Series, Memphis, USA, 2011. ISBN: 9781157644163. www.booksllc.net. Copyright: http://creativecommons.org/licenses/by-sa/3.0/deed.en

Table of Contents

1GOAL Education for All	2
Abatement of debts and legacies	2
Accumulation and Maintenance trust	3
Acts of independent significance	3
Ademption	3
Administration of an estate on death	4
Administrator of an estate	5
Affiliation (family law)	5
Ancillary administration	6
Anti-alienation clause	6
Apertura tabularum	6
Asset-protection trust	7
Attestation clause	10
Australian trust law	11
Barclays Bank Ltd v Quistclose Investments Ltd	11
Bare trust	13
Beach bum trust provision	13
Beneficial interest	13
Beneficiary (trust)	13
Bequest	14
Blind trust	15
Calendars of the Grants of Probate and Letters of Administration	15
Charitable organization	16
Charitable remainder unitrust	19
Charitable trust	21
Codicil (will)	22
Constructive trust	23
Contingent beneficiary	24
Corporate trust	24
Credible witness	25
Crummey trust	25
Cy-près doctrine	26
Delaware statutory trust	27
Disclaimer of interest	28
Discounted gift trust	29
Discretionary trust	29
Dishonest assistance	30
Doctrine of exoneration of liens	34
Elective share	34
English trusts law	35
Estate Planner	37
Estate planning	38
Exempt property	38
Express trust	38
Fiduciary trust	40
Forced heirship	40
Foreign trust	41
Freedom of testation	42
Future interest	42
George Tasker	45
Grantor Retained Annuity Trust	45
Hague Trust Convention	46
Henson trust	48
Holographic will	48
Honorary trust	49
Howe v Earl of Dartmouth	49
Illustrations of the rule against perpetuities	50
Incentive trust	52
Incorporation by reference	52
Inheritance	53
Inquest	55
Insane delusion	56
Inter vivos	56
Interest in possession trust	57
Intestacy	57
Italian trust law	59
Joint wills and mutual wills	59
Knowing receipt	61
Labour Leader's Office Fund	61
Lapse and anti-lapse	61
Last will and testament of Adolf Hitler	62
Last will and testament of Frederica Evelyn Stilwell Cook	63
Laughing heir	63
Legal history of wills	64
Legatee	70
Letter of wishes	70
Letters of Administration	70
Massachusetts business trust	71
Merger doctrine (trust law)	72
National Collegiate Trust	72
No-contest clause	72
Offshore trust	73
Oldland Mill, Keymer	74
Oral will	75
Percy Sladen Memorial Trust	75
Personal injury trust	75
Pet trust	77
Pour-over will	77
Power of appointment	77
Pretermitted heir	78
Private annuity trust	78
Private trustee	80
Probate	80
Probate court	82
Probate research	83
Probate sale	83
Protective trust	83
Protector (trust)	84
Prudent man rule	84
Purpose trust	85
Rabbi trust	87
Real estate investment trust	87
Residuary estate	90
Resulting trust	90
Royal lives clause	92
Rule against perpetuities	92
Rule in Dearle v Hall	95
Satisfaction of legacies	96
Secret trust	96
Settlement (trust)	97
Settlor	97
Simultaneous death	97
Slayer rule	98
Society of Trust and Estate Practitioners	98
Special needs trust	99
Specific devise	99
Specific legacy	99
Spendthrift trust	99
Statute of Wills	101
Succession (conflict)	101
Supplemental Needs Trust	103
Swynfen will case	105
Taxation of trusts (United Kingdom)	106
Testamentary capacity	106
Testamentary disposition	107
Testamentary trust	107
Testator	108
Trust instrument	109
Trust law	109
Trust law in Civil law jurisdictions	116
Trustee de son tort	116

Trusts & Estates (journal) 117	Uniform Simultaneous Death Act ... 120	Will Aid 135
Trusts and estates 117	Unit Valuation System 120	Will contest 136
Trusts of Land and Appointment of Trustees Act 1996 118	United States trust law 122	Will contract 137
	Vesting 130	Wills Act 1837 137
Undue influence 119	Voting trust 131	
Uniform Probate Code 119	Will (law) 132	

Introduction

Purchase of this book entitles you to a free trial membership in the publisher's book club at www.booksllc.net. (Time limited offer.) Simply enter the barcode number from the back cover onto the membership form. The book club entitles you to select from hundreds of thousands of books at no additional charge. You can also download a digital copy of this and related books to read on the go. Simply enter the title or subject onto the search form to find them.

Each chapter in this book ends with a URL to a hyperlinked online version. Type the URL exactly as it appears. If you change the URL's capitalization it won't work. Use the online version to access related pages, websites, footnotes, tables, color photos, updates. Click the version history tab to see the chapter's contributors. Click the edit link to suggest changes.

A large and diverse editor base collaboratively wrote the book, not a single author. After a long process of discussion and debate, the chapters gradually took on a neutral point of view reached through consensus. Additional editors expanded and contributed to chapters striving to achieve balance and comprehensive coverage. This reduced the regional or cultural bias found in many other books and provided access and breadth on subject matter otherwise little documented.

1GOAL Education for All

1GOAL Education for All campaign is run by the Global Campaign for Education. Working with football and the footballing community, 1GOAL raises public awareness and involvement in achieving education for all the 67 million children out of school worldwide. It is supported by over 200 international footballers; over 70 football clubs including Manchester United, Corinthians, LA Galaxy, Chelsea FC, FC Barcelona, Inter Milan, AC Milan, Liverpool FC, FC Porto, Sporting Lisbon and Arsenal; and national and international footballing organisations including the Confederation of African Football, FIFPro, the Professional Footballers' Association and FIFA.

It was launched by Queen Rania of Jordan in August 2009. Alongside Queen Rania, it is co-chaired by FIFA President Sepp Blatter and Nobel prize laureate Archbishop Desmond Tutu.

It campaigns to secure schooling for some 67 million children worldwide in accordance with the Millennium Goal Promise of education for all by 2015. There are several barriers to achieving universal primary education: lack of funds to pay for infrastructure and on-going costs (buildings, teachers' salaries, learning materials); lack of qualified teachers; conflict and the practice of charging school fees in some developing countries.

As of July 2010, "Twelve million people have signed up to support 1Goal - that makes this the biggest campaign for education in history. Football is helping make something very special happen," says ambassador Anthony Baffoe of Ghana.

By September 2010, 18 million people had joined 1GOAL. During the UN Millennium Development Goals Review Summit, held in New York, 20-22 September 2010, Queen Rania delivered this petition directly to UN Secretary General, Ban Ki-moon. At a 1GOAL event during the same summit, the World Bank announced an increase of $750 million to education and the Australian Government announced an increase of c. AUS $5 billion, of which 70% is ringfenced for primary education.

Many world leaders, footballers and celebrities have supported the initiative including Shakira, Cristiano Ronaldo, Pele, Mick Jagger, Jessica Alba, Matt Damon, Patrick Vieira, Michael Essien, Samuel Eto'o, Aaron Mokoena, Quinton Fortune, Rio Ferdinand, Michael Ballack, Sir Bobby Charlton and Marcel Desailly.

Source (edited): "http://en.wikipedia.org/wiki/1GOAL_Education_for_All"

Abatement of debts and legacies

Abatement of debts and legacies is a common law doctrine of wills that holds that when the equitable assets of a deceased person are not sufficient to satisfy fully all the creditors, their debts must abate proportionately, and they must accept a dividend.

In the case of legacies when the funds or assets out of which they are payable are not sufficient to pay them in full, the legacies abate in proportion, unless there is a priority given specially to any particular legacy. Annuities are also subject to the same rule as general legacies.

The order of abatement is usually:
- Intestate property (property not disposed of in the will itself) will abate first
- The residuary estate will abate next
- General devises (gifts of cash) will abate next
- Demonstrative devises (gifts of stock, or orders to sell property and give the proceeds to the beneficiary) will abate next
- Specific devises (gifts of tangible property) will abate last

Definitions

A **specific devise**, is a specific gift in a will to a specific person other than an amount of money. For example, if James's will states that he is leaving his $500,000 yacht to his brother Mike, the yacht would be a specific devise.

A **general devise**, is a monetary gift to a specific person to be satisfied out of the overall estate. For example, if James's will states that he is leaving $500,000 to his son Sam then the money would be a general devise.

A **residual devise** is one left to a devisee after all specific and general devices have been made. For example James's will might say: "I give all the rest, residue and remainder of my estate to my daughter Lilly." Lilly would be the residual devisee.

Source (edited): "http://en.wikipedia.org/wiki/Abatement_of_debts_and_legacies"

Accumulation and Maintenance trust

Accumulation & Maintenance ("A&M") trusts are a type of discretionary trust for the benefit of children and young people in England and Wales.

Development and tax treatment

- The concept of an A&M trust emerged in England and Wales after the enactment of the Capital Taxes Act 1974 (CTA). The CTA discouraged the use of discretionary trusts by introducing new tax rules, but it made a specific exception for trusts designed to help young people (under the age of 25).
- This particular type of trust grew in significance over the years and became known as an Accumulation & Maintenance Trust. They came to fall under the purview of s.71 Inheritance Tax Act 1984 (IHTA), which continued their special tax treatment
- The Finance Act 2006 took A&M Trusts out of the purview of s.71.

Today, A&M Trusts are governed by Pt. III, Ch. III IHTA, and therefore receive exactly the same tax treatment as other types of discretionary trusts.
- As a result, the use of A&M trusts is declining rapidly.
- The new breed of "18-25" trusts are taking their place.

Source (edited): "http://en.wikipedia.org/wiki/Accumulation_and_Maintenance_trust"

Acts of independent significance

The doctrine of **acts of independent significance** at common law permits a testator to effectively change the disposition of his property without changing a will, if acts or events changing the disposition have some significance beyond avoiding the requirements of the will.

The doctrine is frequently applied under the following two circumstances:
- The testator devises assets to a class of beneficiaries where the testator controls membership. For example, Joey leaves the contents of his bank account "to my employees." If Joey then fires some of old employees and hires new ones, the new employees will inherit the contents of the bank account under this provision.
- The testator devises a general type of property, and then changes the specific items of property within that category. For example, Joey writes in his will, "I leave my car to Rachel". Joey drives a 1974 AMC Gremlin at the time of the testamentary instrument, but later sells the Gremlin and purchases a 2009 Rolls-Royce Phantom Drophead Coupé with suicide doors and teak paneling. Because Joey bought a new car to get a more comfortable ride, rather than to change a will without going through the testamentary formalities, the gift to Rachel remains enforceable.

Source (edited): "http://en.wikipedia.org/wiki/Acts_of_independent_significance"

Ademption

Ademption is a term used in the law of wills to determine what happens when property bequeathed under a will is no longer in the testator's estate at the time of the testator's death. For a devise (bequest) of a specific item of property (a specific gift), such property is considered *adeemed*, and the gift fails. For example, if a will bequeathed the testator's car to a specific beneficiary, but the testator owned no car at the time of his or her death, the gift would be *adeemed* and the aforementioned beneficiary would receive no gift at all.

General bequests or **general gifts** - gifts of cash amounts - are never adeemed. If the cash in the testator's estate is not sufficient to satisfy the gift, then other assets in the residuary estate will need to be sold to raise the necessary cash.

Some property lies in a "gray" area, in which the testator's specific intent must be determined. For example, where the testator bequeathes "500 shares of stock" in a company, this may be read as a general bequest (that the estate should purchase and convey the particular stocks to the beneficiary), or it may be read as a specific bequest, particularly if the testator used a possessive ("*my* 500 shares"). Such a gift is deemed to be a demonstrative gift. Such demonstrative gifts are deemed to be a hybrid of both specific and general gifts. If one were to bequeath "500 shares of stock," most states would deem that to be a demonstrative gift. The resultant gift to the heir receiving "500 shares," would be the date of death value of 500 shares of that particular stock.

Ademption may be waived if the property leaves the estate after the testator has been declared incompetent. Furthermore, in some cases the beneficiary will be entitled to the proceeds from the sale of property, or to the insurance payout for property that is lost or destroyed.

To avoid confusion as to what may or may not be adeemed, sometimes the phrase "if owned by me at my death" is placed into the articles of a will in which property is being bequeathed.

As for the sale of land under an executory contract, traditional case law agrees that ademption occurs upon the death of the testator and that the proceeds of sale, when the closing, occurs should not pass to the specific devisee of the property. However, the more modern view and the Uniform Probate Code, which has been adopted by some states, disagrees. These jurisdictions find that when property subject to specific devise is placed under contract of sale before the decedent's death, the proceeds of the sale will pass to the specific devisee.

Statutory variations

Many jurisdictions have ameliorated the effects of the common law doctrine by statute.

In Wisconsin, state law (854.08) attempts to abolish the common law doctrine of ademption by extinction, by, for example, awarding beneficiaries the balance of the purchase price of the item sold (subject to some limitations).

In Virginia, ademption occurs with respect to most forms of property, but if the property at issue is stock certificates, then the fact that the issuer of the stock has been bought out by another company, and that the stocks have been swapped for a new issue by that company, will not adeem the gift of stock. Similarly, if the shares of stock that existed at the time the gift was made have split (for example, where the holder of 500 shares receives a reissue of 1,000 shares each having half the value of the original), then the beneficiary of that gift will be entitled to the number of shares that exist *after* the split.

Source (edited): "http://en.wikipedia.org/wiki/Ademption"

Administration of an estate on death

In English law, **Administration of an estate on death** arises if the deceased is legally intestate. In United States law, the term **Estate Administration** is used.

Where a person dies leaving a will appointing an executor, and that executor validly disposes of the property of the deceased within England and Wales, then the estate will go to probate. However, if no will is left, or the will is invalid or incomplete in some way, then administrators must be appointed. They perform a similar role to the executor of a will but, where there are no instructions in a will, the administrators must distribute the estate of the deceased according to the rules laid down by statute and the common trust.

Certain property falls outside the estate for administration purposes, the most common example probably being houses jointly owned that pass by survivorship on the first death of a couple into the sole name of the survivor. Other examples include discretionary death benefits from pension funds, accounts with certain financial institutions subject to a nomination and the proceeds of life insurance policies which have been written into trust. Trust property will also so frequently fall outside of the estate but this will depend on the terms of the trust.

Since the Land Transfer Act 1897, the administrator (sometimes known as the administratrix, if female) acts as the personal representative of the deceased in relation to land and other property. Consequently, when the estate under administration consists wholly or mainly of land, the court will grant administration to the heir to the exclusion of the next of kin. In the absence of any heir or next of kin, the Crown has the right to property (other than land) as *bona vacantia*, and to the land by virtue of the historic land rights of the Crown (and the Duchy of Cornwall and Duchy of Lancashire in their respective areas). If a creditor claims and obtains a Grant of Administration, the court compels him or her to enter into a bond with two sureties that he or she will not prefer his or her own debt to those of other creditors.

Letter of Administration

Letter of administration: Upon the death of a person intestate, but leaving a will without appointing executors, or when the executors appointed by the will cannot or will not act, the Probate

Division of the High Court of Justice or the local District Probate Registry will appoint an administrator who performs similar duties to an executor. The court does this by granting letters of administration to the person so entitled. Grants of administration may be either general or limited. A general grant occurs where the deceased has died intestate. The order in which the court will make general grants of letters follows the sequence:
- The surviving spouse, or civil partner, as the case may be;
- The next of kin;
- The Crown;
- A creditor;
- A stranger.

Where, under the rules for distribution of estates without a will (the Intestacy Rules), a child under 18 would inherit or a life interest would arise, then the Court or District Probate Registry would normally appoint a minimum of two administrators. On some estates, even under an intestate, it is not clear who are the next-of-kin, and probate research may be required to find the entitled beneficiaries.

Letters of administration

The more important cases of grants of special letters of administration include the following:

Administration cum testamento annexo, where the deceased has left a will but has appointed no executor to it, or the executor appointed has died or refuses to act. In this case the court will make the grant to the person, usually the residuary legatee, with the largest beneficial interest in the estate.

Administration de bonis non administratis occurs in two cases:
- Where the executor dies intestate after probate without having completely administered the estate
- Where an administrator dies.

In the first case the principle of *administration cum testamento* is followed, in the second that of general grants in the selection of the person to whom letters are granted.

- *Administration durante minore aetate,* when the executor or the person entitled to the general grant is under age.
- *Administration durante absentia,* when the executor or administrator is out of the jurisdiction for more than a year.
- *Administration pendente lite,* where there is a dispute as to the person entitled to probate or a general grant of letters the court appoints an administrator till the question has been decided.

Source (edited): "http://en.wikipedia.org/wiki/Administration_of_an_estate_on_death"

Administrator of an estate

The **Administrator of an estate** is a legal term referring to a person appointed by a court to administer the estate of a deceased person who left no will. Where a person dies intestate, i.e., without a will, the court may appoint a person to settle their debts, pay any necessary taxes and funeral expenses, and distribute the remainder according to the procedure set down at law. Such a person is known as the *administrator of the estate* and will enjoy similar powers to those of an executor under a will. A female administrator may be referred to as an *administratrix*, although this sex-specific term is widely considered archaic, obsolete under modern presumptions about equality between sexes, and/or potentially insulting.

Source (edited): "http://en.wikipedia.org/wiki/Administrator_of_an_estate"

Affiliation (family law)

In law, **affiliation** (from Latin *ad-filiare*, to adopt as a son) is the term to describe a partnership between two or more parties.

Affiliation procedures in England

In England a number of statutes on the subject have been passed, the chief being the Bastardy Act of the Parliament of 1845, and the Bastardy Laws Amendment Acts of 1872 and 1873. The mother of a bastard may summon the putative father to petty sessions within 12 months of the birth (or at any later time if he is proved to have contributed to the child's support within 12 months after the birth), and the justices, as after hearing evidence on both sides, may, if the mother's evidence be corroborated in some material particular, adjudge the man to be the putative father] of the child, and order him to pay a sum not exceeding five shillings a week for its maintenance, together with a sum for expenses incidental to the birth, or the funeral expenses, if it has died before the date of order, and the costs of the proceedings.

ceases to be valid after the child reaches the age of 13, but the justices (also referred to as Gold writers under these circumstances) may in the order direct the payments to be continued until the child is 16 years of age.

An appeal to quarter sessions is open to the defendant, and a further appeal on questions of law to the King's Bench by rule *nisi or certiorari*. Should the child afterwards become chargeable to the parish, the sum due by the father may be received by the parish officer.

When a bastard child, whose mother has not obtained an order, becomes chargeable to the parish, the guardians may proceed against the putative father for a contribution.

Any woman who is single, a widow, or a married woman living apart from her husband, may make an application for a summons, and it is immaterial where the child is begotten, provided it is born in England.

An application for a summons may be made before the birth of the child, but in this case the statement of the mother must be in the form of a sworn deposition. The defendant must be over 14 years of age. No agreement on the part of the woman to take a sum down in discharge of the liability of the father is a bar to the making of an affiliation order. In the case of twins it is usual to make separate applications and obtain separate summonses.

The Summary Jurisdiction Act (1879) makes due provision for the enforcement of an order of affiliation. In the case of soldiers an affiliation order cannot be enforced in the usual way, but by the Army Act (1881), if an order has been made against a soldier of the regular forces, and a copy of such order be sent to the secretary of state, he may order a portion of the soldier's pay to be retained. There is no such special legislation with regard to sailors in the Royal Navy.

Affiliation procedures in other countries

In the British colonies, and in the states of the United States (with the (usually termed filiation) akin to that described above, by means of which a mother can obtain a contribution to the support of her illegitimate child from the putative father.

The amount ordered to be paid may subsequently be increased or diminished (1905; 94 N.Y. Supplt. 372). On the continent of Europe, however, the legislation of the various countries differs rather widely. France, Belgium, the Netherlands, Italy, Russia, Serbia and the canton of Geneva provide no means of inquiry into the paternity of an illegitimate child, and consequently all support of the child falls upon the mother; on the other hand, Germany, Austria, Norway, Sweden, Denmark and the majority of the Swiss cantons provide for an inquiry into the paternity of illegitimate children, and the law casts a certain amount of responsibility upon the father.

Affiliation, in France, is a term applied to a species of adoption by which the person adopted succeeds equally with other heirs to the acquired, but not to the inherited, property of the deceased.

In India, affiliation cases are decided by section 125 of Criminal Procedure Code (Cr.P.C.). According to this section - among other things - if a person having sufficient means neglects or refuses to maintain his illegitimate child, a magistrate of the first class may, upon proof of such neglect or refusal, order such person to make a monthly allowance for the maintenance of such child.

Source (edited): "http://en.wikipedia.org/wiki/Affiliation_(family_law)"

Ancillary administration

Ancillary administration is "the administration of a decedent's estate in a state other than the one in which she lived, for the purpose of disposing of property she owned there." Another definition is the "administration of an estate's asset's in another state." This is often a necessary procedure in probate, because the decedent may own property in a state other than his domicile, which is subject to the law of the state in which it sits.

An **ancillary administrator** is the personal representative who handles the property in the other state under ancillary administration. Most major court systems will have forms and checklists for ancillary administrators to use.

Source (edited): "http://en.wikipedia.org/wiki/Ancillary_administration"

Anti-alienation clause

An **Anti-alienation clause** is a provision in the governing document for an arrangement such as a trust that specifies that the beneficial or equitable owner of the property held in that arrangement cannot transfer his or her interest to a third party. This rule is an exception to the general rule in property law that favors free alienability.

The exception is recognized to benefit minors, incompetents, and trust beneficiaries that may otherwise behave as a spendthrift would.

A spendthrift trust is an example of an arrangement containing an anti-alienation provision. The governing document of such a trust provides that the trust corpus may not be reached by creditors while the property is held in the trust. Creditors aware of this legal restriction on alienation may choose not to lend to the spendthrift.

Applied to pensions

Some United States Employee Retirement Income Security Act retirement plans contain anti-alienation provisions requiring that the trusts to which the plans relate be for the exclusive purpose of benefitting plan participants.

Source (edited): "http://en.wikipedia.org/wiki/Anti-alienation_clause"

Apertura tabularum

Apertura tabularum, in ancient law books, signifies the breaking open of a last will and testament.

Source (edited): "http://en.wikipedia. org/wiki/Apertura_tabularum"

Asset-protection trust

An **asset-protection trust** is a term which covers a wide spectrum of legal structures. Any form of trust which provides for funds to be held on a discretionary basis falls within the category. Such trusts are set up in an attempt to avoid or mitigate the effects of taxation, divorce and bankruptcy on the beneficiary. Such trusts are therefore frequently proscribed or limited in their effects by governments and the courts.

History of trusts

Trusts were developed at common law in England originally to minimize the impact of inheritance taxes arising from transfers at death. The essence of the trust was to separate "legal" title, which was given to someone to hold as "trustee", from "equitable title", which was to be retained by the trust beneficiaries.

In the United States and England, a practice developed whereby trust settlors began to use "spendthrift" clauses to prevent trust beneficiaries from alienating their beneficial interests to creditors. Over time, courts were asked to determine the efficacy of spendthrift clauses as against the trust beneficiaries seeking to engage in such assignments, and the creditors of those beneficiaries seeking to reach trust assets. A case law doctrine developed whereby courts may generally recognize the efficacy of spendthrift clauses as against trust beneficiaries and their creditors, but not against creditors of a settlor.

Overview

The asset-protection trust is a trust that splits the beneficial enjoyment of trust assets from their legal ownership. The beneficiaries of a trust are the beneficial owners of equitable interests in the trust assets, but they do not hold legal title to the assets. Thus this kind of trust fulfills the goal of asset protection planning, i.e. to insulate assets from claims of creditors without concealment or tax evasion.

Such trusts must be irrevocable (a revocable trust will not provide asset protection because and to the extent of the settlor's power to revoke). Most of them contain a spendthrift clause preventing a trust beneficiary from alienating his or her expected interest in favor of a creditor. The spendthrift clause has three general exceptions to the protection afforded: the self-settled trusts (if the settlor of a trust is also a beneficiary of a trust), the case when a debtor is the sole beneficiary and the sole trustee of a trust, and the support payments (a court may order the trustee to satisfy a beneficiary's support obligation to a former spouse or minor child). The first general exception, which accounts for the majority of asset protection trusts, no longer applies in several jurisdictions. Certain nations and certain United States now allow self-settled trusts to afford their settlors the protection of the spendthrift clause.

Domestic asset protection trust

Alaska was the first US jurisdiction to enact laws allowing protection for self-settled trusts (in 1997) and was shortly followed by Delaware, Nevada, South Dakota and a few others. These trusts are known as *Domestic Asset Protection Trusts* (DAPTs). Usually, a DAPT must comply with the following requirements:

- the trust must be irrevocable and spendthrift;
- at least one resident trustee must be appointed;
- some administration of the trust must be conducted in respective state;
- the settlor cannot act as a trustee.

Trusts are generally governed by the laws of the jurisdiction that is designated by the settlor as the governing jurisdiction. There are two exceptions to the general rule, which may create conflicts of law: (i) states will not recognize laws of sister states that violate their own public policy, and (ii) if the trust owns real property, such property will be governed by the law of jurisdiction that is the property's situs. Additionally, the Full Faith and Credit clause of the Constitution provides that each state must give full faith and credit to the laws of every other state. This means that if a court from another state refuses to recognize the protection of a DAPT and enters a judgment for the creditor, the creditor may be able to enforce the judgment against the trustee of the DAPT, even if that trustee was located in the DAPT jurisdiction. The efficacy of a DAPT may also be challenged under the Supremacy clause of the U.S. Constitution, under the applicable fraudulent transfer statute, or because the settlor retained some prohibited control over the trust.

These jurisdictions are also known as *United States Asset Protection Trusts* (USAPTs), from the point of view of the non-US settlors. The issues that would seem to apply on a USAPT established by a non-US settlor are: 1) whether a non-US court has jurisdiction over the USAPT; 2) the conflict of US versus non-US laws (i.e., which jurisdiction's laws will apply to the trust and the protection it purports to offer); 3) which fraudulent transfer law would apply; and 4) whether the US state court will recognize the non-US judgment.

The context of a non-US settlor has a few advantages over that of a US settlor. The issue of the Full Faith and Credit clause doctrine of the US Constitution would not apply to a non-US settlor facing a non-US judgment. Creditors of non-US settlors would have to first obtain a judgment in their home jurisdiction and then attempt to enforce that "foreign" judgment in the US against the trustee of the USAPT, who was not a party to the original action. Therefore, except in unusual cases, this would mean that the only issues to litigate would be whether a fraudulent transfer has taken place, and in turn, which jurisdiction's fraudulent transfer laws would

South Dakota

apply. Despite that, the non-US creditor must still seek to first have the foreign judgment recognized, because without formal legal acknowledgment of the judgment in the US court, there would be no basis on which to question the transfer.

South Dakota is the top choice for a trust company because of the state's advantageous trust and tax laws, its cost-efficient and dedicated workforce, the founders' previous favorable experience and their market recognition with the state. South Dakota was one of the first states (1983) to allow a trust to endure perpetually, essentially jumping outside the onerous federal transfer (gift, estate and generation-skipping) tax system theoretically forever. Currently, twenty-four other states have joined the ranks of offering a long-term trust. Nineteen of these states, including South Dakota, allow for a trust to go on in perpetuity.

South Dakota can be distinguished from these other states by its modern trust laws coupled with the fact that it does not impose any form of state taxation on the assets that comprise a trust located there. This includes, but is not limited to: no state income, capital gains, dividend/interest and/or intangible's taxes. Additionally, South Dakota has the lowest insurance premium tax of any state (i.e. 8 basis points or 8/100ths of 1%) and also offers other very favorable insurance legislation. South Dakota also has both excellent self-settled trust as well as Third Party Discretionary trust statutes, both allowing for domestic asset protection planning with trusts.

South Dakota is the first and only state in the U.S. with a Third Party Discretionary Trust statute for asset protection, which states that a discretionary interest in third party trust, limited power of appointments, and remainder interests are not considered property interests. This statute is extremely important to properly asset protect trusts set up to benefit one's family. South Dakota also has some of the top-rated Asset Protection statutes for LLCs and LPs based upon a powerful "sole remedy charging order statute". Consequently, most of the unique and creative trust strategies for the wealthy involve trust administration in South Dakota without the necessity of having the trust's family reside there.

Offshore jurisdictions

In 1989, the Cook Islands enacted the world's first asset-protection trust law. A key feature of the Cook Islands International Trusts Act (1984) is that the settlor of a trust may establish a spendthrift trust in which the settlor is a beneficiary. In the United States and England, a common law doctrine developed to prevent trust settlors from enjoying the benefits of a spendthrift trust; it was regarded as void against public policy for a trust settlor to avoid his own debts by the mere act of establishing a trust. The Cook Islands asset protection trust law has now been implemented in one form or another in 13 countries and eight U.S. states.

According to Jacob Stein's treatise on asset protection, common provisions enacted among some, but not all, of these countries are: (i) there is no recognition of foreign judgments with respect to trusts; (ii) there is a very short statute of limitations on fraudulent transfers; (iii) to establish a fraudulent transfer the creditor must show that the debtor was insolvent, and must establish the debtor's intent to "hinder, delay or defraud" beyond a reasonable doubt; (iv) the anti-duress provisions are incorporated into the statutes; and (v) spendthrift protection is extended to self-settled trusts. These jurisdictions also offer the additional advantages of (i) not being subject to the U.S. constitutional issues like the Full Faith and Credit clause; (ii) using the English common-law legal system; (iii) having abolished the rule against perpetuities; and (iv) not allowing trusts to be pierced for child or spousal support.

Cook Islands

The Cook Islands is an independent country joined in "free association" with New Zealand. While the Cook Islands has its own government and court system, it uses the New Zealand dollar as its functional currency, and its citizens carry New Zealand passports. It has a population of roughly 35,000, with more than half residing on its primary island, Rarotonga.

With a British common law tradition and English as the primary language, the Cook Islands has an active offshore banking sector attractive to Asians and North Americans. Major offshore-licensed banks in the Cook Islands include Australia and New Zealand Banking Group (ANZ) and Capital Security Bank. The confidentiality laws of the Cook Islands prohibit the disclosure of trust and banking relationships except with the consent of the customer, ensuring that no creditor or foreign government can gain access to bank or trust information except in cases of preventing money laundering or averting the financing of terrorism.

The Cook Islands was the first country to enact an explicit asset protection law, implementing particular provisions in 1989 to its International Trusts Act. Several of these changes have been adopted in one form or another in several other countries and a handful of a U.S. states. The most important of these changes permits the settlor of a trust to be named as a spendthrift beneficiary.

The trust laws of the Cook Islands provide a shortened statute of limitations on fraudulent transfer claims. While most U.S. states have a four year statute of limitations (and the Statute of Elizabeth in some common law jurisdictions has no statute of limitations), the general statute of limitations in the Cook Islands is reduced to two years for fraudulent transfers; in certain circumstances, it may be as short as one year. If the trust is funded while the settlor is solvent, then the transfer cannot be challenged (i.e., there is no time period for the creditor to challenge the transfer).

Several provisions of the Cook Islands law specify the form of pleading that a creditor must establish in order for its claim to be heard in a Cook Islands court. The effect of these provisions is to raise the burden of proof to "beyond a reasonable doubt," something akin to a criminal law standard, in order for a creditor to establish a fraudulent transfer. The "constructive" fraudulent transfer theories are eliminated under Cook Islands law, requiring the creditor to prove that the transfer was made with specific intent to avoid the creditor's claim.

It is believed that the Cook Islands now has more registered asset protection trusts than any other country. Along with a body of case law that has interpreted major provisions of its trust law, many lawyers find the Cook Islands to be the premier jurisdiction for asset protection planning. Recently enacted LLC legislation in the Cook Islands includes some asset protection features that are likely to keep the Cook Islands popular among asset protection attorneys.

Nevis
Nevis was one of the first countries to follow the Cook Islands, duplicating an older version of the Cook Islands law and naming it the Nevis International Exempt Trust Ordinance, 1994. One distinguishing feature of the Nevis legislation is that a creditor must post a bond of ECB 25,000 (roughly USD 13,000) to lodge a complaint against a trust registered in Nevis.

Very little case law exists in Nevis, which many attorneys interpret to mean that creditors are effectively deterred from bringing suit in Nevis. It has a small offshore banking industry, with St. Kitts Nevis Anguilla Bank and Bank of Nevis International as the only licensed offshore banks.

LLC legislation modeled after the Delaware LLC Act was passed in 1996. This has enabled Nevis to distinguish itself as a primary offshore jurisdiction for LLC formations, as opposed to other countries that are well known for IBC formations (British Virgin Islands) or trust formations (Cook Islands). A Nevis LLC is often used in conjunction with an asset protection trust because it gives the creator of the trust direct control over the assets if the creator is listed as the manager of the Nevis LLC. This gives the creator added security in that it keeps the assets one step removed from the trustee of the asset protection trust. Because the managers and members of a Nevis LLC are not public information, the creator of the trust is able to assume control over the assets without making disclosing his control on any public records.

Belize
Belize, for example, offers immediate protection from court action initiated by creditors which challenges the settlor's transfer of property into the trust. However, due to the paucity of credible offshore banks in Belize, many trusts established in Belize hold assets with a second trustee or third-party financial institution in another country.

Bahamas
The Bahamas have traditionally been associated with offshore planning. However, the Bahamas are probably more noteworthy for offshore banking and IBC formations than for asset protection trusts. The Bahamas do not recognize self-settled spendthrift trusts, unlike the Cook Islands, Nevis, or Belize. For this reason, the Bahamas are not regarded as an asset-protection trust jurisdiction.

Channel Islands (Guernsey and Jersey)
The Channel Islands have captured the imagination of UK residents longing for offshore asset protection and safe havens to hide assets. However, modern case law indicates that creditors are routinely able to invade trust assets in the Channel Islands. Furthermore, tax law initiatives in the UK have largely eliminated the tax advantages of placing assets in trust in the Channel Islands. While the Channel Islands enjoys a modern banking sector, most attorneys do not regard the Channel Islands as appropriate for asset protection planning.

Switzerland and Liechtenstein
Switzerland and Liechtenstein are noteworthy for large banking sectors and sophisticated wealth management services. While both countries now recognize trusts (particularly trusts established under the laws of another jurisdiction, such as Nevis), there is as of yet no available case law indicating how the courts of those two countries will enforce offshore asset protection trust laws.

Many attorneys establish asset protection trusts under the laws of another country and deposit the trust assets in Switzerland or Liechtenstein. One question raised by this approach is whether a creditor can seize assets in Switzerland or Liechtenstein without having to bring a claim in the trust-protective jurisdiction. Again, a lack of precedent suggests that this is an open issue in Switzerland and Liechtenstein.

Both countries are also known for offering asset protection annuities, with a six-month statute of limitations on fraudulent transfers into an annuity. Unfortunately for most Americans, these annuities cannot invest in US securities without punitive taxation due to the offshore status of the insurance carriers that offer these annuity products. Furthermore, many lawyers peddling these annuity products to their clients collect commissions from the insurance carriers. These reasons, among others, may help explain why annuities offered in these two countries are not particularly popular with U.S. persons. This does not mean that taxpayers of other jurisdictions may not significantly benefit from holding a Swiss or Liechtenstein annuity. Also, U.S. persons may benefit from holding an annuity issued by a carrier in an asset-protective jurisdiction (such as the Cook Islands), particularly if the carrier is an electing 953(d) carrier (a reference to a provision of US tax law).

Challenges
Whether such a trust is a spendthrift trust on the U.S. model, a protective trust on the Commonwealth model or another form of discretionary trust, it is more likely to be subject to challenge under the common law doctrine of sham or under specific statutory provisions if any person setting up the trust (or their spouse and their spouse in turn as in a reciprocal trust):

- can benefit under its provisions;

- is the person under risk financially;
- benefits (whether permitted or not) from the trust; or
- if the person setting up the trust is at risk financially, if bankruptcy or divorce occurs soon after the establishment of the trust (fraudulent conveyance).

Offshore trusts and other asset protection vehicles typically do not prevent action against the individual concerned in his or her home country. Orders under divorce and creditor protection laws can typically be made against that individual notwithstanding the alleged independence of such trustees. If a judge determines that the trust settlor controls the assets of the offshore trust, the judge may order the settlor to repatriate the trust assets. Failure to comply with the court's order may lead to a finding of contempt of court and imprisonment. For this reason, a properly established asset protection trust should provide a clear separation between the settlor and those who exercise control over the trust assets.

US v. Grant

The most recent case to rule on the merits of a contempt order is *US v. Grant*. In 2005, a federal district court in Miami ordered a domestic protector of an offshore asset protection trust, under threat of contempt, to exercise her power to replace the foreign trustee with a domestic trustee chosen by the court. The ruling, *U.S. v. Grant* Case No. 00-08986-Civ-Jordan (D.C. So. Fla. 2005), threatened to draw into question the viability of an asset-protection trust if a domestic protector could be compelled to appoint a domestic trustee to marshal the assets and bring them within the purview of the domestic court proceedings.

In May 2008, the U.S. government sought to hold the domestic protector in contempt of court for failing to secure the cooperation of the foreign trustee to resign and repatriate the trust assets. The U.S. District Court for the Southern District of Florida ruled against the government, finding that the domestic protector could not be held in contempt for failure to gain the cooperation of the offshore trustee. In denying the government's contempt motion, the judge observed:

"I understand that it has been more than two years since the repatriation order was issued and that the funds had not yet been repatriated. But this failure is not for a lack of effort. I am reluctant to fault Mrs. Grant for her trustees' denial of her requests to repatriate the funds." *U.S. v. Grant*, 2008 U.S. Dist. LEXIS 51332, 101 A.F. T.R.2d (RIA) 2676 (D.C. So. Fla. 2008).

For years, lawyers have vigorously debated the vulnerability of an asset protection trust with a domestic protector. The Grant case stands for the proposition that no vulnerability exists if the domestic protector complies with the court's orders. While a domestic protector may be required to make an effort to repatriate trust assets, failure to achieve repatriation should not entail any dire consequences to the trust or to the domestic protector. As long as a duress clause permits the foreign trustee to ignore the pleas of a domestic protector acting under threat of a contempt order, the selection of a domestic protector should not jeopardize the integrity of the offshore asset protection trust.

While most attorneys draft trust agreements to limit the domestic protector's powers to those of a negative nature (i.e., the domestic protector may veto trustee decisions, but a domestic protector cannot order a trustee to do anything), the ruling in *Grant* implies that even positive powers exercisable by a domestic protector may not jeopardize an offshore asset protection trust containing a duress clause. Whether this leads attorneys to be more cavalier in their trust drafting remains to be seen. At least we know that traditional offshore asset protection trust planning works as anticipated.

Taxation

There are rigorous US tax reporting requirements that apply to taxpayers who establish offshore trusts. While no additional tax is usually imposed, certain forms of asset protection trusts require full disclosure of all trust assets and activities on the U.S. contributor's tax returns. Confidentiality is usually not enjoyed under these arrangements.

Most asset protection trusts established by U.S. settlors are considered "grantor trusts" under U.S. income tax law, meaning that all income of the trust is reportable on the grantor's (i.e., the settlor's) individual income tax return. Asset-protection trusts do not, in and of themselves, offer any tax advantages under U.S. income tax law.

Source (edited): "http://en.wikipedia.org/wiki/Asset_protection_trust"

Attestation clause

In the statutory law of wills and trusts, an **attestation clause** is a clause that is typically appended to a will, often just below the place of the testator's signature.

Attestation clauses were introduced into probate law with the promulgation of the first version of the Model Probate Code in the 1940s. A typical attestation clause reads:

We, the undersigned testator and the undersigned witnesses, respectively, whose names are signed to the attached or foregoing instrument declare:
(1) that the testator executed the instrument as the testator's will;
(2) that, in the presence of both witnesses, the testator signed or acknowledged the signature already made or directed another to sign for the testator in the testator's presence;
(3) that the testator executed the will as a free and voluntary act for the purposes expressed in it;
(4) that each of the witnesses, in the presence of the testator and of each other, signed the will as a witness;

(5) that the testator was of sound mind when the will was executed; and
(6) that to the best knowledge of each of the witnesses the testator was, at the time the will was executed, at least eighteen (18) years of age or was a member of the armed forces or of the merchant marine of the United States or its allies.

This attestation clause is modeled on the Model Probate Code's version. Statutes that authorize self-proved wills typically provide that a will that contains this language will be admitted to probate without affidavits from the attesting witnesses. In order to issue an attestation report, Active CPA status is required by federal law.

The validity and form of an attestation clause is usually a matter of U.S. state law, and will vary from state to state. Many states allow attestation clauses to be added as codicils to wills that were originally drafted without them.

Source (edited): "http://en.wikipedia.org/wiki/Attestation_clause"

Australian trust law

Trust law in Australia

In Australia, trust law is under the jurisdiction of state governments, and the legislation often interacts with Corporations law and Family tax law. Equity still regulates trust law to a significant extent, and Australian law has often followed English developments.

There are a variety of trusts recognised and used in Australia, including Unit trusts, Discretionary trusts and Hybrid trusts. Testamentary trust are also sometimes used.

Often referred to as a "family trust" in Australia, is a discretionary trust where the trustee has made a family trust election. Family trusts provide flexibility in relation to distributions of income and assets among members of the family, while at the same time permitting the family to maintain either direct or indirect control over funds or other assets that have become the property of the family members. Streaming a category of trust income to a particular beneficiary provides tax planning opportunities. For example: foreign tax credits can be best utilised bny resident individual beneficiaries with high marginal tax rates and net capital gains can be best utilised by beneficiaries with carried forward losses, low income beneficiaries with carried forward revenue losses and minors able to receive excepted trust income. However, discretionary trusts are usually unsuitable for accumulation of profits as the undistributed income will generally be taxed at 45% under s99A of the ITAA36.

Family Trusts are often used to distribute income to beneficiaries in an attempt to achieve the most desirable tax outcomes available to the members of the trust. Discretionary or "Family" trusts also protect assets when individual members become insolvent or bankrupt. Asset protection also extends to other types of liabilities.

The power of appointment of the trustee of a discretionary trust is held by the Appointor.In some trust deeds the person holding the power of appointment of the trustee is called the Custodian.The only difference is in the name. The Appointor is usually a natural person but can be a company. Generally upon the death of the Appointor, in the absence of an alternate appointment in the trust deed,the personal legal representative (executor) of the Appointor becomes the Appointor.The real power in relation to the control of the trust rests with the Appointor because of the ability to terminate the appointment of the trustee and appoint a different trustee. This must be kept in mind when considering succession and estate planning involving assets held in a discretionary trust.

Source (edited): "http://en.wikipedia.org/wiki/Australian_trust_law"

Barclays Bank Ltd v Quistclose Investments Ltd

Barclays Bank Ltd v Quistclose Investments Ltd AC 567 (sub nom *Quistclose Investments v Rolls Razor*) is a leading property, unjust enrichment and trusts case, which invented a new species of proprietary interest. What is now known as a "Quistclose trust" means that when an asset is given to somebody for a specific purpose and for whatever reason the purpose for the transfer fails, the transferor may take back the asset.

Suppose a debtor undertakes to use the loan in a particular way, and segregates the creditor's money from his general assets. Consequently, if the debtor becomes insolvent, the creditor's money is refundable, and not available to pay the debtor's other creditors, i.e. if the trust fails (because the purpose is not, or cannot, be fulfilled), then the sums become subject to a resulting trust in favour of the person who originally advanced the credit, and the person to whom the sums were advanced holds them as trustee.

Facts

Rolls Razor was deeply indebted to Barclays. It needed further additional sums to be able to pay a dividend which it had declared. Rolls Razor borrowed funds from Quistclose in order to satisfy the dividend declared. The terms of the loan were such that the funds would only be used for the sole purpose of paying the dividend. The loan was paid into an account with Barclays, and Barclays was given notice of the arrangement.

However, between the time that the loan was advanced and the dividend being paid, Rolls Razor went into liquidation. Barclays Bank claimed that they were entitled to exercise a set-off of the money in the account against the debts that Rolls Razor owed with respect of

Barclays. Quistclose claimed that the moneys had to be returned to them, as the purpose for which they had been lent had now failed and were incapable of being fulfilled (as Rolls Razor was now in liquidation).

Judgment

The House of Lords (with the leading judgment being given by Lord Wilberforce) unanimously held that the money was held by Rolls Razor on trust for the payment of the dividends; that purpose having failed, the money was held on trust for Quistclose. The fact that the transaction was a loan did not exclude the implication of a trust. The legal rights (to call for repayment) and equitable rights (to claim title) could co-exist. Barclays, having notice of the trust, could not retain the money as against Quistclose. Similarly, the liquidator of Rolls Razor could not claim title to the money, as the assets did not form part the beneficial estate of Rolls Razor.

Significance

The conceptual analysis underpinning *Quistclose* trusts was the source of some debate. Shortly after the decision, an article appeared in the Law Quarterly Review written by Peter Millett QC suggesting how the traditional trust need for certainty of objects (beneficiary) could be squared with the decision of the House of Lords, and the refusal to accept new categories of purpose trust in equity. In *Twinsectra v Yardley* the House of Lords reviewed the law and the leading judgment was given by Lord Millett, whose judicial analysis, unsurprisingly, closely mirrored that which he suggested twenty years previously.

The key issue, according to Lord Millett, in upholding the trust concept is ascertaining where the beneficial interest in the money lies. Lord Millett suggests that there are four possible answers: (1) the lender, (2) the borrower, (3) the ultimate purpose, and (4) no-one, in the sense that the beneficial interest remains "in suspense". Lord Millett then analysed all of the foregoing, and determined that the beneficial interest remains with the lender, until the purpose for which the funds are lent is fulfilled. The only other reasoned decision was Lord Hoffmann, who agreed with Lord Millett, though disagreed as to whether it was an express or resulting trust.

Some have suggested that this means a *Quistclose* trust, whilst it is indubitably a trust, it would not be a resulting trust as the beneficial interest never 'results back' to the lender; it was with him all the time. However, others point out that there are many resulting trusts where the beneficial interest never leaves the donor: the classic example of a trust failing for uncertain objects, for example.

Requirements

It is sometimes argued that *Quistclose* trusts are not a separate species of trust at all, but merely a simple trust, which has certain characteristics. However, *Quistclose* trusts are often regarded as somewhat special and distinct. The English Court of Appeal in *Twinsectra v Yardley* Lloyd's Rep 438 suggested, *obiter dictum*, that it was in fact a 'quasi-trust' which is not required to satisfy "the usually strict requirements for a valid trust so far as 'certainty of object[s]' is concerned. However, the House of Lords, on appeal, declined to endorse those comments.

Purpose

However, what differentiates the *Quistclose* trust from other trusts, is the existence of the specific purpose for which the sums on credit must be applied, and the failure of which gives rise to the trust. It must also be clear that, if that specific purpose fails, the sums will revert to the person who originally advanced them.

The situations in which *Quistclose* trusts have been upheld are varied. They have been upheld in cases of:
- sums advanced for the specific payment of a dividend;
- sums advanced for the specific payment of a creditor;
- sums advanced on the basis of an undertaking for a specific project, and
- advance payments made on credit for the purchase of specific goods.

One issue that has escaped notice in the judicial consideration of *Quistclose* trusts to date is how narrowly the purpose has to be defined. Suggestions have been made to the effect that the general law in relation to powers would apply (such that if the purpose is sufficiently well defined to be a power, a *Quistclose* trust may arise), but others have argued that to take tests from one branch of the law and apply it to another may not be appropriate. The lower courts in *Twinsectra* suggested that the purpose must be sufficiently well defined, but Lord Millett distanced himself from that position, claiming that "uncertainty works in favour of the lender, not the borrower."

Certainty of intention

In *Twinsectra v Yardley*, Lord Millett spent some time considering the necessary intention. It has long been settled law that a person need not have a specific intention to create an express trust, so long as the court can determine from the person's intention that a beneficial entitlement should be conferred which the law (or equity) will enforce. So in *Twinsectra* where there was a solicitor's undertaking that the money should only be used for one purpose, this was held to be sufficient intent. In *Quistclose* itself and in *Carreras Rothmans v Freeman Mathews Treasure* where loans were made for a specific purpose, this may also amount to sufficient intention. Where a loan is advanced for the borrower to use as he will, no *Quistclose* trust can arise.

Criticisms

In the early stages of development of the *Quistclose* trust, it was suggested that the concept was unambiguously good. In *Re Kayford* it was suggested that a segregated account for customers' money to be placed in to guard against the insolvency of the company was a proper and responsible thing to do.

However, more recently criticism has been mounted that giving a proprietary claim to a lender which enables the lender to reclaim the loan ahead of unsecured creditors has the effect of putting the lender in the position of a secured creditor, but without the need to register any security interest against the borrower (and thus meaning that other creditors would not be aware of the preferential status of the lender's claim).

Quistclose trusts still remain relatively uncommon, and as yet there has been no clamour for legislation or regulation (*Quistclose* trusts were not even addressed under English law when the insolvency law was last revised in the Enterprise Act 2002). However, should the courts start finding them with increasing frequency, it may be that regulation, or judicial revision, follows.

Source (edited): "http://en.wikipedia.org/wiki/Barclays_Bank_Ltd_v_Quistclose_Investments_Ltd"

Bare trust

A **bare trust** (sometimes referred to as a **simple trust**) is a trust in which the beneficiary has a right to both income and capital and may call for both to be remitted into his own name. He is also entitled to take actual ownership and control of the trust property. Although there are trustees, they are only effectively nominees and must act according to the beneficiary's instructions.

Source (edited): "http://en.wikipedia.org/wiki/Bare_trust"

Beach bum trust provision

A **beach bum trust provision**, in the law of trusts, ties the ability of a trust beneficiary to take from the trust to the beneficiary's own earnings. Such a provision serves to prevent a beneficiary from lazily living off the trust funds (i.e. a "beach bum"). If the beneficiary earns no income, then he reaps nothing from the trust.

Source (edited): "http://en.wikipedia.org/wiki/Beach_bum_trust_provision"

Beneficial interest

A **beneficial interest** is "that right which a person has in a contract made with another" (third) person. The typical example is "if A makes a contract with B that he will pay C a certain sum of money, B has the legal interest in the contract, and C the beneficial interest."

More generally, a **beneficial interest** is any "interest of value, worth, or use in property one does not own," for example, "the interest that a beneficiary of a trust has in the trust." More specifically, it could be:

- "A property interest that inures solely to the benefit of the owner," or
- Property that "remains of an estate after the payment of debts and the expenses of administration", or
- The right of a person having a power of appointment to appoint himself."

Black's Law Dictionary defines *beneficial interest* as "Profit, benefit or advantage resulting from a contract, or the ownership of an estate as distinct from the legal ownership or control." Examples of beneficial interests in mining claims include unrecorded deeds and agreements to share profits, *but not* mortgages and other liens. A beneficial interest is also "distinguished from the rights of someone like a trustee or official who has responsibility to perform and/or title to the assets but does not share in the benefits."

Source (edited): "http://en.wikipedia.org/wiki/Beneficial_interest"

Beneficiary (trust)

"Cestui que use" redirects here. See also, Cestui que.

In trust law, a **beneficiary** or ***cestui que use***, a.k.a. ***cestui que trust***, is the person or persons who are entitled to the benefit of any trust arrangement. A beneficiary will normally be a natural person, but it is perfectly possible to have a company as the beneficiary of a trust, and this often happens in sophisticated commercial transaction structures. With the exception of charitable trusts, and some specific anomalous non-charitable purpose trusts, all trusts are required to have ascertainable beneficiaries.

Generally speaking, there are no strictures as to who may be a beneficiary of a trust; a beneficiary can be a minor, or under a mental disability (in fact many trusts are created specifically for persons with those legal disadvantages). It is also possible to have trusts for unborn children, although the trusts must vest within the applicable perpetuity period.

Categorisation

There are various ways in which beneficiaries of trusts can be categorised, depending upon the nature and need of the categorisation.

From the perspective of the trustees' duties, it is most common to differentiate between:

- fixed beneficiaries, who have a simple fixed entitlement to income and capital; and
- discretionary beneficiaries, whom the trustees must make decisions as to the respective entitlements.

Where a trust gives rise to sequential interests, from a tax perspective (and also from the point of view of trustee's duties), it is often necessary to differentiate beneficiaries sequentially, between:

- those with a vested interest, such as tenants for life; and
- those with a contingent interest, such as remaindermen

For the purposes of various exercise of beneficiaries' rights, it is often necessary to distinguish between:

- beneficiaries under a bare trust (including a constructive or resulting trust), to whom the trustee owes basic duties arising by law; and
- beneficiaries under an express trust (either an *inter vivos trust* or a testamentary trust), where the trustee owes additional duties and has additional powers specified by the trust instrument.

Rights and interest

The nature of a beneficiaries' interest in the trust fund varies according to the type of trust.

In the case of a fixed trust, the beneficiaries' interest is proprietary; they are the owners of an equitable interest in the property held under the trust.

The position is slightly different in the case of a discretionary trust; in such cases the beneficiaries are dependent upon the exercise by the trustees of their powers under the trust instrument in their favour.

Similarly, where a trust gives rise to successive interest, the title of a remainderman is a prospective, or contingent, interest; although unlike a discretionary beneficiary, this is still a species of property that can be dealt with, much in the same was as a contingent or prospective debt.

Taxation

Tax planning usually plays a considerable role in relating to the use of trusts.

Historically, whilst the courts have been fairly amenable to the use of trusts in tax planning, as tax planning schemes have become more aggressive, so the courts have increasingly taken a restrictive view of the tax treatment of trusts.

Although individual countries tend to have very detailed rules about the taxation of trusts, the three mechanisms whereby taxation is usually assessed is by either treating (i) the trust as a separately taxable entity in its own right, (ii) treating the trust property as still the property of the settlor, and (iii) treating the trust property as belonging absolutely to the beneficiaries. Some jurisdictions apply different combinations of the rules in income tax, capital gains tax and inheritance tax.

Beneficiaries' powers

Because an interest under a trust is a species of property, adult beneficiaries of sound mind are able to deal with their rights under the trust fund as they could with any other species of property. They can sell it, assign it, exchange it, release it, mortgage it, and do most other things that they could do with a *chose in action*.

If all of the beneficiaries of the trust are adults and of sound mind, then they can terminate the trust under the rule in *Saunders v Vautier*, and require the trustees to transfer absolute legal title to the trust assets to the beneficiaries.

Source (edited): "http://en.wikipedia.org/wiki/Beneficiary_(trust)"

Bequest

A **bequest** is the act of giving (not the act of receiving) property by will. Strictly, "bequest" is used of personal property, and "devise" of real property. In legal terminology, "bequeath" is a verb form meaning "to make a bequest."

(From Old English *becwethan*, to declare or express in words; cf. "quoth")

Interpreting bequests

The general repetition of the ballet (La répétition générale du ballet, *by par Edgar Degas is a bequest of Count Isaac de Camondo, (Musée d'Orsay)*

Part of the process of probate involves interpreting the instructions in a will. Some wordings that define the scope of a bequest have specific interpretations. "All the estate I own" would involve all of the decedent's possessions at the moment of death.

A *conditional bequest* is a bequest which will only be granted if a particular event has occurred by the time of its operation. For example, a testator might write in their will that "Mary will receive the house held in trust if she is married" or "...if she has children," etc.

An *executory bequest* is a bequest which will be granted when a particular event occurs in the future, if it happens. For example, a testator might write in their will that "Mary will receive the house held in trust set when she marries" or "when she has children," etc.

Explaining bequests

In microeconomics theorists have engaged the issue of bequest from the perspective of consumption theory, in which they seek to explain the phenomenon in terms of a bequest motive.

For the Recipient
In order to calculate a taxpayer's income tax obligation, the gross income of the taxpayer must be determined. Under Section 61 of the U.S. Internal Revenue Code gross income is "all income from whatever source derived". On its face, the receipt of a bequest would seemingly fall within gross income and thus be subject to tax. However, in other sections of the code, exceptions are made for a variety of things that do not need to be included in gross income. Section 102(a) of the Code makes an exception for bequests stating that "Gross income does not include the value of property acquired by gift, bequest, or inheritance." In general this means that the value or amount of the bequest does not need to be included in a taxpayer's gross income. This rule is not exclusive, however, and there are some exceptions under Section 102(b) of the code where the amount of value must be included. There is great debate about whether or not bequests should be included in gross income and subject to income taxes, however there has been some type of exclusion for bequests in every Federal Income Tax Act.

For the Donor
One reason that the recipient of a bequest is usually not taxed on the bequest is because the donor may be taxed on it. Donors of bequests may be taxed through other mechanisms such as federal wealth transfer taxes. Wealth Transfer taxes, however, are usually imposed against only the very wealthy.
Source (edited): "http://en.wikipedia.org/wiki/Bequest"

Blind trust

A **blind trust** is a trust in which the fiduciaries, namely the trustees or those who have been given power of attorney, have full discretion over the assets, and the trust beneficiaries have no knowledge of the holdings of the trust and no right to intervene in their handling. Blind trusts are generally used when a settlor (sometimes called a trustor or donor) wishes to keep the beneficiary unaware of the specific assets in the trust, such as to avoid conflict of interest between the beneficiary and the investments. Politicians or others in sensitive positions often place their personal assets (including investment income) into blind trusts, to avoid public scrutiny and accusations of conflicts of interest when they direct government funds to the private sector.

British party funding

In the United Kingdom, while the Labour Party was in opposition in 1992–97, its front bench received funding from blind trusts. One set up to fund its campaign in the 1997 general election received donations from wealthy supporters, some of whose names leaked out, and some of whom received life peerages into the House of Lords after Labour won the election. The Neill Committee's report in 1998 found the use of blind trusts to be "inconsistent with the principles of openness and accountability" and recommended that such trusts be "prohibited as a mechanism for funding political parties, party leaders or their offices, Members of Parliament or parliamentary candidates" This was incorporated into the Political Parties, Elections and Referendums Act 2000 as section 57 "Return of donations where donor unidentifiable".
Source (edited): "http://en.wikipedia.org/wiki/Blind_trust"

Calendars of the Grants of Probate and Letters of Administration

Calendars of the Grants of Probate and Letters of Administration or **CGPLA** was an index published in the United Kingdom and Ireland that lists an alphabetical summary of probate documents such as wills. The correct full title for Ireland is *Calendars of the Grants of Probate and Letters of Administration Made in the Principal Registry and in the Several District Registries 1858-1920.*

Every year from 1858, volumes of short summaries of grants of probate and of letters of administration were created, in alphabetical order by surname. For each grant of probate, these include the name, address, and occupation (or other description) of the deceased, the place and date of the death, the date on which probate was granted and the value of the estate, and the names and addresses of any executors.

For 1858 to 1877, there is also a consolidated index.
Source (edited): "http://en.wikipedia.org/wiki/Calendars_of_the_Grants_of_Probate_and_Letters_of_Administration"

Charitable organization

American Cancer Society offices in Washington, D.C.

A **charitable organization** is a type of non-profit organization (NPO). The term is relatively general and can technically refer to a public charity (also called "charitable foundation," "public foundation" or simply "foundation") or a private foundation. It differs from other types of NPOs in that its focus is centered around goals of a general philanthropic nature (e.g. charitable, educational, religious, or other activities serving the public interest or common good).

The legal definition of charitable organization (and of charity) varies according to the country and in some instances the region of the country in which the charitable organization operates. The regulation, tax treatment, and the way in which charity law affects charitable organizations also varies.

Australia

Definition of charity

The definition of charity in Australia is derived through English common law, originally from the Charitable Uses Act 1601, and then through several centuries of case law based upon it. In 2002, the Federal Government establish an inquiry into the definition of a charity. That inquiry proposed that the government should legislate a definition of a charity, based on the principles developed through case law. This resulted in the Charities Bill 2003. The Bill incorporated a number of provisions, such as limitations on charities being involved in political campaigning, which many charities saw as an unwelcome departure from the case law. The government then appointed a Board of the Taxation inquiry to consult with charities on the Bill. As a result of widespread criticism from charities, the Government decided to abandon the Bill.

As a result, the government then introduced what became the Extension of Charitable Purpose Act 2004. This Bill did not attempt to codify the definition of a charitable purpose; it merely sought to clarify that certain purposes were indeed charitable, whose charitable status had been subject to legal doubts. These purposes were: childcare; self-help groups; closed/contemplative religious orders.

To publicly raise money, charities in Australia are required to register under the State jurisdiction within which they intend to raise funds and must be registered in each and any State within which they intend to publicly raise funds. For example, in Queensland charities must register with the QLD Office of Fair Trading. An example of a registered charity in Queensland, Australia is Sunnykids so whilst Sunnykids can publicly raise funds for charitable purposes, and whilst such donations are tax deductible in every Australian State and Territory - the funds themselves may only be raised in QLD as this is the only State within which the charity is registered to raise funds. In order for the charity to raise funds in the remaining seven Australian States and Territories it would need to register in each State or Territory individually. Needless to say, Many Australian charities are calling on Federal, State and Territory governments to unify legislation to allow registration in a single State or Territory to allow charities to raise funds in all 8 Australian States and Territories.

Canada

Charities in Canada must be registered with the Charities Directorate of the Canada Revenue Agency. According to the Canada Revenue Agency:
A registered charity is an organization established and operated for charitable purposes, and must devote its resources to charitable activities. The charity must be resident in Canada, and cannot use its income to benefit its members. A charity also has to meet a public benefit test. To qualify under this test, an organization must show that:
- its activities and purposes provide a tangible benefit to the public
- those people who are eligible for benefits are either the public as a whole, or a significant section of it, in that they are not a restricted group or one where members share a private connection, such as social clubs or professional associations with specific membership
- the charity's activities must be legal and must not be contrary to public policy

To register as a charity, the organization has to be either incorporated or governed by a legal document called a trust or a constitution. This document has to explain the organization's purposes and structure.

United Kingdom

England and Wales

Definition of charitable organization

A charity, or charitable organization, in England and Wales is a particular type of voluntary organization. A voluntary organization is an organization set up for charitable, social, philanthropic or other purposes. It is required to use any profit or surplus only for the organization's purposes, and it is not a part of any governing department, local authority or other statutory body. All charities are voluntary organizations, but not all voluntary organizations in England and Wales are charities.

For a voluntary organization to be a charitable organization or charity, its overall goals, sometimes called the "purposes" of the organization, must be charitable. All the purposes of the organization must be charitable, as a charity cannot have some purposes which are charitable and some which are not. The

Charities Act 2006 provides the following list of charitable purposes.
- the prevention or relief of poverty
- the advancement of education
- the advancement of religion
- the advancement of health or the saving of lives
- the advancement of citizenship or community development
- the advancement of the arts, culture, heritage or science
- the advancement of amateur sport
- the advancement of human rights, conflict resolution or reconciliation or the promotion of religious or racial harmony or equality and diversity
- the advancement of environmental protection or improvement
- the relief of those in need, by reason of youth, age, ill-health, disability, financial hardship or other disadvantage
- the advancement of animal welfare
- the promotion of the efficiency of the armed forces of the Crown or of the police, fire and rescue services or ambulance services
- other purposes currently recognised as charitable and any new charitable purposes which are similar to another charitable purpose.

A charity must also provide a public benefit.

Legally, all charities must also comply with:
- the Charities Acts 1992 (Part III), 1993, 2006: trustees of smaller organisations 2006 Act (the Office of the Third Sector)
- the Trustees Acts 1925, 2000: the most recent Act concerns the powers of trustees regarding investments and delegation.
- Charity Commission regulation: requires compliance (depending on annual income) on the submission of annual returns, reports and accounts
- the Statement of Recommended Practice (SORP) 2005: published by the Charity Commission, regarding published annual reports
- laws on trading, political activities and fundraising
- regulation covering people who are disbarred from acting as trustees under the Charities Act 1993 or your Memorandum and Articles.

Before the Charities Act 2006 the definition of charity arose from a list of charitable purposes in the Charitable Uses Act 1601 (also known as the Statute of Elizabeth), which had been interpreted and expanded into a considerable body of case law. In *Commissioners for Special Purposes of Income Tax v Pemsel* (1891), Lord McNaughten identified four categories of charity which could be extracted from the Charitable Uses Act and which were the accepted definition of charity prior to the Charities Act 2006.
- the relief of poverty,
- the advancement of education,
- the advancement of religion, and
- other purposes considered beneficial to the community.

Charitable organization structure

In 2008 there are a number of types of legal structure for a charity in England and Wales.
- Unincorporated association
- Trust
- Company limited by guarantee
- Another incorporation, such as by Royal Charter

The unincorporated association is the most common form of organization within the voluntary sector in England and Wales. An unincorporated association is essentially a contractual arrangement between individuals who have agreed to come together to form an organization for a particular purpose. An unincorporated association will normally have as its governing document, a constitution or set of rules, which will deal with such matters as the appointment of office bearers, and the rules governing membership. The organization is not though a separate legal entity. So it cannot start legal action, it cannot borrow money, and it cannot enter into contracts in its own name. Also the officers can be personally liable if the charity is sued or has debts.

A Trust is essentially a relationship between three parties, the donor of some assets, the trustees who hold the assets and the beneficiaries (those people who are eligible to benefit from the charity). When the trust has charitable purposes, and is a charity, the trust is known as a charitable trust. The governing document is the Trust Deed or Declaration of Trust, which comes into operation once it is signed by all the trustees. The main disadvantage of a trust is that, as with an unincorporated association, it does not have a separate legal entity and the trustees must themselves own property and enter into contracts. The trustees are also liable if the charity is sued or incurs liability.

A company limited by guarantee is a private limited company where the liability of members is limited. A guarantee company does not have a share capital, but instead has members who are guarantors instead of shareholders. In the event of the company being wound up the members agree to pay a nominal sum which can be as little as £1. A company limited by guarantee is a useful structure for a charity where it is desirable for the Trustees to have the protection of limited liability. Also, the charity has a clear legal identity, and so can enter into contracts, such as employment contracts in its own name.

A small number of charities are incorporated by Royal Charter, a document which creates a corporation with legal personality (or, in some instances, transforms a charity incorporated as a company into a charity incorporated by Royal Charter). The Charter must be approved by the Privy Council before receiving Royal Assent. Although the nature of the charity will vary depending on the clauses enacted, generally a Royal Chartered will offer a charity the same limited liability as a company and the ability to enter into contracts.

The Charities Act 2006 introduced a new legal form of incorporation designed specifically for charities, the Charitable Incorporated Organisation. This is not yet available for charities to use.

The word Foundation is not generally used in England and Wales. Occasionally a charity will use the word Foundation as part of its name e.g. British Heart Foundation, but this has no legal significance and does not provide any information about either the work of the charity or how it is legally structured. The structure of the organization will be one of the three types of structure described above.

Charity registration

Charitable organizations that have an income of more than £5,000, and for whom the law of England and Wales applies, must register with the Charity Commission for England and Wales. For companies, the law of England and Wales will normally apply if the company itself is registered in England and Wales. In other cases if the governing document does not make it clear, the law which applies will be the country with which the organization is most connected.

Where an organization's income does not exceed £5,000 it is not able to register as a charity with the Charity Commission for England and Wales. It can, however, register as a charity with HM Revenue and Customs for Tax purposes only. With the rise in mandatory registration level, to £5,000 by The Charities Act 2006, smaller charities can be reliant upon HMRC recognition to evidence their charitable purpose and confirm their not-for-profit principles.

Some charities which are called exempt charities are not required to register with the Charity Commission and are not subject to any of the Charity Commission's supervisory powers. These charities include most universities and national museums and some other educational institutions. Other charities are excepted from the need to register, but are still subject to the supervision of the Charity Commission. The regulations on excepted charities have however been changed by the Charities Act 2006. Many excepted charities are religious charities.

Northern Ireland

Charities in Northern Ireland are registered with the UK HM Revenue and Customs. The **Charity Commission for Northern Ireland** has now been established and has received the names and details of over 7,000 organisations that have previously been granted charitable status for tax purposes. The entering of these organisations onto a new and temporary list under the heading of **"Organisations that have previously been known as charities"** is continuing. This list is not the new register, but will be made publicly available on the CCNI website.

Scotland

The 20,000 or so charities in Scotland are registered with the Office of the Scottish Charity Regulator (OSCR), which also publishes a Register of charities online. Scotland has the highest number of charities per capita in the world.

Taxation of Charities

Charitable organisations, including charitable trusts, are eligible for a complex set of reliefs and exemptions from taxation in the UK. These include reliefs and exemptions in relation to income tax, capital gains tax, inheritance tax, stamp duty land tax and value added tax.

United States

In the United States a charitable organization is an organization that is organized and operated for purposes that are beneficial to the public interest, however a distinction is made between types of charitable organizations.

Every U.S. and foreign charity that qualifies as tax-exempt under Section 501(c)(3) of the Internal Revenue Code is considered a "private foundation" *unless* it demonstrates to the IRS that it falls into another category. In a general sense, any organization that is not a private foundation (i.e. it qualifies as something else) is usually a public charity as described in Section 509(a) of the Internal Revenue Code.

In addition, a private foundation usually derives its principal fund from an individual, family, corporation, or some other single source and is more often than not a grantmaker and does not solicit funds from the public. In contrast, a foundation or public charity generally receives grants from individuals, government, and private foundations and although some public charities engage in grantmaking activities, most conduct direct service or other tax-exempt activities.

This leads to another distinction: Foundations that are generally grantmakers (i.e. they use their endowment to make grants to other organizations, which in turn carry out the goals of the foundation indirectly) are usually referred to as "grantmaker" or "non-operating" foundations. These of course tend to be private foundations. Some private foundations however, (and most public charities) use their received funds to directly engage in service activities themselves and achieve their goals "personally," so-to-speak.

Examples of a non-operating private foundation would be the Rockefeller Foundation and the Bill & Melinda Gates Foundation.

Examples of operating foundations or public charities include the Elizabeth Glaser Pediatric AIDS Foundation, American Cancer Society, Inc., and the World Wildlife Fund.

The requirements and procedures for forming charitable organizations vary from state to state, as do the registration and filing requirements for charitable organizations that conduct charitable activities or solicit charitable contributions. So effectively in practice the detailed definition of charitable organization is determined by the requirements of state law of the state in which the charitable organization operates, and the requirements for federal tax relief set by the IRS.

Federal tax relief

Federal tax law provides tax benefits to non profit organizations recognized as exempt from federal income tax under section 501(c)(3) of the Internal Revenue Code (IRC). The benefits of 501(c)(3) status include exemption from federal income tax as well as eligibility to receive tax deductible charitable contributions. To qualify for 501(c)(3) status most organizations must apply to the Internal Revenue Service (IRS) for such status.

There are several requirements that must be met for a charitable organization to obtain 501(c)(3) status. These include the organization being organized as a corporation, trust, or unincorporated association, and the organization's organizing document (such as the articles of incorporation, trust documents, or articles of association) must limit its purposes to being charitable, and permanently dedicate its assets to charitable purposes. The organization must refrain from undertaking a number of other activities such as participating in the political campaigns of candidates for local, state or federal office, and must ensure that its earnings do not benefit any individual.

The types of charitable organization that are considered by the IRS to be organized for the public benefit include those that are organized for:
- Relief of the poor, the distressed, or the underprivileged,
- Advancement of religion,
- Advancement of education or science,
- Erection or maintenance of public buildings, monuments, or works,
- Lessening the burdens of government,
- Lessening of neighborhood tensions,
- Elimination of prejudice and discrimination,
- Defense of human and civil rights secured by law, and
- Combating community deterioration and juvenile delinquency.

A number of other organizations, including those organized for religious, scientific, literary and educational purposes, as well as those for testing for public safety and for fostering national or international amateur sports competition, and for the prevention of cruelty to children or animals, may also qualify for exempt status.

The IRS, except in rare circumstances, refers to all organizations qualifying for exemption under 501(c)(3) as charities.

List of relevant organizations

Charity regulating bodies
- Australian Taxation Office
- Canada Revenue Agency
- Inland Revenue Department (Hong Kong)
- Public Trustee (Ontario)
- Charity Commission for England and Wales
- Office of the Scottish Charity Regulator
- Charity Commission for Northern Ireland
- United States Internal Revenue Service
- SHATAC-Pakistan

Source (edited): "http://en.wikipedia.org/wiki/Charitable_organization"

Charitable remainder unitrust

A **charitable remainder unitrust** is an irrevocable trust created under the authority of Internal Revenue Code §664 ("Code"). This special, irrevocable trust (known as a "CRUT") has two primary characteristics: (1) Once established, the CRUT distributes a fixed percentage of the value of its assets (on an annual or more frequent basis) to a non-charitable beneficiary (usually the settlor of the trust); and (2) At the expiration of a specified time (usually the death of the settlor), the remaining balance of the CRUTs assets are distributed to charity. The trustee determines the fair market value of the CRUT's assets at the time of contribution, and thereafter on the applicable valuation date. The fixed annuity percentage must be at least 5% and no more than 50% of the fair market value of the assets in the corpus. The remainder (the amount expected to go to charity) must be at least 10% of the fair market value of the assets contributed to the CRUT. Code Section 664(d)(1) sets the federal income tax requirements for a charitable remainder unitrust.

Example

Assume an individual, Mr. Smith, has $1 million of publicly traded stock and would like to establish a CRUT. Assume the CRUT is set up to pay the annuity to Mr. Smith over his lifetime. Mr. Smith selects a 10% CRUT. The CRUT will pay Mr. Smith 10% of its assets (initially $100,000) per year until Mr. Smith passes away. At that time, any balance remaining in the CRUT will be distributed to charity. The term "unitrust" means the annuity *percentage* is fixed; the CRUT will distribute 10% of the value of the CRUT's assets each year, which may increase or decrease over time.

History

Code §664 (authorizing CRUTs) was added to the Code in 1969, as part of the Tax Reform Act of 1969 (Pub. L. No. 91-172).

Requirements

A charitable remainder unitrust is a trust that which meets both: (1) The applicable rules under state law for a valid Charitable Trust; and (2) the requirements set forth in Code Section §664(d)(2).

State Law Requirements

First, a CRUT is formed like any other kind of trust, and must be valid under state law. Most states require CRUTs to be registered with the state. For example, California requires charitable trusts to be registered by filing a form CT-1 with the state attorney general. This is because the state attorney general represents the charitable interests involved with CRUT.

Income Tax Requirements

Code Section 664 imposes the following requirements on CRUTs:

Fixed percentage payment

The CRUT must distribute a fixed percentage annuity to the non-charitable beneficiary. This percentage may not be less than 5 percent nor more than 50 percent of the net fair market value of the CRUT's assets. The CRUT's assets are valued annually, and the annuity amount is determined at that time. As may be seen, the amount of the annuity might vary from year to year, but the percentage always stays the same. For example, assume a 10% CRUT is established, and assume the value of its portfolio holdings in year 1 is $1 million. The annuity that year is $100,000. Assume the portfolio drops in value, and in year 2 is worth $900,000. The annuity in year 2 will be reduced to $90,000 (10% of the value of the CRUT's assets).

The annuity must be distributed not less often than annually to one or more persons. The "person" may be an organization, however, it may not be a charity described in section 170(c). The CRUT is usually set up so that annuity is paid to the settlor of the trust. In the case of natural persons, payments may be made only to those who are living at the time of the creation of the trust. The annuity is paid to that non-charitable beneficiary for his or her lifetime, or for a fixed term of years (not to exceed 20 years).

No other payments

The CRUT may not distribute any of its assets to anyone other than the annuity recipient or the qualified charity beneficiary. The CRUT may not let any of its assets be used for the benefit of anyone other than the annuity recipient or the qualified charitable beneficiary. Code Section 664(d)(2)(B).

Transfer remainder interest when termination of payments

Once the annuity period is over (i.e., at the death of the non-charitable beneficiary, or at the expiration of the term of years), the remainder of the CRUT principal is distributed to charity. The charity must be an organization described in Section 170(c).

Portion of remainder interest in contributions to trusts

At least 10% of the statistical fair market value of each contribution of property to the trust, must be a part of the remainder interest that will pass to charity once the annuity term expires.

Treasury Regulations have imposed several other conditions relating to CRUTs:

NIMCRUTS

Treas. Reg. §1.664-3 authorizes CRUTs to be drafted so that the annuity can be the *lesser of:*

1. The annuity percentage, multiplied by the fair market value of the CRUT's assets (i.e., the normal annuity amount); or
2. The amount of the CRUT's "trust income" for the year.

This is known as a "net income CRUT", or NICRUT. For example, assume a 10% CRUT holds $1 million in assets. Assume the CRUT has only $70,000 of income that year. A NICRUT would distribute $70,000, because that is lesser than the ordinary $100,000 annuity.

Furthermore, Treas. Reg. §1.664-3(a)(1)(i)(b)(2) allows the CRUT to pay a "makeup amount", which means if the trust income is lower than the selected fixed percentage, the trustee can distribute a "make up amount" from the trust's income in subsequent years. This is known as a "net income/makeup CRUT", or "NIMCRUT". For example, assume the NICRUT above distributed $70,000, and had $130,000 of trust income the following year. Assume the NICRUT included the makeup provision (making it a NIMCRUT). The NIMCRUT would distribute the $130,000 to the annuity beneficiary.

The IRS has issued a series of sample CRUT forms since 1989, the latest series in 2005, known as Revenue Procedures 2005-52, 2005-53, 2005-54, 2005-55, 2005-56, 2005-57, 2005-58, and 2005-59. It is not recommended, however, that these sample forms be used verbatim and without any additional supplemented provisions.

Income, Gift, and Estate Tax Consequences

Charitable Deductions

A donor is entitled to a Charitable Deduction based on the present value of the remainder interest in a CRUT. Regs. § 1.664-4(e)(3)and (4). The method of determining the charitable deduction is complicated, and is generally stated in Treas. Regs. § 1.664-4(e)(3) and (4). Various factors are taken into consideration, including the adjusted payout rate, the value of the remainder interest, the age of the measuring life (the annuitant), the term of the CRUT, the date of trust creation, and federal interest rates.

Gift Tax Implications

The grantor/donor does not make a taxable gift if he or she is the recipient of the CRUT income for life or term of years. However, the creation of a CRUT will have a gift tax consequence if an individual other than the grantor/donor (or his or her spouse) is the designated beneficiary of the CRUT income.

Estate Tax

Section 2055(a) provides for a deduction from the value of the gross estate of bequest for public, charitable, and religious purposes. Therefore, the amount of principal contributed to a CRUT is not considered for estate tax purposes. Furthermore, the corpus is not subject to probate.

Unrelated Business Taxable Income

If a CRUT has any unrelated business taxable income (UBTI), the trust becomes a taxable entity subject to a 100% excise tax. UBTI is generally income earned from an active business. Accordingly, it loses its status as a CRUT.

WIFO

The annuity paid from the CRUT is taxable to the person receiving the payment. The annuity is taxed in the so-called "Worst-In, First-Out" (WIFO)method. Roughly, the annuity is taxed in the following order of the

CRUTs income: ordinary income, capital gain, other income, and trust corpus. The trust's income, for the year it is required to be taken into account by the trust, is assigned to one of three categories: the ordinary income, the capital gains category, or the other income.

Tax Planning

CRUTs are used for a variety of reasons. Often, CRUTs can be used to save income, gift, and/or estate tax. Because the CRUT is a tax-exempt entity a CRUT can be used to sell highly appreciated assets at greatly reduced tax consequences.

For example, assume an individual purchases publicly traded stock for $50,000.00. Assume that, over time, the stock appreciates in value to $1 million. If this individual taxpayer were to sell the stock, the taxpayer would have a $950,000.00 capital gain for income tax purposes, and would be subject to a substantial capital gains tax (this example will assume a combined federal and state capital gains tax rate of 20%, or $190,000.00 of capital gains tax). One tax planning idea would be for this individual to contribute the stock to a CRUT prior to the sale of the stock. The CRUT would then sell the stock. Assuming no other activity in the CRUT account, the $190,000.00 capital gains tax on the $950,000.00 gain would be paid over the lifetime of the taxpayer (without the CRUT, the taxpayer would have to pay the $190,000.00 all at once). The taxpayer would receive an annuity from the CRUT based on the full $1 million dollars of sales proceeds, rather than an annuity (or income stream) based on the $810,000.00 after-tax proceeds.

One possible concern for the taxpayer in the above situation is the risk of death shortly after setting up the CRUT. In such instance, the CRUT proceeds would pay to charity before the taxpayer has received much benefit from the annuity. In addition, at the taxpayer's death, charity receives the assets that might have otherwise passed to children or other heirs. Because of this, tax planners often suggest that their clients purchase life insurance, to be held separately from the CRUT. Using life insurance mitigates the risk of an early death.

For example, assume the same taxpayer above were to set up a CRUT and were to pass away quickly. In such instance, the balance of the CRUT would pay to charity. If this taxpayer purchased a $1 million dollar life insurance policy, in the event of the taxpayer's premature death, the taxpayer's family would receive the $1 million dollar life insurance proceeds and charity would receive the balance of the CRUT.

With proper planning, the life insurance proceeds received by the family would be free from all income tax and estate tax.

Source (edited): "http://en.wikipedia.org/wiki/Charitable_remainder_unitrust"

Charitable trust

A **charitable trust** is an irrevocable trust established for charitable purposes, and is a more specific term than "charitable organization".

Charitable trusts may be set up inter vivos, during a donor's life, or as a part of a trust or will at death, as testamentary.

Charitable **remainder** trusts are irrevocable structures established by a donor to provide an income stream to the income beneficiary, while the public charity or private foundation receives the remainder value when the trust terminates. These "split interest" trusts are defined in §664 of the Internal Revenue Code of 1986 as amended and are normally tax-exempt. A section 664 trust makes its payments, either of a fixed amount (charitable remainder annuity trust §664(d)(1)(D)) or a percentage of trust principal (charitable remainder unitrust), to whomever the donor chooses to receive income. *Normally, the donor may claim a charitable income tax deduction, and may not have to pay an immediate capital gains tax when the charitable remainder trust disposes of the appreciated asset and purchases other property as it diversifies its portfolio of trust property. At the end of the trust term, which may be based on either lives or a term of years, the charity receives whatever amount is left in the trust.* Charitable remainder unitrusts (§664(d)(2)(D)- paying a fixed percentage) provide some flexibility in the distribution of income, and may be helpful in retirement planning, while charitable remainder annuity trusts paying a fixed dollar amount are more rigid and usually appeal to much older donors unconcerned about inflation's impact on income distributions who are using cash or marketable securities to fund the trust.

Charitable **lead** trusts make payments, either of a fixed amount (charitable lead annuity trust) or a percentage of trust principal (charitable lead unitrust), to charity during its term. At the end of the trust term, the remainder can either go back to the donor or to heirs named by the donor. The donor may sometimes claim a charitable income tax deduction or a gift/estate tax deduction for making a lead trust gift, depending on the type of a charitable lead trust. Generally, a non-grantor lead trust does not generate a current income tax deduction, but it eliminates the asset (or part of the asset's value) from the donor's estate.

If the trust has qualified under laws such as Internal Revenue Code section 501(c), donations to the trust may be deductible to an individual taxpayer or corporate donor.

United Kingdom

In England and Wales, charitable trusts are a form of express trust dedicated to charitable goals. There are a variety of advantages to charitable trust status, including exception from most forms of tax and freedom for the trustees not found in other types of English trust. To be a valid charitable trust, the organisation must demonstrate both a charitable purpose and a public benefit. Applicable charitable purposes are normally divided into four categories; trusts for the relief of poverty, trusts for the promotion of education, trusts for the promotion of religion and all other types of trust recognised by the law, which includes trusts for the benefit of animals and a locality. There is also a requirement that the trust's purposes benefit the public (or some section of the public), and not simply a group of private individuals.

Such trusts will be invalid in several circumstances; charitable trusts are not allowed to be run for profit, nor can they have purposes that are not charitable (unless these are ancillary to the charitable purpose). In addition, it is considered unacceptable for charitable trusts to campaign for political or legal change, although discussing political issues in a neutral manner is acceptable. Charitable trusts, as with other trusts, are administered by trustees, but there is no relationship between the trustees and the beneficiaries. This results in two things; firstly, the trustees of a charitable trust are far freer to act than other trustees and secondly, beneficiaries cannot bring a court case against the trustees. Rather, the beneficiaries are represented by the Attorney General for England and Wales as a *parens patriae*, who appears on the part of The Crown.

Jurisdiction over charitable disputes is shared equally between the High Court of Justice and the Charity Commission. The Commission, the first port of call, is tasked with regulating and promoting charitable trusts, as well as providing advice and opinions to trustees on administrative matters. Where the Commission feels there has been mismanagement or maladministration, it can sanction the trustees, removing them, appointing new ones or temporarily taking the trust property itself to prevent harm being done. Where there are flaws with a charity, the High Court can administer schemes directing the function of the charity.

India

In India, trusts set up for the social causes and approved by the Income Tax Department, get not only exemption from payment of tax but also the donors to such trusts can deduct the amount of donation to the trust from their taxable income. The legal framework in India recognizes activities including "relief of the poor, education, medical relief, and the advancement of any other object of general public utility" as charitable purposes. Companies formed under Section 25 of the Companies Act, 1956 for promoting charity also receive benefits under law including exemption from various procedural provisions of the Companies Act, either fully or in part, and are also entitled to such other exemptions that the Central Government may accord through its orders.

Iran

Currently, in the Islamic Republic of Iran, religious charitable trusts, or Bonyads make up a substantial part of the country's economy, controlling an estimated 20% of Iran's GDP. Unlike some other Muslim-majority countries, the bonyads receive large and controversial subsidies from the Iranian government.

Source (edited): "http://en.wikipedia.org/wiki/Charitable_trust"

Codicil (will)

A **codicil** is a document that amends, rather than replaces, a previously executed will. Amendments made by a codicil may add or revoke small provisions (e.g., changing executors), or may completely change the majority, or all, of the gifts under the will. Each codicil must conform to the same legal requirements as the original will, such as the signatures of the testator and, typically, two or three (depending on the jurisdiction) disinterested witnesses.

When confronted with testamentary writings executed after the date of the original will, a probate court may need to decipher whether the document is a codicil or a new will. As a rule of thumb, if the second document neither expressly revokes the prior will in its entirety nor supersedes it for all purposes by making a complete disposition of the testator's property, it will be presumed to be a codicil, leaving the validity of the earlier will unchanged with respect to the property whose disposition the codicil does not address.

In some jurisdictions, acting as a witness to the execution of the codicil may invalidate a gift to a beneficiary under the original will. This rule extends such a jurisdiction's "disinterested-witnesses" requirement to those subsequent documents that might affect what a beneficiary receives from the probate process. For example, if a codicil revokes a bequest in a prior will or adds one not in the prior will, it thereby increases or decreases the value of the residuum of the estate, and it thereby affects any residuary beneficiaries' interest in the estate, such that a residuary beneficiary in a will is an interested party with respect to any codicil.

As an alternative to a codicil, a testator may modify a Last Will & Testament by writing a new, dated will revoking any previous wills and codicils. With the advent of word-processors this is now becoming recommended practice (as suggested by the international specialist body in this field, STEP) even for relatively minor changes to avoid the difficulties of interpretation which can arise from a chain of (possibly mutually inconsistent) codicils. Particular difficulties in interpreting chains of codicils arise in jurisdictions such as England and Wales which do not require wills or codicils to be dated (although this is common practice).

In completion of a codicil, a form must be created specifying the modifications to the existing last will and testament. As with a last will and testament, it is necessary to witness amendments to the will since they may override the relevant sections of the original will.

Source (edited): "http://en.wikipedia.

org/wiki/Codicil_(will)"

Constructive trust

A **constructive trust** is an equitable remedy resembling a trust imposed by a court to benefit a party that has been wrongfully deprived of its rights due to either a person obtaining or holding legal right to property which they should not possess due to unjust enrichment or interference . There is considerable debate as to whether a constructive trust is a real trust.

Events generating constructive trusts

In a constructive trust the defendant breaches a duty owed to the plaintiff. The most common such breach is a breach of fiduciary duty. A controversial example is the case of *Attorney-General for Hong Kong v Reid*, in which a senior prosecutor took bribes not to prosecute certain offenders. With the bribe money, he purchased property in New Zealand. His employer, the Attorney-General, sought a declaration that the property was held on constructive trust for it, on the basis of breach of fiduciary duty. The Privy Council awarded a constructive trust. The case is different from *Regal (Hastings)* because there was no interference with a profit-making opportunity that properly belonged to the prosecutor.

This area is highly controversial and may not represent the law in England because of the previous Court of Appeal case of *Lister v Stubbs* which held the opposite, partially because a trust is a very strong remedy that gives proprietary rights to the claimant not enjoyed by the defendant's other creditors. In the event of the defendant's insolvency, the trust assets are untouchable by the general creditors. Supporters of *Lister v Stubbs* suggest that there is no good reason to put the victim of wrongdoing ahead of other creditors of the estate. However, being a Privy Council decision Reid's case did not overrule the decision in Lister v Stubbs, which is still good law in England and Wales, but not in some of its former colonies, such as Australia. There is a tension in English law between Lister and Reid which has been highlighted in the recent cases such as Sinclair Investments (UK) Ltd v Versailles Trade Finance Ltd.

Property interference

In *Foskett v McKeown* a trustee used trust money together with some of his own money to purchase a life insurance policy. Then he committed suicide. The insurance company paid out to his family. The defrauded beneficiaries of the trust sought a declaration that the proceeds were held on constructive trust for them. The House of Lords said that the beneficiaries could choose between either: (a) a constructive trust over the proceeds for the proportion of the life insurance payout purchased with their money; or (b) an equitable lien over the fund for the repayment of that amount.

There is controversy as to what the true basis is of this trust. The House of Lords said that it was to vindicate the plaintiffs' original proprietary rights. However, this reasoning has been criticized as tautologous by some scholars who suggest the better basis is unjust enrichment (see below). This is because there must be a reason why a new property right is created (i.e. the trust) and that must be because otherwise the family would be unjustly enriched by receiving the proceeds of the insurance policy purchased with the beneficiaries' money. "Interference with the plaintiff's property" can justify why the plaintiff can get its property back from a thief, but it cannot explain why new rights are generated in property for which the plaintiff's original property is swapped.

In *Foskett v McKeown*, the plaintiff's original property was an interest in the trust fund. The remedy they obtained was a constructive trust over an insurance payout. It is not obvious why such a new right should be awarded without saying it is to reverse the family's unjust enrichment.

Unjust enrichment

In *Chase Manhattan Bank NA v Israel-British Bank (London) Ltd* one bank paid another bank a large sum of money by mistake (note that the recipient Bank did not do anything wrong - it just received money not owing to it). Goulding J held that the money was held on (constructive) trust for the first bank. The reasoning in this case has been doubted, and in *Westdeutsche Landesbank Girozentrale v Islington London Borough Council* the House of Lords distanced itself from the idea that unjust enrichment raises trusts in the claimant's favour. This remains an area of intense controversy.

These type of trusts are called '"institutional" constructive trusts'. They arise the moment the relevant conduct (breach of duty, unjust enrichment etc) occurs. They can be contrasted with '"remedial" constructive trusts', which arise on the date of judgment as a remedy awarded by the court to do justice in the particular case.

An example is the Australian case *Muschinski v Dodds*. A de facto couple lived in a house owned by the man. They agreed to make improvements to the property by building a pottery shed for the woman to do arts and crafts work in. The woman paid for part of this. They then broke up. The High Court held that the man held the property on constructive trust for himself and the woman in the proportions in which they had contributed to the improvements to the land. This trust did not arise the moment the woman commenced improvements - that conduct did not involve a breach of duty or an unjust enrichment etc. The trust arose at the date of judgment, to do justice in the case.

Remedial constructive trusts do not exist in England and Wales, and the High Court of Australia has also distanced itself from *Muschinski v Dodds* in the later case of *Bathurst City Council v PWC Properties*.

For example, if the defendant steals

$100,000 from the plaintiff and uses that money to buy a house, the court can trace the house back to the plaintiff's money, and can deem the house to be held in trust for the plaintiff; the defendant must then convey title to the house to the plaintiff - even if rising property values had appreciated the value of the house to $120,000 by the time the transaction occurred. If the value of the house had instead *depreciated* to $80,000, the plaintiff could demand a remedy at law (money damages equal to the amount stolen) instead of an equitable remedy.

The situation would be different if the defendant had mixed his own property with that of the plaintiff, for example, adding $50,000 of his own money to the $100,000 stolen from the plaintiff and buying a $150,000 house; or using plaintiff's $100,000 to add a room to defendant's existing house. The constructive trust would still be available, but in the proportions of the contributions, not wholly in the claimant's favour. Alternatively, the claimant could elect for an equitable lien instead, which is like a mortgage over the asset to secure repayment.

Because a constructive trust is an equitable device, the defendant can raise all of the available equitable defenses against it - including unclean hands, laches, detrimental reliance, and undue hardship.

Source (edited): "http://en.wikipedia.org/wiki/Constructive_trust"

Contingent beneficiary

A **contingent beneficiary** on a will or insurance contract is a person who receives the benefits only if predetermined conditions have been met. Until that time, the property interest is regarded as a contingent interest.

In the context of an insurance policy, the condition is generally the death of the insurance contract holder, who is regarded as the primary beneficiary.

Source (edited): "http://en.wikipedia.org/wiki/Contingent_beneficiary"

Corporate trust

In the most basic sense of the term, A **corporate trust** is a trust created by a corporation.

However, the term in the United States is most often used to describe the business activities of many financial services companies and banks that involve acting in a fiduciary capacity for investors in a particular security (ie. stock investors or bond investors). For example, instead of borrowing funds from a bank, a company might borrow funds from the general public in the form of a bond. When a bank lends money to a company, it may often inspect the companies financial statements to ensure that the company follows the rules (known as covenants) of the loan agreement, and may also attempt to negotiate a settlement if the company has problems and stops repaying its loan. In the situation of a public bond issuance (the company borrowing from anyone in the general public who chooses to lend the funds), there would be no one clear person who would be capable to monitor the loans on their own, and the investors would find it difficult to agree and communicate their agreement to the company to settle any problems with the loan repayments. Therefore, they agree as a condition of their bond borrowing to appoint a financial institution, known as a "corporate trustee", to be the responsible party for monitoring compliance with the loan terms, acting in interests of the general public who have purchased the bond. Another aspect of this service, which is often performed by a different party, is the distribution of the repayment from the company to the bondholders, this function is known as a "paying agent". In fact, modern bonds often appoint many different financial institutions to have special roles, based on their area of expertise (such as corporate trustee with an expertise in bankruptcy who is only called in if the company stops paying back the bond). Financial institutions receive fees for their services.

Large corporate trust providers include Citi, Deutsche Bank, The Bank of New York Mellon, Wells Fargo ,One Investment Group and BNP Paribas Securities Services

Reasons

A corporation with little or no financial expertise may seek the services of a financial institution (often a corporation as well) through the creation of a corporate trust. By doing so, they are entrusting the finances of their corporation to that particular financial institution.

Services Offered

Corporate trust providers offer a wide range of services, which include but are not limited to:
- Escrow services
- Public finance
- Project finance
- Corporate finance
- Money market services
- Loan Agency and Administration services
- Structured finance
- Document Custody services

url=http://www.citi.com/transactionservices/home/securities_svcs/agency/index.jsp title=Corporate Trust| date=September 13, 2010| accessdate=2010-09-13| publisher=Citi}}</ref> url=http://www.usbank.com/cgi_w/cfm/commercial_business/products_and_services/corp_trust/comm_bus_corp_trust_ps.cfm%7C title=Corporate Trust| date=January 1, 2007| accessdate=2007-03-10| publisher=U.S. Bancorp}}</ref>

Source (edited): "http://en.wikipedia.org/wiki/Corporate_trust"

Credible witness

In the law of evidence, a **credible witness** is a person making testimony in a court or other tribunal, or acting otherwise as a witness, whose credibility is unimpeachable. A witness may have more or less credibility, or no credibility at all. In the common law system, the term 'credible witness' may be used generally, to refer to testimony, or for the witnessing of certain documents.

A credible witness is "competent to give evidence, and is worthy of belief."

Testifying in court

In a wide variety of cases that use the rules of evidence, testimony must be given by credible witnesses.

In Scottish law, a credible witness is one "whose credibility commends itself to the presiding magistrate ... the trustworthiness" of whom is good.

In English law, a credible witness is one who is *not* "speaking from hearsay." In English:
Credible seems here to be used in the way that people have employed it ever since it appeared in the English language in the fourteenth century: of something that is convincing or is capable of being believed. (It came from Latin *credibilis*, worthy of being believed, from the verb *credere*, to believe.)
—Michael Quinion (*italics in original*)
In the United States, such a witness is "more than likely to be true based on his/her experience, knowledge, training and appearance of honesty and forthrightness...." Some factors for determining the credibility of testimony in U.S. courts include: (1) the witness had personal knowledge, (2) he or she was actually present at the scene, (3) the witness paid attention at the scene, and (4) he or she told the whole truth. The probative value of a credible witness is *not* a required element in any criminal case. However, credibility is always a factor in civil cases. The number of witnesses does *not* matter for credibility: "The question for the jury is not which side has more witnesses, but what testimony they believe." Only the "quality or power" of believability matters.

In Australian law, the reliability of every witness in a criminal case must be taken into account.

Witnessing of Wills and documents

Credible witnesses must be used to give meaning or existence to certain types of documents, such as a Last will and testament, codicil, apostille, deposition, interrogatories, certified document, or government record.

For example, in most common law jurisdictions, two or three witnesses must sign their names to the Will at the attestation clause below the testimonium clause that is executed by the testator. The exact number of witnesses depend on the state or local law. Under the English Statute of Wills of 1540, it was three witnesses. Under modern New York law, only two witnesses are required. In Canada, a credible witness to a Will "means a witness not incapacitated by mental inbecility (sic), interest or crime."

For authentication of a document, a credible witness is needed, whose major duty is identify to a notary public who signed the document.

Source (edited): "http://en.wikipedia.org/wiki/Credible_witness"

Crummey trust

In the United States a **Crummey trust** (named for the first person to use such a structure) is a trust for the benefit of a minor into which gifts are made in a manner qualifying them for exclusion from the unified gift and estate tax.

Normally, gifts to minors are subject to parental / guardian control until the age of majority. In order to delay the transfer of control beyond the age of 18, the funds must be placed in trust. However, the annual gift exclusion ($13,000 as of 2009) from the gift tax is only available for gifts of so-called *current interests*. Normally, a gift into a trust that comes under control of the beneficiary at a future date does not constitute a current interest.

A Crummey trust achieves the desired treatment by offering the recipient a window of time (often 30 days) to take immediate control of the gift. (The control offered only applies to the current gift--by assumption, an amount no greater than the annual exclusion amount--not the entire trust.) If the recipient fails to do so during that window, the gift becomes part of the trust, and is subject to the trust's distribution conditions. However, since the recipient had the opportunity to receive the funds outside of the trust, the gift is deemed to be a current interest, subjecting it to the annual exclusion.

The expectation of future annual gifts under the same mechanism (or the expectation of the withholding of such future gifts if the recipient exerts control over the gift) may motivate the recipient to relinquish control of the funds into the trust.

Use in life insurance trusts

In addition, similar provisions are often added to life insurance trusts or "ILITs" in order to maintain the annual gift tax exclusion by funding the ILIT using Crummey powers. This way additional gifts and beneficiaries can be taken advantage of to fund the life insurance trust. If executed properly the beneficia-

Cy-près doctrine

The **cy-près doctrine** (pronounced /ˌsiːˈpreɪ/ *see-pray*) is a legal doctrine that first arose in courts of equity. The term can be translated (from old Norman French to English) as "as near as possible" or "as near as may be." The doctrine originated in the law of charitable trusts, but has been applied in the context of class action settlements in the United States.

When the original objective of the settlor or the testator became impossible, impracticable, or illegal to perform, the cy-près doctrine allows the court to amend the terms of the charitable trust as closely as possible to the original intention of the testator or settlor, to prevent the trust from failing.

A typical example would be a trust established to turn public opinion against slavery. Once slavery was abolished, the trust's stated purpose had become impossible to effect. The court will then modify the particular purpose of the trust, leaving it within the same general charitable purpose.

In *Jackson v. Phillips*, the testator bequeathed to trustees money to be used to "create a public sentiment that will put an end to negro slavery in this country." Thereafter, slavery was abolished by the Thirteenth Amendment to the United States Constitution. The funds were nevertheless applied cy-près to the "use of necessitous persons of African descent in the city of Boston and its vicinity."

Application in England and Wales

The cy-près doctrine applied in England and Wales limited the strictness of the rules of mortmain under which property disposed of otherwise than to a legal heir was subject to forfeiture in certain circumstances. Following abolition of mortmain, the modern application of the cy-près doctrine has predominantly occurred in relation to charities as these are the most important trusts for a general purpose (not private benefit) permitted under English law.

The Charity Commission for England and Wales has the statutory power to apply the cy-près doctrine on behalf of a charity where, for example, no trustees remain in a charity or the necessary mandate cannot be agreed. These powers extend to a corporate charity or unincorporated association (which the common law rules may not cover). Similar powers apply to the equivalent bodies in Northern Ireland and Scotland. The cy-près doctrine will not be applied where a charity has alternative powers to redirect its funds under its constitution.

In jurisdictions which have retained the English cy-près doctrine but do not have an equivalent state body to the Charity Commission (or in relation to foreign charities' assets in the United Kingdom), charity trustees may seek the approval of the Court to their entry into cy-près arrangements to avoid later accusations of breach of trust.

Model Code

In the United States there is a Uniform Trust Code ("UTC"), which is a model code that various jurisdictions (e.g. states) may adopt by statute.

The UTC codifies that cy-près applies only to charitable trusts where the original particular purpose of the trust has become impossible or impracticable, and the terms of the trust do not specify what is to happen in such a situation.

The UTC provides, in part, that "if a particular charitable purpose becomes unlawful, impracticable, impossible to achieve, or wasteful ... the court may apply cy-près to modify or terminate the trust ... in a manner consistent with the settlor's charitable purposes."

However, the UTC further provides that the court may not apply cy-près where "[a] provision in the terms of a charitable trust ... would result in distribution of the trust property to a non-charitable beneficiary" and also that cy-près may not be used to violate the rule against perpetuities.

The UTC also contains a cy-près rule for noncharitable trusts. It provides that "[t]he court may modify the administrative or dispositive terms of a trust or terminate the trust if, because of circumstances not anticipated by the settlor, modification or termination will further the purposes of the trust." This power over trusts other than charitable trusts is not found in English law, or in most common law jurisdictions outside the United States.

United States class actions

In 1986, the California Supreme Court endorsed cy-près mechanisms in class action settlements, and other American courts followed. Cy-près mechanisms allow money to be used to promote the interests of class members, rather than reverting to a defendant, which could be seen as a windfall to a defendant charged with breaking the law. Judge Richard Posner has argued that the term is a misnomer in the class action context, because cy-près awards serve a punitive effect. Some commentators have criticized the use of cy-près settlements; the American Law Institute's Draft of the Principles of the Law of Aggregate Litigation proposes limiting cy-près to "circumstances in which direct distribution to individual class members is not economically feasible, or where funds remain after class members are given a full opportunity to make a claim."

Source (edited): "http://en.wikipedia.org/wiki/Cy-pr%C3%A8s_doctrine"

Delaware statutory trust

A **Delaware statutory trust** (DST) is a legally recognized trust that is set up for the purpose of business, but not necessarily in the State of Delaware. It may also be referred to as an **Unincorporated Business Trust** or **UBO**.

Delaware statutory trusts are formed as private governing agreements under which either a) property (real, tangible, and intangible) is held, managed, administered, invested and/or operated, or b) business or professional activities for profit are carried on by a trustee(s) for the benefit of the trustor who is entitled to a beneficial interest in the trust property.

History

The concept for business trusts, especially those that involve the holding of property, dates back as early as 16th century English Common Law. In Delaware, it was not until 1947 that Common Law began recognizing statutory trusts. No legal recognition of statutory trusts existed until the passage of the **Delaware Statutory Trust Act (DSTA), 12 Del. C. 3801 et. Seq.**, in 1988. Under The Act, developed on the premise of trust law, statutory trusts were now recognized as their own legal entity, separate from their trustee(s), offering freedom from the corporate law template. Within the tradition of trust law, freedom of contract allows the trustee(s) to structure their entity in a way that is most beneficial to the relationship of all parties and their expertise, while offering liability protection similar to that of a Limited liability company or Partnership. Since the year 2000, Delaware statutory trusts have increasingly been used as a form of tax deferral, asset protection, and balance sheet advantages in real estate, securitization, mezzanine financing, Real estate investment trusts (REITs), and mutual funds. Massachusetts, another state that has trust law, refers to its legal entity as a Massachusetts business trust. Most states, however, still rely on Common Law to oversee the trusts within their jurisdiction.

Formation requirements

Delaware Certificate of Statutory Trust form & official State Seal.

The formation of a Delaware statutory trust is relatively simple and inexpensive, when compared to that of the more complex filings of other entity types. To form a statutory trust, a private trust agreement must be developed by all involved parties to ensure that individual interests are protected. The private trust agreement need not be shown to any official of the State. Once the agreement is completed, a Certificate of Trust can be obtained from the Delaware Division of Corporations and completed. The signatures of the trustee(s) involved are then required, followed by submission of the forms to the Division of Corporations, along with a one-time $200 processing fee. If the statutory trust is, or will become, a registered investment company, it must maintain a registered agent and a registered office within the State of Delaware. If no desire for the statutory trust to be an investment company exists, the only remaining requirement is that it must have at least one trustee who resides in, or has a principal place of business within the State of Delaware.

Legal and tax implications

Federal/1031 Exchange

On August 16, 2004 **Internal Revenue Bulletin 2004-33** was published in reference to **Rev. Rul. 2004-86**. This involved a Delaware Statutory Trust that came before the Internal Revenue Service (IRS) and Treasury Department, who offered a ruling on the following two issues:

- "[H]ow is a Delaware statutory trust, described in **Del. Code Ann. title 12, §§ 3801 - 3824**, classified for federal tax purposes?"
"The Delaware statutory trust described above is an investment trust, under **§ 301.7701-4(c)**, that will be classified as a trust for federal tax purposes."
- "[M]ay a taxpayer exchange real property for an interest in a Delaware statutory trust without recognition of gain or loss under **§ 1031** of the Internal Revenue Code?"
"A taxpayer may exchange real property for an interest in the Delaware statutory trust described above without recognition of gain or loss under **§ 1031**, if the other requirements of **§ 1031** are satisfied."

These holdings of the Federal Government offered a clearer notion that Delaware statutory trusts are legal entities, separate from their trustee(s), offering them limited liability. In addition, Delaware statutory trusts were shown to be considered a trust for federal tax purposes, making them a pass through entity that mitigates taxation for their trustee(s). The second holding offers the opinion that real property, being held under a Delaware statutory trust, is eligible to use a 1031 exchange, without the recognition of gain or loss, as long as the following seven restrictions are met:

- Once the offering is closed, there can be no future contributions to the DST by either current or new beneficiaries.
- The trustee cannot renegotiate the terms of the existing loans and cannot borrow any new funds from any party, unless a loan default exists as a result of a tenant bankruptcy or insolvency.
- The trustee cannot reinvest the proceeds from the sale of its real estate.

- The trustee is limited to making capital expenditures with respect to the property for normal repair and maintenance, minor nonstructural capital improvements, and those required by law.
- Any reserves or cash held between distribution dates can only be invested in short-term debt obligations.
- All cash, other than necessary reserves, must be distributed on a current basis.
- The trustee cannot enter into new leases, or renegotiate the current leases unless there is a need due to a tenant bankruptcy or insolvency.

Local

As an entity that was created within the boundaries of Delaware and is written into the Delaware state charter, Title 12 Chapter 38, there is no question as to where the state stands on the backing of the Delaware statutory trust. Limited liability is offered for DSTs, affording each trustee the benefit of personal asset protection. DSTs can be structured as a pass through entity, so that any income will go straight to each individual trustee's Form 1040 and state's tax returns, thus avoiding income tax at the entity level.

Many say that the features of a Delaware statutory trust read like a holiday wish list when it comes to business entities. These features include:
- liability protection for the trustee(s)
- asset protection for the beneficial owner
- delegation of management
- low minimum investment requirements
- cash investors may complete a 1031 exchange upon sale
- one-time registration
- no need for annual meetings
- no franchise tax
- no limit on the number of investors
- availability of indemnification
- recognition of separate series

Source (edited): "http://en.wikipedia.org/wiki/Delaware_statutory_trust"

Disclaimer of interest

Disclaimer of interest (also called a **renunciation**), in the law of inheritance, wills and trusts, is a term that describes an attempt by a person to renounce their legal right to benefit from an inheritance (either under a will or through intestacy) or through a trust.

There are a number of reasons why a person might wish to avoid an inheritance, particularly if the proceeds would only go to their creditors, or if it would drastically affect their income tax liabilities. Under the common law, a person who disclaimed their interest would be treated as though they had died before the trust or will came into effect. This was a sensible option if the disclaiming party was an heir by descent, whose own children would then take in his place and without the imposition of a gift tax.

The disclaimer must be in writing and submitted to the court overseeing the disposition of the estate within a legally specified time period, which is usually nine months after the death of the person from whom the disclaiming party stands to inherit, or twelve months after the creation of a trust by a living person. An affidavit may be required in which the disclaiming party must swear that he has not received any consideration (i.e., compensation) for the disclaimer. The disclaimer must also occur before the disclaiming party has enjoyed any benefits of the trust or inheritance. Many jurisdictions now have statutes that prohibit a disclaimer when the individual is insolvent or receiving certain public benefits due to low income.

A disclaimer of interest is irrevocable. It must be a complete, and not a partial disclaimer. Such a disclaimer can be made by a legal guardian on behalf of a person who lacks the capacity to make the disclaimer themselves, but this usually requires the finding by a court that the disclaimer is in the ward's best interest.

Disclaimers and Deeds of Variation: England and Wales

In England and Wales a disclaimer is likewise irrevocable and covers the entire testamentary gift. It may be a unilateral act but should be communicated in writing to the persons administering the estate. It does not need to be registered with the court; the persons administering the estate are obliged to retain the communication as they may be required to provide an account to the court of their actions in the administration.

A similar effect to a disclaimer (including for inheritance tax and capital gains tax purposes) can be achieved with a greater degree of flexibility through the use of a **deed of variation** (or **deed of family arrangement**). A person or persons due to inherit property may enter into such a deed with the personal representatives (executors or administrators of an intestate estate) and redirect property due to the persons entering into the deed to whomsoever they wish. However one cannot vary one's entitlement under a deed of variation! A deed of variation may be revocable or irrevocable. Disclaimers and deeds of variation may be overturned by the bankruptcy court and assets traced.

Disclaimer of other interests

In addition to the more typical disclaimer under wills, an individual may also be able to disclaim his interest as the beneficiary of a life insurance policy or employee benefit plans. It may also apply to concurrent interests in real property that automatically transfer after death by operation of law rather than by the rules of inheritance (such as joint tenancies or tenancies by the entirety).

Source (edited): "http://en.wikipedia.org/wiki/Disclaimer_of_interest"

Discounted gift trust

A **Discounted Gift Trust** (DGT) is a type of UK trust arrangement usually set up in connection with an investment in either an onshore or offshore investment bond (insurance bond). It allows the gifting of a lump sum into a trust whilst retaining a life-long 'income' from that money (technically withdrawals of capital), with the over-arching aim of reducing the eventual IHT (inheritance tax) bill on death.

The name Discounted Gift Trust was coined by the life insurance industry. In strict legal terms, it is a type of Carve Out Trust.

Furthermore, provided the settlor (the person making the gift into the trust) is in reasonable health, a calculation is made as to the likely total amount of 'income' that will be paid back to them by the trustees. This "bag of rights", normally known as the "discount", is deemed to be retained by the client. The remainder will be treated like any other gift into trust (a chargeable transfer (CT) in the case of a discretionary trust, or a potentially exempt transfer (PET) for a bare trust), leaving the IHT net after 7 years (or 14 years in some cases).

In the event of the settlor dying within seven years, this retained "bag of rights" should in theory be returned to their personal representatives. However, the accepted IHT treatment, as has been tested many times and accepted by HMRC, is that this right to an income for life has no value once the settlor has died, and **therefore no money has to be returned**.

The effect is that the discount is deemed to leave their estate on day one of settlement of monies into the trust- the remainder will be treated like any other gift into trust and brought back into calculations if death occurs within 7 (in some cases 14) years. In effect, there is an **immediate IHT reduction** upon creation of a discounted gift trust

A discounted gift trust is a very powerful planning tool for anyone in later life whose intentions are to draw income from their investments throughout their lifetime, then to pass on the remainder to their beneficiaries, as it allows for this and helps to reduce the amount of Inheritance Tax that might eventually have to be paid.

Example

This is a simplified example:

Mr Smith gifts £100,000 into a discounted gift trust.

He selects £4,000 per year 'income' (withdrawals) for life.

Based on his age and gender and on HMRC guidelines (drafted with reference to mortality tables), his life expectancy is deemed to be 15 years.

£4,000 x 15 = £60,000 is the discount, or the amount of the gift which has technically been 'carved out' and retained (in reality this would be lowered a little to reflect the real cost of providing £4,000 over fifteen years assuming there is some return on capital held).

If he dies within seven years:

- The £40,000 is brought back into the calculation for inheritance tax, reducing his nil rate band by this amount
- The value of the "right to withdrawals for life", which started as £60,000, is now deemed to be nil (as he is dead). Thus, the £60,000 does not come back into play in the IHT calculation.

Note - importantly - that Mr Smith will have no future access to any of the £100,000 capital - rather his only benefit will be the £4,000 per annum 'income'. Also, this 'income' is dependent on there being sufficient capital remaining in the investment so in this example 4% per annum net growth is needed just to stand still.

Source (edited): "http://en.wikipedia.org/wiki/Discounted_gift_trust"

Discretionary trust

In British and Canadian law, a **discretionary trust** is a trust where the beneficiaries and/or their entitlements to the trust fund are not fixed, but are determined by the criteria set out in the trust instrument by the settlor. It is sometimes referred to as a **family trust** in Australia. Where the discretionary trust is a testamentary trust, it is common for the settlor to leave a letter of wishes for the trustees to guide them as to the settlor's wishes in the exercise of their discretion. Letters of wishes are not legally binding documents.

Discretionary trusts can only arise as express trusts. It is not possible for a constructive trust or a resulting trust to arise as a discretionary trust.

Discretionary trusts can be discretionary in two respects. First, the trustees usually have the power to determine which beneficiaries (from within the class) will receive payments from the trust. Second, trustees can select the amount of trust property that the beneficiary receives. Although most discretionary trusts allow both types of discretion, either can be allowed on its own. It is permissible in most legal systems for a trust to have a fixed number of beneficiaries and for the trustees to have discretion as to how much each beneficiary receives, or to have a class of beneficiaries from whom they could select members, but provide that the amount to be provided is fixed. Most well-drafted trust instruments also provide for a power to add or exclude beneficiaries from the class; this allows the trustees greater flexibility to deal with changes in circumstances (and, in particular, changes in the revenue laws of the applicable jurisdiction).

Characteristically, discretionary trusts provide for a discretionary distribution of income only, but in some cases the trustees also have a power of appointment with respect to the capital in the trust, i.e. the corpus.

Discretionary trusts are usually subdivided into two types:

- *exhaustive*, where the trustees must distribute all income accruing to the trust fund; and
- *non-exhaustive*, where the trustees have a power to accumulate income.

Analysis

In a fixed trust the beneficiary has a specific proprietary right in relation to the trust fund. Each beneficiary of a discretionary trust, in contrast, is dependent upon the trustees to exercise their power of selection favourably. In *Gartside v IRC* AC 553 the Inland Revenue argued that as each beneficiary might be entitled to income from the trust fund, each should be charged as if he were entitled to the whole of the fund. Perhaps unsurprisingly, the House of Lords rejected this argument. Even where there is a sole member of the class remaining, so long as there is a possibility that another member of the class could come into existence, that member is not considered a sole beneficiary for purposes of taxation liability.

Gartside v IRC concerned a non-exhaustive discretionary trust; however, in *Re Weir's Settlement* 1 Ch 657 and *Sainsbury v IRC* Ch 712, the courts held that the same analysis was equally applicable to exhaustive discretionary trusts.

The rights of individual beneficiaries under a discretionary trust being uncertain, it was open to question to what extent the beneficiaries of a discretionary trust (if all of adult age and sound mind) could utilise the rule in *Saunders v Vautier*. It had been held that beneficiaries under a discretionary trust could do so, although that authority was decided pre-*McPhail v Doulton*, where to be valid the trustees had to be able to draw up a "complete list" of beneficiaries. That notwithstanding, leading commentators have suggested that provided all of the beneficiaries could be ascertained, they should still retain the right to terminate the trust under the rule, so long as it is an exhaustive discretionary trust.

Duties

The ordinary correlation between beneficiaries' rights and trustees' duties which arises in fixed trusts is absent in discretionary trusts. Although there are clearly duties, it is less clear whether there are any correlating rights. However, it seems clear that the trustees' duty is limited to (a) determining whether to exercise their discretion, and (b) exercising their discretion lawfully under the terms of the trust. Whilst the beneficiaries will have standing to sue the trustees for failing to fulfill their duties, it is not clear that they would gain by such action.

In *Re Locker's Settlement* 1 WLR 1323 the trustees of a discretionary trust did not make any distributions for a number of years based upon the expressed wishes of the settlor. The trust then fell dormant, and after several more years, the trustees sought directions. The court held that their discretionary powers continued, and that they should exercise it in respect of the dormant years now as they should have done at the time. The court reaffirmed that if trustees refuse to distribute income, or refuse to exercise their discretion, although the court could not compel it be exercised in a particular manner, it could order that the trustees be replaced.

The position with a duty to consider exercising discretion in non-exhaustive discretionary trusts is more complicated, as the duty to exercise discretion can be satisfied by deciding to accumulate.

Purposes

Discretionary trusts still serve a useful function, despite their original source of popularity (tax savings) having diminished in most countries. They still continue to be used for these reasons, among others:

- to protect improvident beneficiaries against creditors - as the beneficiary has no claim to any specific part of the trust fund, none of the trust fund is vulnerable to attachment by the trustee in bankruptcy of any beneficiary
- to exercise control over young or improvident beneficiaries
- to create flexibility to react to changes in circumstances
- in certain jurisdictions, a discretionary trust can be used to protect family assets from forming part of any divorce settlement.

Popularity and decline

The popularity of discretionary trusts rose sharply after the decision of the House of Lords in *McPhail v Doulton* AC 424 where Lord Wilberforce restated the test for certainty of objects in connection with discretionary trusts. Previously, it had been understood that for the trust to be valid, the trustees had to be able to draw up a "complete list" of all the possible beneficiaries, and if they could not do so, the trust was void. But Lord Wilberforce held that provided it could be said of any person whether they were "in or out" of the class, as described by the settlor, the trust would be valid.

Because under a discretionary trust, no one beneficiary could be said to have title to any trust assets prior to a distribution, this made discretionary trusts a powerful weapon for tax planners. Inevitably, the surge in popularity has led to a legislative response in most jurisdictions, thus in many countries there are now considerable tax disadvantages to discretionary trusts, which has predictably hampered their use outside the scope of charitable trusts.

Source (edited): "http://en.wikipedia.org/wiki/Discretionary_trust"

Dishonest assistance

Dishonest assistance, or knowing assistance, is a type of third party liability under trust law. It is usually seen as one of two liabilities established in *Barnes v Addy*, the other one being knowing receipt. To be liable for dishonest assistance, there must be a breach of trust or fiduciary duty by someone other than the defendant, the defendant must have helped that person in the breach, and the defendant must have a dishonest state of mind. The liability itself is well established, but the mental element of dishonesty is subject to considerable controversy which sprang from the House of Lords case *Twinsectra Ltd v Yardley*. It is a common belief that dishonest or knowing assistance originates from Lord Selbourne's judgment in *Barnes v Addy*:

[S]trangers are not to be made constructive trustees merely because they act as the agents of trustees in transactions, … unless those agents received and become chargeable with some part of the trust property, or unless they assist with knowledge in a dishonest and fraudulent design on the part of the trustees.

As can be seen, the judgment laid down two heads of liability: one based on receipt of trust property (knowing receipt) and the other on assisting with knowledge in a dishonest and fraudulent design (knowing assistance).

Lord Selbourne's statement has been heavily criticized, particularly on the requirement that the defaulting fiduciary / trustee has to be dishonest or fraudulent. A commentator noted that *Fyler v Fyler* and *AG v The Corporation of Leicester*, two decisions on knowing assistance in the 1840s which predated *Barnes v Addy*, did not mention the moral quality of the breach induced or assisted at all.

Another debate was regarding the type of knowledge that would suffice to impose liability. Peter Gibson J in *Baden v Société Générale* identified 5 categories of knowledge which was subject to much debate and led the courts into "tortuous convolutions".

Nature

Secondary

The prevalent view is that liability for dishonest assistance is secondary. Therefore, the liability of the assistant is premised on that of the defaulting fiduciary / trustee and he/she will be jointly and severally liable with the fiduciary / trustee whom he/she assisted. However, Charles Mitchell recognized possible difficulties with this categorization:

firstly, secondary liability means that the dishonest assistant will be liable for the disgorgement gains of the defaulting fiduciary / trustee, while the fiduciary / trustee will not be liable for secret profits of the dishonest assistant; secondly, the assessment of exemplary damages against the dishonest assistant will be based on that of the fiduciary / trustee which can be undesirable.

There are also views that liability for dishonest assistance should be primary. However, such views have yet to receive judicial endorsement.

Constructive trusteeship

Dishonest assistants have been frequently described by courts as constructive trustees. However, such classification is not without difficulty: dishonest assistance is often imposed even if there is no obviously identifiable property subject to the trust; also, in many cases of dishonest assistance property has reached the hands of innocent third parties who may not be under any obligation to restore it. Some commentators have sought to explain this on the basis that there is a type of constructive trust which can arise even if there is no identifiable trust property.

However, the prevalent view is that dishonest assistance is a personal liability that does not result in an imposition of constructive trust. This view has the support of Lord Millett who remarked in *Dubai Aluminium Co v Salaam*:

" Equity gives relief against fraud by making any person sufficiently implicated in the fraud accountable in equity. In such a case he is traditionally (and I have suggested unfortunately) described as a 'constructive trustee' and is said to be 'liable to account as a constructive trustee'. But he is not in fact a trustee at all, even though he may be liable to account as if he were. He never claims to assume the position of trustee on behalf of others, and he may be liable without ever receiving or handling the trust proper- " ty... In this second class of case the expressions 'constructive trust' and 'constructive trustee' create a trap... The expressions are nothing more than a formula for equitable relief'... I think we should now discard the words 'accountable as constructive trustee' in this context and substitute the words 'accountable in equity'.

Elements

Breach of trust

The trustee or fiduciary of the claimant must be liable for a breach of trust or fiduciary duty. It is sufficient if the trust in question is a resulting trust or constructive trust.

Previously, it was thought that the dishonest assistant would not be liable unless the defaulting trustee was also dishonest or fraudulent, but *Royal Brunei Airlines v Tan* confirmed that there is no such requirement in English law. However, the requirement of dishonest or fraudulent design on the part of the defaulting fiduciary / trustee is still part of the law in Australia.

Whether a breach of trust should be required at all has been queried by a commentator, since no breach is required for the analogous tort of interference with contractual relations and if the fiduciary reasonably relies on the probity and competence of the dishonest assistant, the claimant would be left with no remedy.

Assistance by defendant

This element is a question of fact as to whether the defendant has been accessory to the misfeasance or breach of trust in question.

Dishonesty

The test

In the seminal case *Royal Brunei Airlines v Tan*, Royal Brunei Airlines appointed Borneo Leisure Travel ('BLT') to act in Sabah and Sarawak as its general travel agent. The arrangement constituted BLT a trustee for the airline of the money it received from the sale of passenger and cargo transportation. The money received by BLT on behalf of the airline was paid into BLT's ordinary current account. Any balance in its current account in excess of a stated amount was transferred at times to a fixed deposit account of Mr. Tan, who was BLT's managing director and principal shareholder. BLT was required to pay the airline within 30 days, but at times from 1988 onwards, it was in arrears. In August 1992, the airline terminated the agreement and subsequently claimed against Mr. Tan in respect of the unpaid money.

Historically in England, liability would be imposed on persons who assisted in a breach of trust or fiduciary duty "with knowledge". Hence its previous name of "knowing assistance". It should be noted that knowledge is still the cornerstone of the liability in Australia and Canada.

The modern English terminology emerged in *Royal Brunei Airlines v Tan* in which the Privy Council rejected knowledge as an element of the liability and replaced it with a requirement for dishonesty. After opting for the imposition of fault-based liability, Lord Nicholls said,

" Drawing the threads together, their Lordships' overall conclusion is that dishonesty is a necessary ingredient of accessory liability. It is also a sufficient ingredient. A liability in equity to make good resulting loss attaches to a person who dishonestly procures or assists in a breach of trust or fiduciary obligation. It is not necessary that, in addition, the trustee or fiduciary was acting dishonestly...'Knowingly' is better avoided as a defining ingredient of the principle...

His Lordship went on to articulate a test for dishonesty, which is generally perceived to be an objective test with some subjective characteristics:

" Whatever may be the position in some criminal or other contexts (see, for instance, *R v Ghosh*), in the context of the accessory liability principle acting dishonestly, or with a lack of probity, which is synonymous, means simply not acting as an honest person would in the circumstances. This is an objective standard. At first sight this may seem surprising. Honesty has a connotation of subjectivity, as distinct from the objectivity of negligence. Honesty, indeed, does have a strong subjective element in that it is a description of a type of conduct assessed in the light of what a person actually knew at the time, as distinct from what a reasonable person would have known or appreciated. Further, honesty and its counterpart dishonesty are mostly concerned with advertent conduct, not inadvertent conduct. Carelessness is not dishonesty. Thus for the most part dishonesty is to be equated with conscious impropriety. However, these subjective characteristics of honesty do not mean that individuals are free to set their own standards of honesty in particular circumstances. The standard of what constitutes honest conduct is not subjective. Honesty is not an optional scale, with higher or lower values according to the moral standards of each individual. If a person knowingly appropriates another's property, he will not escape a finding of dishonesty simply because he sees nothing wrong in such behaviour.

Hence, the conduct of the defendant is to be assessed according to an objective standard of dishonesty in light of the actual knowledge of the defendant. When undertaking such exercise, the court will also have regard to personal attributes of the defendant, such as his experience and intelligence, and the reason why he acted as he did. His Lordship then gave a few examples of dishonesty, such as deception, knowingly taking the property of others, participation in a transaction in light of knowledge that it involves a misapplication of trust assets, willful blindness etc.

The issue was later reconsidered in *Twinsectra Ltd v Yardley* in the House of Lords, which unfortunately returned a different answer. The majority in that case held that Lord Nicholls in *Royal Brunei* meant to say that, for a person to be held liable as an accessory to a breach of trust, he had to have acted dishonestly by the ordinary standards of reasonable and honest people and have been himself aware that by those standards he was acting dishonestly. This became known as the "combined test", namely a standard which requires both subjective and objective states of mind. Lord Hutton's reason for adopting the combined test is that a finding by a judge that a defendant has been dishonest is a grave finding, and it is particularly grave against a professional man. Therefore, in his view, a higher level of blameworthiness is required to impose liability in dishonest assistance.

Lord Millett delivered a dissenting judgment, maintaining that *Royal*

Brunei decided that the test of dishonesty is objective, although account must be taken of subjective considerations such as the defendant's experience and intelligence and his actual state of knowledge at the relevant time. But it is not necessary that he should actually have appreciated that he was acting dishonestly; it is sufficient that he was. The question is whether an honest person would appreciate that what he was doing was wrong or improper, not whether the defendant himself actually appreciated this. His Lordship gave 3 reasons for this:

- Consciousness of wrongdoing is an aspect of *mens rea* and an appropriate condition of criminal liability: it is not an appropriate condition of civil liability.
- The objective test is in accordance with *Barnes v Addy* and the traditional doctrine.
- The claim for "knowing assistance" is the equitable counterpart of the economic torts. These are intentional torts; negligence is not sufficient and dishonesty is not necessary. Liability depends on knowledge. A requirement of subjective dishonesty introduces an unnecessary and unjustified distinction between the elements of the equitable claim and those of the tort of wrongful interference with the performance of a contract.

What Lord Hutton said in *Twinsectra* has now been reinterpreted and restated by the Privy Council in *Barlow Clowes International v Eurotrust International*. In that case, Lord Hoffmann reaffirmed the objective test, i.e. the one maintained by Lord Millett in *Twinsectra*, as the correct test for dishonesty. His Lordship interpreted Lord Hutton's reference to 'what he knows would offend normally acceptable standards of honest conduct' as meaning only that his knowledge of the transaction had to be such as to render his participation contrary to normally acceptable standards of honest conduct. His Lordship said that it is no necessary for the defendant to have reflections what those normally acceptable standards of honest conduct were.

Subsequently, the lower English courts have adopted the test laid down in *Barlow Clowes*, although theoretically it is not open to them to refuse to follow the House of Lords decision in *Twinsectra*. In *Abou-Rahmah v Abacha* before the English Court of Appeal, Arden LJ endorsed *Barlow Clowes* as representing the current English law for 4 reasons:

- *Barlow Clowes* did not require a departure from *Twinsectra*, but merely give guidance as to the proper interpretation to be given to *Twinsectra* as a matter of English law.
- *Barlow Clowes* drew no distinction between the law of Isle of Man and English law
- Members of the Privy Council in *Barlow Clowes* were all member of House of Lords, and included 2 members of the majority from *Twinsectra*. The House of Lords is unlikely to come to a different view as to the proper interpretation of *Twinsectra*.
- There are no overriding reasons why in the context of civil liability (as opposed to criminal liability) the law should take account of the defendant's subjective views of the morality of his actions.

However, the other two judges, Pill LJ and Rix LJ, refused to get drawn into the controversy as it was unnecessary to decide on the proper test for dishonesty to dispose of the appeal. In fact, some commentators have suggested that Pill LJ seems to support the combined test in *Twinsectra*, although he did not make it explicit.

In *AG of Zambia v Meer Care & Desai*, Peter Smith J at the Chancery Division opined that the question of objective/subjective test is an over elaboration and endorsed the test set out in *Royal Brunei*, which he regards as another way of posing the jury question "was the defendant dishonest". He disagreed with Lord Hutton's view in Twinsectra that Lord Millett was articulating a purely objective test. He also regarded Lord Hutton's justification for the combined test, that dishonesty is a grave finding against professionals, as erroneous since it is no less grave for a non profession to be accused of dishonesty and there had been plenty of dishonest professionals.

The test in *Royal Brunei* and *Barlow Clowes* has been accepted as the law in New Zealand in the New Zealand Court of Appeal case *US International Marketing Ltd v National Bank of NZ Ltd*. However, one of the three judges (Tipping J) applied a reasonable person test as opposed to the honest person test in determining the question of dishonesty.

What knowledge constitutes dishonesty

In *Agip (Africa) Ltd v Jackson* and *Twinsectra v Yardley*, Lord Millett remarked that it is not necessary the dishonest assistant should be aware of the identity of the victim or nature of the breach and knowledge that the money is not at the free disposal of the assisted person suffices to impose liability. Similarly, in *Barlow Clowes*, Lord Hoffmann said it is unnecessary for the dishonest assistant to know of the existence of breach or the facts; it is enough if he /she knows or suspects he is assisting in misappropriation of money without knowing money is held on trust.

What level of suspicion suffice to trigger the liability continues to trouble the courts. In *Abou-Rahmah*, Arden LJ opined that the dishonest assistant is not dishonest if he only has general suspicions about impropriety as opposed to particular suspicions regarding specific transactions. However, Rix LJ thought otherwise and said that general suspicion is enough to trigger the liability.

Relationship with knowing receipt

Traditionally, dishonest assistance and knowing receipt are seen as two distinct heads of liability: one is fault based, while the other is receipt based. However, there has been academic discussion as to whether they can be grouped together. Charles Mitchell proposes that if we adopt Peter Birk's view regarding knowing receipt (that knowing receipt can be based on unjust enrichment as well as fault), there is a strong case for treating liability for dishonest assistance and fault-based knowing receipt as aspects of a single equitable wrong of interfering with another's equitable rights – a wrong he called "equitable conversion". Furthermore, Lord Nicholls has proposed extra-judicially that dishonesty is one of the bases for the liability for knowing receipt and that dishonest receipt can be grouped with dishonest assistance into dishonest participation in breach of trust.

Source (edited): "http://en.wikipedia.org/wiki/Dishonest_assistance"

Doctrine of exoneration of liens

The **doctrine of exoneration of liens** (sometimes simply referred to as "**doctrine of exoneration**") refers to a common law rule. The rule says that encumbrances (i.e. a mortgage) of a property conveyed by a will is discharged with funds from the originating estate, not from the property itself.

Source (edited): "http://en.wikipedia.org/wiki/Doctrine_of_exoneration_of_liens"

Elective share

An **elective share** is a term used in American law relating to inheritance, which describes a proportion of an estate which the surviving spouse of the deceased may claim in place of what they were left in the decedent's will. It may also be called a **widow's share**, **statutory share**, **election against the will**, or **forced share**.

Function and operation

The elective share is the modern version of the English common law concepts of dower and curtesy, both of which reserved certain portions of a decedent's estate which were reserved for the surviving spouse, in order to prevent them from falling into poverty and becoming a burden on the community.

Currently, the amount to be reserved for a spouse is determined by the law of the state where the estate is located. In most states, the elective share is between ⅓ and ½ of all the property in the estate, although many states require the marriage to have lasted a certain number of years for the elective share to be claimed, or adjust the share based on the length of the marriage, and the presence of minor children. Some states also reduce the elective share if the surviving spouse is independently wealthy.

In some jurisdictions, if the spouse claims the elective share, they get that amount, but nothing else from the estate. In other states, claiming an elective share has no effect on gifts under a will or through a trust (though things given by will or trust may fulfill in part the elective share portion). Obviously, there would be no point in seeking an elective share if the surviving spouse has already been willed more than they would receive under the statute. Furthermore, some assets held by the estate may be exempt from becoming part of the elective share, so their value is subtracted from the total value of the estate before the elective share is calculated.

Some states also permit children of the deceased to claim an elective share.

Calculation of the augmented estate

The elective share is usually calculated from assets beyond those in the probate estate alone, and the assets that are added together to make this calculation are referred to as an **augmented estate**. This calculation serves two functions. First, it prevents the decedent from effectively disinheriting the surviving spouse by either gifting away assets before death, or by tying up assets in devices such as trusts or joint accounts that benefit third parties after the decedent's death. Second, it prevents the surviving *spouse* from taking too large of an elective share, if the decedent had already transferred substantial assets to the spouse.

In order to accomplish this, the augmented estate is calculated by combining the value of the probate estate with such things as the value of gifts given by the decedent to third parties, property or accounts held in survivorship estates (such as a joint bank account, the proceeds of which would pass to the survivor among the account holders), the value of life insurance policies over which the decedent had the power to name the beneficiary, as well as gifts to the surviving spouse, and property held jointly with the surviving spouse.

The elective share in Florida gives a surviving spouse 30% of the elective estate, which includes all property owned by the decedent, property given away within one year of death, property inside a revocable trust (also known as a Living Trust), and pay on death accounts.

Source (edited): "http://en.wikipedia.org/wiki/Elective_share"

English trusts law

The Royal Exchange, adjacent to the Bank of England has been the centre of the City of London's financial activity since 1565, much involving trading of wealth among trust funds.

English trusts law is the original and foundational law of trusts in the world, and a unique contribution of English law to the legal system. Trusts are part of the law of property, and arise where one person (a "settlor") gives assets (e.g. some land) to another person (a "trustee") to keep safe or to manage on behalf of another person (a "beneficiary").

The law of trusts developed in the Middle Ages from the time of the crusades under the jurisdiction of the King of England. The "common law" regarded property as an indivisible entity, as it had been done through Roman law and the continental version of civil law. Where it seemed "inequitable" (i.e. unfair) to let someone with legal title hold onto it, the King's representative, the Lord Chancellor who established the Courts of Chancery, had the discretion to declare that the real owner "in equity" (i.e. in all fairness) was another person.

History
- *fideicommissum*
- Feudalism and crusades
- Court of Chancery
- Charity and the British Museum
- Judicature Acts
- Indian Trusts Act 1882
- Welfare state and retirement
- UK company law and UK insolvency law
- Offshore tax haven and tax avoidance

Formation

Three certainties

For a valid trust, the "three certainties" must be present, see *Knight v Knight*. In *Milroy v Lord*, Turner LJ stated that: "...to render a voluntary settlement valid and effectual, the settlor must have done everything which, according to the nature of the property comprised in the settlement, was necessary to be done in order to transfer the property, and render the settlement binding upon himself."

He went on to say that the settlor may constitute an express trust by either transferring the property to the trustee or by a self-declaration of trust. In the latter case, no transfer is needed.

Depending on what type of property is involved, certain formalities need to be satisfied before the property is validly transferred, and the general principle is that equity will not perfect an imperfect gift. Thus, in the case of land, there needs to be a deed, and in the case of shares, ss 182-183 of the Companies Act 1985 provides that in general, a share transfer form must be executed and delivered with the share certificates followed by entry of the name of the new owner in the company books.

- *Jones v Lock* (1865) 1 Ch App 25
- *Paul v Constance* 1 WLR 527
- *Hunter v Moss* 1 WLR 452
- *Re Barlow's Will Trusts* 1 WLR 278
- *McPhail v Doulton* AC 424
- *Re Baden's Deed Trusts (no 2)* Ch 9
- *Re Tuck's Settlement Trusts* Ch 49

Purpose trusts
- *Morice v Bishop of Durham* (1805) 10 Ves 522
- *Re Bowes* 1 Ch 507
- *Re Endacott* Ch 232
- *Re Denley's Trust Deed* 1 Ch 373
- *Leahy v Attorney-General for New South Wales* AC 457
- *Re Recher's Will Trusts* Ch 526
- *Re Lipinski's Will Trusts* Ch 235
- *Re Grant's Will Trusts* All ER 359
- *Re Bucks Constabulary Widows and Orphans Fund Friendly Society (no 2)* 1 All ER 623

Charitable trusts
- Charities Act 2006

Pension trusts
- Goode Report (1993)
- Pensions Act 2004
- Pensions Act 2008

Formalities

There are several formality requirements that have been imposed on express trusts by, inter alia, Wills Act 1837 s 9 and the Law of Property Act 1925 s 53.

Section 9 of the Wills Act 1837 provides that all testamentary trusts must be in writing, signed by the testator or by someone in his presence and by his direction, and be attested by two witnesses. However, secret trusts and now half secret trusts are recognised exceptions to this requirement. A full secret trust occurs when a testator leaves what appears to be an absolute gift in his will, but has communicated to the legatee that she is to hold the property on trust for purposes communicated to her. A half secret trust occurs when a testator leaves property on trust in his will, but communicates the terms of the will to the trustee privately.

The two leading justifications for allowing these exceptions to s 9 are the fraud theory and the modern theoretical approach. The fraud theory was laid down in *McCormick v Grogan* and is based on the idea that to disregard evidence of an oral testamentary trust and allow the legatee to take the property absolutely would be against the testator's intent and would unjustly enrich the legatee. The modern theoretical approach is based on the analysis that the testator validly declared the trust in his lifetime, and it became constituted by the vesting of the property in the trustee on his death.

The Law of Property Act 1925 s 53(1)(b) states that 'a declaration of trust respecting any land or any interest therein must be manifested and proved by some writing signed by some person who is able to declare such trust or by his will.' The declaration itself need not be in writing. The writing required is that of evidence of the declaration and failure to comply with this requirement will render the declaration of trust unenforceable (*Leroux v Brown*).

Dispositions of equitable interests are void unless they are in writing signed by the person disposing of the interests or by an agent authorised by that person (LPA 1925 s 53(1)(c)). By contrast to s 53(1)(b), the requirement here is that the disposition itself must be in writing. The requirement here also applies to dispositions of equitable interests in both land and personalty, as in *Grey v IRC*.

As mentioned above, to constitute a trust, there usually needs to be a transfer of trust assets to the trustees and in the course of doing so, there might be certain formalities that have to be complied with. Otherwise, because equity will not perfect an imperfect gift, the trust will not be constituted.

However, since *Milroy v Lord*, the court have at times appeared to have added the qualification that although legal title to trust property remains vested in the settlor, an attempted transfer by the settlor to the trustee might be effective in equity even though not all the formalities required for a valid transfer have been complied with. This might be the case where the settlor has done everything in his power to divest himself of trust property. In such cases, it is therefore possible for a trust to be constituted even though certain formalities have not been complied with.

An illustration of this principle is seen in *Re Rose*. Here, the settlor had by voluntary deed transferred shares in a private company to be held on certain trusts. Under the company constitution, however, the directors of the company have the right to refuse to register transfers. Accordingly, they delayed registration by some two months after the deed had been executed. The question faced by the court was when were the shares transferred? Section 182 and s.183 of the Companies Act 1985 would suggest that the shares were only transferred when the directors registered the transfer. However, the court held that the shares were transferred when then the settlor executed the deed and the trust was constituted on that date. This is because the settlor had done everything in his power to divest himself of the shares.

Re Rose was applied subsequently in a number of cases including *Mascall v Mascall* which concerned the transfer of registered land. More importantly, the *Re Rose* principle was reviewed in *Pennington v Waine*. Here the donor intended for her nephew to take up directorship in a private company. To do so, he needed to own shares in the company. Therefore, she executed a share transfer form concerning shares in the company in favour of her nephew. In contravention of the companies act, she had not delivered the share transfer form to her nephew. Neither had he been registered as a shareholder. The donor had sent the forms to her agent, the company auditor, who then told the nephew the he need not take further steps as regards the shares. The nephew then took up directorship of the company. The court held that the shares did not from part of the donor's estate on her death as there was an equitable assignment of those shares. This was so despite the fact that the donor had not done everything in her power to transfer the shares. The court reached its decision partly on the basis that clearly the donor intended the transfer to have immediate effect and it would have been unconscionable for the donor to retract. Unconscionability would depend on the circumstances in each particular case but in this case, the court felt that it was because the Donor had told the nephew of her intentions and he, in taking up directorship, had acted detrimentally.

- Secret trusts in English law

Content

Duties of trustees include:
- a duty to consider the proper investment of the trust assets
- a duty to prepare annual accounts except where the assets are held in specie
- a duty to keep adult beneficiaries informed at least annually

Trustees must be unanimous in their decisions and are personally responsible to the beneficiaries for those decisions. In the event of dispute can apply to the Court of Chancery for directions as to the correct course of action.

Administration

- Appointment and removal of trustees
- Delegation
- Variation of the trust deed
- Power of maintenance
- Power of advancement
- *Saunders v Vautier* (1841) 4 Beav 115, the sole beneficiary of a trust of East India Company stock could take the money when he reached adulthood, rather than wait till age 25 as the trust stipulated
- *Re Duke of Norfolk's Settlement Trusts* Ch 61, the court had the power to pay a trustee more for unforeseen work, as it had been necessary for the trust's administration

Duty of loyalty

- Trustee de son tort
- Trustee Act 2000
- *Armitage v Nurse* Ch 241
- *Bristol and West Building Society v Mothew* 1 Ch 1
- *Morley v Morley* (1678) 22 ER 817, Lord Nottingham LC held that if a trustee performed his duties then he was not liable for loss, as in this case where the trustee was robbed of £40 of the beneficiary's gold.
- *Keech v Sandford* EWHC Ch J76

- *Meinhard v Salmon*, 164 NE 545 (NY 1928)
- *Boardman v Phipps* 2 AC 46
- *Holder v Holder* Ch 353

Duty of care

- *Speight v Gaunt* (1883-84) LR 9 App Cas 1, trustees who employed a dishonest broker that stole £15,000 were not liable to repay the money to the beneficiaries because they acted in the ordinary course of business
- *Learoyd v Whiteley* (1887) 12 AC 727, trustees liable for loss of money when investing in a spurious brickfield business because they failed to exercise the care of a prudent person
- *In re Lucking's Will Trusts* 1 WLR 866, trustees with 70% shares in a company should have had representatives in management to stop director thieving company property
- *Bartlett v Barclays Bank Trust Co Ltd* 1 Ch 515, corporate trustee with 99% of company should have intervened in management to prevent disastrous speculation
- *Nestlé v National Westminster Bank plc* 1 WLR 1260, trustees investing only in tax exempt gilts were not liable for failure to take care because although they should follow modern portfolio theory now, their actions were not to be judged with the benefit of hindsight
- *Cowan v Scargill* Ch 270, trustees of miners' pensions were not allowed to disregard the potentially disastrous financial implications of investing all the trust money in the UK mines, even though this might serve an objective of propping up the industry
- *Harries v Church Commissioners for England* 1 WLR 1241, unless financial performance can be shown to be harmed, a trustee for church clergy retirement could take ethical considerations into account when investing money, and so avoid investments contrary to the religion's principles
- *Re Londonderry's Settlement* Ch 918, a beneficiary of a family trust was not entitled to information about a decision for why small sums were distributed to her
- *Schmidt v Rosewood Trust Ltd* UKPC 26, a discretionary beneficiary could get information about a trust's accounts, set up by his father
- *Sieff v Fox* 1 WLR 3811

Breach and remedies

Breach of trust

- *Target Holdings Ltd v Redferns* AC 421
- *Re Hallett's Estate* (1880) 13 Ch D 696
- *Re Oatway* Ch 356
- *Barlow Clowes International Ltd v Vaughan* 4 All ER 22
- Dishonest assistance

Tracing

Beneficiaries who feel the trustees are not (properly) fulfilling their obligations have the right to take the trustees to the Court of Chancery for a declaration concerning the proper actions of the trustees.

- *Bishopsgate Investment Management Ltd v Homan* Ch 211
- *Foskett v McKeown* 1 AC 102
- *Bank of Credit and Commerce International (Overseas) Ltd v Akindele* Ch 437
- *Twinsectra Ltd v Yardley* 2 AC 164
- *Barlow Clowes International Ltd v Eurotrust International Ltd* 1 All ER 333

Constructive trusts

- *Pennington v Waine* 1 WLR 2075
- *Bannister v Bannister* 2 All ER 133
- *Lloyds Bank plc v Rosset* AC 107
- *Boardman v Phipps* 2 AC 46
- *Attorney-General for Hong Kong v Reid* AC 713
- *Westdeutsche Landesbank Girozentrale v Islington London Borough Council* AC 669

Resulting trusts

- *Vandervell v Inland Revenue Commissioners* 2 AC 291
- *Re Vandervell's Trusts (no 2)* Ch 269
- *Tinsley v Milligan* 1 AC 340
- *Tribe v Tribe* Ch 107
- *Westdeutsche Landesbank Girozentrale v Islington London Borough Council* AC 669
- *Air Jamaica Ltd v Charlton* 1 WLR 1399
- *Barclays Bank Ltd v Quistclose Investments Ltd* AC 567
- *Twinsectra Ltd v Yardley* 2 AC 164
- Quistclose trusts in English law

Theory

- Unjust enrichment and restitution
- Consent and autonomy
- Law of obligations and property

Source (edited): "http://en.wikipedia.org/wiki/English_trusts_law"

Estate Planner

Estate Planner, a professional that creates an estate plan. This professional works with an estate owner to maximize their goals. This is a legal and tax specialty for an attorney or an accountant. Further, the key to estate planning is to help the family to avoid federal estate taxes and have adequate assets after the death of a loved one to continue a business, send children to college, and pay major expenses such as a mortgage.

Professional Credentials

Many advisors, lawyers, and CPAs also earn advanced credentials such as the CTEP Chartered Trust and Estate Planner designation from organizations such as the American Academy of Financial Management or the STEP Society of Trust and Estate Planning Professionals.

Source (edited): "http://en.wikipedia.org/wiki/Estate_Planner"

Estate planning

Estate planning is the process of anticipating and arranging for the disposal of an estate. Estate planning typically attempts to eliminate uncertainties over the administration of a probate and maximize the value of the estate by reducing taxes and other expenses. Guardians are often designated for minor children and beneficiaries in incapacity.

Estate planning devices

Estate planning involves the will, trusts, beneficiary designations, powers of appointment, property ownership (joint tenancy with rights of survivorship, tenancy in common, tenancy by the entirety), gift, and powers of attorney, specifically the durable financial power of attorney and the durable medical power of attorney. After widespread litigation and media coverage surrounding the Terri Schiavo case, many estate planning attorneys now advise clients to also create a living will. Specific final arrangements, such as whether to be buried or cremated, are also often part of the documents. More sophisticated estate plans may even cover deferring or decreasing estate taxes or winding up a business.

Many people (and even some attorneys) confuse a living will with a durable medical power of attorney. A living will sets out directives concerning end of life decisions, whereas a durable power of attorney gives all medical decision making authority to an appointed individual upon incapacity, including end of life decisions. Some people have both a living will and a health care power of attorney. In some countries, legal trust lawyers and estate planning attorneys may require or prefer to have some form of accreditation or licensing, such as an MTI or CSEP designation.

==Remainder== The tax code allows people to set up charitable remainder trusts and set up qualified personal residence trusts to own their personal residence yet leave it to their children without estate tax.

Tax

Because the United States tax code does not tax life insurance proceeds as income, a life insurance trust could be used to pay estate taxes. However, if the decedent holds any incidents of ownership like the ability to remove or change beneficiary, the proceeds will remain in his estate. For this reason, the trust vehicle is used to own the life insurance policy and it must be irrevocable to avoid inclusion in the estate.

Mediation

Mediation serves as an alternative to a full-scale litigation to settle disputes. At a mediation, family members and beneficiaries discuss plans on transfer of assets. Because of the potential conflicts associated with blended families, step siblings, and multiple marriages, creating an estate plan through mediation allows people to confront the issues head-on and design a plan that will minimize the chance of future family conflict and meet their financial goals.

Source (edited): "http://en.wikipedia.org/wiki/Estate_planning"

Exempt property

Exempt property, under the law of property in many jurisdictions, is property that can neither be passed by will nor claimed by creditors of the deceased in the event that a decedent leaves a surviving spouse or surviving descendants. Typically, exempt property includes a family car, and a certain amount of cash (perhaps $10,000-$20,000), or the equivalent value in personal property.

Source (edited): "http://en.wikipedia.org/wiki/Exempt_property"

Express trust

Where property is passed from an owner to a person an implied express trust, but no gift is made by the owner to that person, it is therefore held for the owner by the person, and this is the Resulting trust; where property should for some reason of public policy or rule of Equity be held by a person for someone other than the legal owner, this is either the Statutory trust or the Constructive trust; but where legal title to property is held by someone 'on trust', this is the **Ex-**

press trust.

Terms

Law generally requires only a simple formality to create an express trust. In certain jurisdictions, an express trust may even be established orally. Typically, a settlor would record the disposition, where real property is to be held in trust or the value of property in trust is large. Where legal title to property is being passed to a trustee, a "deed of settlement" or "Trust Instrument" (for jurisdictions that do not recognise Deeds) may be used. Where property is to continue to be held by the person making the trust, a "declaration of trust" will be appropriate.

Often, a trust corporation or more than one trustee are appointed to allow for uninterrupted administration of the trust in the event of a trustee's resignation, death, bankruptcy or incapacity. Additionally a Protector may be appointed who, for example, is authorized to appoint new trustees and to review the trustees' annual accounts.

To be valid at common law, a trust instrument must ascertain its beneficiaries, as well as the res, or subject matter of the trust, unless it is a charitable trust which does not provide specific beneficiaries.

Common forms of express trust

Bare trust

property transferred to another to hold e.g. for a third person absolutely. May be of use where property is to be held and invested on behalf of a minor child or mentally incapacitated person.

Life Interest trust

the income from property transferred is paid to one person "the life tenant" (e.g. a widow/er) during their lifetime and thereafter is transferred to another person (who may take absolutely or a second life interest according to the terms of the trust, in the second case a third beneficiary would come into play). The trustees may have power to pay capital as well as income to the life tenant; alternatively they may have rights to transfer ("appoint") property to other beneficiaries ahead of their entitlement.

Discretionary trust

the trustees may pay out income to whichever of the beneficiaries they, in the reasonable exercise of their discretion, think fit. They will normally also have a power to pay out capital. They may have extensive powers, even to add new beneficiaries, but such powers may normally only be exercised bona fide in the interests of the beneficiaries as a whole.

Charitable trusts

trusts for a purpose (as opposed to for individuals) are generally invalid at common law however charities are an exception. Persons wishing to pass money to causes not recognised as charitable may instead make gifts to established companies or associations or may establish trusts or trust-like structures in jurisdictions which do not restrict non-charitable purpose trusts (e.g. Jersey trusts, Danish and US foundations and Liechtenstein Anstallts).

Protective trusts and Spendthrift trusts

can be established to provide an income for persons who cannot be trusted with it.

Variation of Trusts in English Law

The Variation of Trusts Act 1958 gave the courts the power to vary trusts in the following circumstances

- s1(1)(a) Any person having, directly or indirectly, an interest, whether vested or contingent, under the trusts who by reason of infancy or other incapacity is incapable of assenting; or
- s1(1)(b) Any person (whether ascertained or not) who may become entitled, directly or indirectly, to an interest under the trusts as being at a future date or on the happening of a future event a person of any specified description or a member of any specified class of persons, so however that this paragraph shall not include any person who would be of that description, or a member of that class, as the case may be, if the said date had fallen or the said event had happened at the date of the application to the court; or
- s1(1)(c) Any person unborn; or
- s1(1)(d) Any person in respect of any discretionary interest of his under protective trusts where the interest of the principal beneficiary has not failed or determined.

The court does not have the power to consent to the variation of a trust on behalf of an ascertained individual who is sui juris.(Someone above the age of consent and of sound mind)

Forms of trust used by UK taxpayers

Accumulation and Maintenance trust

A variation on the discretionary trust, the A&M does not carry the Inheritance tax disadvantages of a discretionary settlement but can only be established for persons under 25 who must be entitled to income at that age. Allows the accumulation of income within the trust until 25.

Disabled Trust

Similar to an A&M trust but established for a disabled person.

Reverter to Settlor trust

A trust where, on the death of the life tenant, the property reverts to the person making the gift.

Nil Rate Band Discretionary trust

UK inheritance tax is payable at 40% on estates worth over £325,000 for the 2009-2010 tax year. If assets up to that value are placed in a discretionary trust during a person's lifetime, the trust will not be taken into account for inheritance tax if the person survives for a further 7 years. Likewise in a will, many persons leave a legacy on discretionary trusts so as to take full advantage of their nil rate band (gifts to spouses and registered civil partners being wholly exempt).

Forms of trust used by US persons

Certain US jurisdictions and other jurisdictions have developed a radically different interpretation of the trust. Valid trusts can be established by persons who then continue to deal with property as if it were their own during their lifetime, the trust crystallising on death. Trust funds can be taxed as legal entites by election ("checking the box").

Source (edited): "http://en.wikipedia. org/wiki/Express_trust"

Fiduciary trust

A **fiduciary trust** is a fiduciary relationship in which a trustee holds the title to assets for the beneficiary. The trust's creator is called the grantor.

Source (edited): "http://en.wikipedia. org/wiki/Fiduciary_trust"

Forced heirship

Forced heirship is a form of partible inheritance whereby a deceased's estate is separated into (1) an indefeasible portion, the forced estate, passing to those the deceased is survived by, and (2) a disposable portion, or free estate, to be freely disposed of by will. Forced heirship is generally a feature of Civil law legal systems which do not recognize total freedom of testation. Normally, the deceased's estate is in-gathered and wound up without discharging liabilities, which means accepting inheritance includes accepting the liabilities attached to inherited property. The forced estate is divided into shares which include the share of issue (legitime or child's share) and the spousal share. This provides a minimum protection that cannot be defeated by will. The free estate, on the other hand, is at the discretion of a testator to be distributed by will on death to whomsoever he or she chooses. Takers in the forced estate are known as forced heirs.

Forced heirship laws are most prevalent among Civil law jurisdictions and in Islamic countries; these include major countries such as France, Saudi Arabia, Japan, and most other countries in the world. Reckoning shares in instances of multiple or no children and lack of surviving spouse vary from country to country.

The institution began as a Germanic custom for intestate inheritance according to which all of a deceased's personalty was divided into thirds - the widow's part, bairn's part/legitim, and dead's part - the last of which, consisting of clothes, weapons, farm animals and implements, was usually buried with the deceased. In time, after the revival of the will, and consequently of testation, the dead's part came to be freely disposable. Realty, or heritable property, on the other hand, was originally inherited in joint tenancy, termed gavelkind, and passed on to the kin group as a whole. However, after the household superseded the kin group in importance in the late Middle Ages, preference was given to the deceased's immediate family, specifically any surviving sons. Gavelkind inheritance gave rise to inter-family rivalries, so primogeniture laws arose in some areas of feudal Europe giving preference to the eldest son in order to stem feuding. Widows were universally disinherited, though they were varyingly entitled to a dower and/or a terce (or curtesy in the case of widowers), that is, one third of the heritable marital estate. The terce was earliest known as *tertia collaborationis* and first appears in the Ripuarian law code, making it also a localized Germanic institution. Eventually, these elements were all consolidated into the modern form of forced heirship most notably in Revolutionary France, which restored gavelkind inheritance and innovatively extended the system of thirds to realty.

Advocates of forced heirship contend that it is perfectly proper for testators to be required to make adequate provision for their dependents, and that most countries in the world permit wills to be varied where they would leave dependents destitute. Critics suggest that there is a great difference between varying wills to the minimum degree to provide sufficient financial support for dependents and prohibiting the testator from distributing the estate or a proportion of the estate to any female children, or younger male children, and that it cannot be any less repugnant to force a deceased person to distribute their assets in a certain manner on their death than it would be to tell them how they may do so during their lifetime.

Wealthy individuals sometimes seek to circumvent forced heirship laws by transferring assets into an offshore company and seeking to settle the shares in the offshore company in a trust governed by the laws of a jurisdiction outside their domicile.

Louisiana

In Louisiana, Civil Code Article 1493 dictates that children under 24 at the time of death and interdicts (individuals permanently incapable of caring for themselves) who are not disinherited (Civil Code Art. 1494) qualify as forced heirs. The legitime is equal to 25% of the patrimony (if one forced heir); or 50% (if more than one); and each forced heir will receive the lesser of an equal proportion of the legitime or what they would have received through intestacy (Civil Code Art. 1495, Succession of Greenlaw). If a person who would have otherwise qualified as a forced heir dies before the parent, rights to that share may pass to that person's children, although how that share is distributed among them if one or more is an interdict remains unsettled law. Forced heirs may demand collation, whereby certain gifts received by a forced heir within three years of the death of the parent may be subtracted from their share. Louisiana does not have a forced heirship provision for spouses, however at death the spouse's interest in any community property is converted to his or her separate property; and a usufruct is granted over the remaining community (with the forced heirs as naked owners of their respective shares). That usufruct terminates at death or remarriage.

Source (edited): "http://en.wikipedia.org/wiki/Forced_heirship"

Foreign trust

Foreign trust commonly refers to a trust that is governed by the laws of a jurisdiction other than the United States. These trusts may be used for investment, estate planning and succession planning purposes, but are most commonly used for asset protection.

Here are some reason why foreign trusts may be used for asset protection.

The commonly understood meaning of the term "foreign trust" is a trust governed by the laws of a foreign jurisdiction. However, as discussed below, the term "foreign trust" has a very specific meaning under the Code. Whenever the term "foreign trust" appears in this text, it refers simply to a trust governed by the laws of a foreign jurisdiction.

A foreign trust, per se, does not have any asset protection benefits. The benefits come from the jurisdiction which governs the trust. To understand more fully the benefits of foreign trusts and the reasons why they are so commonly used in asset protection planning the reader must return briefly to (i) domestic trusts, and (ii) fraudulent transfer laws.

A domestic discretionary trust, set up for a beneficiary by a third party, has great asset protection benefit. A domestic spendthrift trust also has certain asset protection benefits. In some states, including California, there are statutory limitations placed on the protective benefits of these trusts.

The most important statutory limitation is the prohibition against self-settled trusts. That one factor severely limits the use of domestic trusts for asset protection purposes, as most asset protection trusts are self-settled. Several states have now passed legislation allowing self-settled trusts as a protective shield. But questions remain, as these jurisdictions are a part of the United States and are subject to the constitutional restrictions, such as the full faith and credit clause, requiring one state to recognize a judgment from a sister state, and are further hampered by the choice of law analysis.

Even assuming that these domestic asset protection trusts manage to overcome such issues, or a debtor establishes a California discretionary trust for the benefit of a third party, there is always a potential of a fraudulent transfer challenge. No matter how protective a domestic trust is, even if it is fully discretional, in the case of a fraudulent transfer the trustee will have to distribute the trust assets to the creditor.

It is in light of these challenges that the efficacy of foreign trusts becomes obvious. Foreign jurisdictions are not subject to the constitutional restrictions placed on U. S. states. Some jurisdictions do not recognize foreign judgments against trusts and have very debtor friendly fraudulent transfer laws. For example, St.Vincent (in the West Indies) requires creditors to establish a fraudulent transfer beyond a reasonable doubt and has a one-year statute of limitations on fraudulent transfers that begins running from the date of the transfer.

Foreign trusts are truly efficient for asset protection purposes only if liquid assets are used to fund the trust, and such assets are, at some point, transferred offshore. While a foreign asset protection trust can hold any property, including personal and real property in the U. S., the ability of a U. S. court to reach U. S. property suggests the benefits of holding offshore assets in the foreign trust.

Foreign trusts are usually treated as "foreign trusts" for the purposes of the Internal Revenue Code. This means that transfers of assets to the trust will be treated as a sale for tax purposes. To avoid the sale treatment on the funding of the trust, most foreign trusts are drafted as grantor trusts. Being grantor trusts, they avoid sale treatment on funding, and remain tax neutral during their existence. Foreign asset protection trusts are usually established solely for asset protection purposes, and almost never for tax purposes.

Generally, when contrasted with a domestic trust, a foreign trust offers the following benefits:

1. Increased ability of the settlor to retain benefit and control; 2. Less likely to be pursued by a creditor; 3. Foreign jurisdictions usually have more beneficial to the debtor statute of limitations, burden of proof, and other important provisions; 4. No full faith and credit, comity or supremacy clause issues; 5. Favorable to the debtor spendthrift provision laws; 6. Confidentiality and privacy; and 7. Flexibility.

It is very important to pick the right jurisdiction as the trust's situs. Over the past decade, certain foreign jurisdictions have implemented trust legislation specifically designed to provide added asset protection to settlers and beneficiaries. Other jurisdictions, while not focusing on asset protection per se, have made their trust laws more flexible in other respects.

The following factors should be considered when evaluating a foreign trust situs jurisdiction:

1. Nonrecognition of foreign judgments, 2. Recognition of self-settled trusts, 3. No local taxation, 4. Debtor friendly fraudulent transfer laws, including short statute of limitations and high burden of proof, 5. Availability of competent and reliable trustees, 6. Availability of competent local attorneys and banks, 7. British Commonwealth based culture and legal system, 8. Trust assets are not reachable by creditors, include for alimony or child support, and 9. Stable political environment.

Also, in some cases secrecy may be an important consideration, but it is not a factor in most asset protection cases.

From an asset protection standpoint three jurisdictions stand out from the rest of the pack: (i) the Cook Islands (in the South Pacific), (ii) St. Vincent and the Grenadines (in the West Indies), and (iii) Nevis (in the West Indies). Certain other offshore jurisdictions also offer asset protection benefits to trusts, but not to the same extent. These jurisdictions include the Cayman Islands, Bermuda, Bahamas, the Channel Islands (Isle of Man, Jersey and Guernsey) and Gibraltar.

For example, Cook Islands, St. Vincent and the Grenadines and Nevis have the following favorable to the debtor provisions: (i) nonrecognition of foreign judgments with respect to trusts; (ii) "beyond a reasonable doubt" standard for fraudulent transfers; (iii) a short statute of limitations for fraudulent transfers; (iv) requirement of showing actual fraud and constructive fraud to prove a fraudulent transfer; (v) allowance of self-settled trusts; and (vi) ability by the settlor/beneficiary to retain some control. All three, particularly St. Vincent, have a long established financial services industry and legal system.

Bahamas lacks clauses (i), (ii) and (iii). Bermuda and Cayman Islands lack clauses (i), (ii), (iv), (v) and (vi). Mauritius lacks clause (i).

Interestingly, New Zealand has been recently gaining popularity as an asset protection destination. New Zealand is closely tied to the Cook Islands (which were a former New Zealand protectorate) and its trust laws are at the forefront of other developed nations. New Zealand does not tax trusts that generate their income elsewhere, but it does recognize self-settled trusts. In eyes of some practitioners, New Zealand is not a "notorious" asset protection jurisdiction, and makes planning easier.

There are several disadvantages to using New Zealand for asset protection purposes. New Zealand has a relatively long statute of limitations on fraudulent transfers (four years), it will recognize a U. S. judgment, and there is no established history of protecting trust settlors and beneficiaries from creditors. (At least not to the same extent as in St. Vincent, the Cook Islands and Nevis.) Because foreign asset protection trusts should be used openly, and they are extremely effective if established in the right jurisdiction, perceptions by creditors (and even judges) are not very important.

Source (edited): "http://en.wikipedia.org/wiki/Foreign_trust"

Freedom of testation

Freedom of testation, is the power of a person to choose the heir(s) of her/his properties upon her/his death. This especially implies the freedom of making provision for charity.

After the Norman Conquest of England, The Church succeeded in allowing a person to leave part of his property to the church to use them as funds for its activities. This was a turning point in its history, which took a long time to develop to its present day form.

Source (edited): "http://en.wikipedia.org/wiki/Freedom_of_testation"

Future interest

In property law and real estate, a **future interest** is a legal right to property ownership that does not include the right to present possession or enjoyment of the property. Future interests are created on the formation of a defeasible estate; that is, an estate with a condition or event triggering transfer of possessory ownership. A common example is the landlord-tenant relationship. The landlord may own a house, but has no general right to enter it while it is being rented. The conditions triggering the transfer of possession, first to the tenant then back to the landlord, are usually detailed in a lease.

As a slightly more complicated example, suppose O is the owner of Blackacre. Consider what happens when O transfers the property "to A for life, then to B." Person A acquires possession of Blackacre. Person B does not receive any right to possess Blackacre immediately; however, once person A dies, possession will fall to person B (or his estate, if he died before person A). Person B has a *future* interest in the property. In this example, the event triggering the transfer is person A's death.

Because they convey ownership rights, future interests can usually be sold, gifted, willed, or otherwise disposed of by the beneficiary (but see *Vesting* below). Because the rights vest in the future, any such disposition will occur before the beneficiary actually takes possession of the property.

There are five kinds of future interests recognized at common law: three in the transferor and two in the transferee.

Vesting

Vesting means granting a person an immediate right to present or future enjoyment of property. In plain English, one has a right to a vested asset that cannot be taken away by any third party, even though one may not yet possess the asset. When the right, interest or title to the present or future possession of a legal estate can be transferred to any other party, it is termed a **vested interest**.

A vested interest may be one of three types:

- A future interest is **absolutely (or indefeasibly) vested** if its beneficiary must (legally) eventually take possessory ownership.
- A future interest is **vested subject to open** if it belongs to a class of beneficiaries, where that class can expand. A common example is a grant from O "to A's children": the class of A's children can't be **closed** until approximately thirty eight weeks after A dies, so any children alive at the time of the grant are vested subject to open. This interest is also sometimes referred to as

being **vested subject to partial divestment**.
- A future interest is **vested subject to divestment** if something can occur that would divest the remainder of his interest. For example "From O to A for life, then to B, but if A stops growing corn, then to C" B would have a vested remainder subject to divestment because he could be divested of his interest before it becomes possessory by an act of A.

A person may divest themselves of, or alienate, only those interests that are *guaranteed* to vest. This rule aligns with the policy that a person should not be allowed to sell a thing that he or she does not own outright. Interests that are not guaranteed to vest are subject to the rule against perpetuities.

Future interests in the transferor

Reversion

A reversion occurs when a granted estate is absolutely vested in the grantor.
- Example: "O grants Blackacre to A for life."
- Analysis (O): A is guaranteed to die (eventually), at which point Blackacre returns to O. This future interest is absolutely (*indefeasibly*) vested in O.
- Analysis (A): A has a life estate.
- Alienation: O can alienate her future interest. A can alienate his rights in the property, but only to the extent that those rights were granted him (i.e., as a life estate). So A can sell Blackacre to B, but once A dies it returns to O. Notice that B has no control over this kind of vesting.

Reversion is not subject to the rule against perpetuities, because O's future interest is absolutely vested.

Possibility of reverter

There is a possibility of reverter when an estate will return to the grantor if a condition is violated. The possibility of reverter can only follow a fee simple determinable.
- Example: "O grants Blackacre to A, as long as A refrains from drinking alcohol."
- Analysis: If A never drinks after the grant (and never sells the property), then Blackacre will belong to A at A's death, and be distributed according to the rules of probate. If A does drink after the grant, then the property returns to O.
- Language used: Durational. Examples include "for as long as", "while", and "during".
- Alienation: A's interest is freely transferable.

This type of future interest can only follow the *fee simple determinable*. The vesting of the future interest is determinable at the time of the grant, because reverter is automatic if the condition is broken.

Right of entry (or power of termination)

This type of future interest follows a *fee simple subject to a condition subsequent*. A grantor has the power of termination when an estate may return to the grantor if a condition is violated *and* the grantor decides to reclaim the estate. This type of grant may occur when the grantor wants the option of deciding the severity of the violation.
- Example: "O grants Blackacre to A, on condition that A refrains from drinking alcohol."
- Analysis: If A never drinks after the grant (and never sells the property), then Blackacre will belong to A at A's death, and be distributed according to the rules of probate. If A does drink after the grant, then A's rights in Blackacre end, although A is still in possession of Blackacre.
- Language used: Conditional. Examples include "on condition", "if used for", and "provided that".
- Alienation: A's interest is vested. This interest is never subject to the rule against perpetuities. A's interest cannot be transferred *inter vivos* ("between living people"); can only be transferred by will or by intestate succession upon death of the grantor.

This type of future interest follows a *fee simple subject to a condition subsequent*. To see why, consider that in order to retain Blackacre, A must continue to perform under the terms of the grant (by not drinking). If A fails to "not drink", that condition will trigger the subsequent loss of A's rights in Blackacre.

Future interests in a transferee

Remainders

A **remainder** is a future interest in a third party that vests upon the natural conclusion of the grant to the original grantee. It is the interest in the property that is "left over", or remains, after the original grantee is finished possessing it. For example, O's grant "to A for life, then to B" creates a remainder in B. There are two types of remainders: vested and contingent.

Vested remainders

A **vested remainder** is created when property is granted to both a direct grantee and a named third party, and is not subject to a condition precedent to the third party taking possession.
- Example: "O grants Blackacre to A for life, then to B".
- Analysis (A): A has a life estate.
- Analysis (B): B has a vested remainder, because Blackacre will vest in B after A dies, with no further conditions.
- Alienation: B may divest his (absolutely) vested remainder, which is not subject to the rule against perpetuities. A is subject to the rules regarding divestiture of a life estate, as noted above.
- Example(2): "O grants Blackacre to A for life, then to B" and B dies before A. Who takes possession?
- Answer: B's heirs. The terms "and his heirs" are assumed to be part of the conveyance.

Contingent remainders

A **contingent remainder** is created when a remainder cannot fully vest at the time of granting. This normally occurs in two situations:
- when the property can't vest because the beneficiary is unknown (for example, if the beneficiary is a class subject to open), or
- when the property can't vest because

the (known) beneficiary is subject to a condition precedent which has not yet occurred.

Remainders subject to open
- Example: "O grants Blackacre to A for life, then to B's children".
- Analysis: The class of B's children can't be determined until approximately thirty-eight weeks after B dies, so any children who are unborn at the time of the grant have a remainder contingent upon B having offspring. Children of B are fully vested as soon as they are born, provided A is still alive. B's children who are born have vested remainder subject to open, because the conveyance was given to a class of persons (B's Children) and B could still have more children. If A dies before B, then the class is closed, and only those children alive at A's death will have an interest.

Remainders subject to condition precedent
- Example: "O grants Blackacre to A for life, then to B if B is married to C (at the time A dies)".
- Analysis (O): If B is married to C when A dies, B will own Blackacre. If B isn't married to C, then the property will vest in O (or O's estate) without O having to make a claim for it. So O has a reversion.
- Analysis (A): A has a life estate.
- Analysis (B): B has a contingent remainder subject to condition precedent, because Blackacre will vest in B, but only if B is married to C at the moment A dies.
- Alienation: B does not vest unless he is married to C at the moment of A's death. In other words, he will have to wait until A dies to divest.

Note: a different result would be reached if the grant was "O to A for life, then to B if B *has married* C". In this case, B could marry C to obtain a fully vested interest, then divorce C without affecting his rights to Blackacre.

Legislatures and courts tend to prefer vested remainders over contingent remainders, to reduce uncertainty in ambiguous grants, and to speed up probate.

Executory interests

An **executory interest** is a future interest, held by a third party transferee (i.e. someone other than the grantee), which either cuts off another's interest or begins after the natural termination of a preceding estate. An executory interest vests upon any condition subsequent except the natural termination of the original grantee's rights. In other words, an executory interest is any future interest held by a third party that isn't a remainder.

Executory interests usually arise when a grantor gives property to one person, provided that they use it a certain way. If the person fails to use it properly, the property transfers to a third party. There are two different types of executory interests: **shifting** and **springing**. Executory limitations transferring ownership from the grantor to a third party are called *springing executory interests*, and those that transfer from the grantee to a third party are called *shifting executory interests*.

Shifting executory interest

A shifting executory interest cuts short someone other than the grantor. For example, if O conveys property "To A, but if B returns from Florida within the next year, to B"; here, B has a shifting executory interest, and A has a fee simple subject to this shifting executory interest. A shifting executory interest may be premised on any event, irrespective of whether that event is under the control of one party or the other, or if it is an external event under the control of neither party. For example, a conveyance "To A, but if the property is ever used as a commercial dairy, to B" would leave A in control of the condition; so long as A does not use the property in the proscribed manner it will remain hers. Conversely, a conveyance "To A, but if the B receives a law degree, to B" places B entirely in control of the dispensation of the property; if B is able to fulfill the condition, B will get the property irrespective of what A does. Finally, the interest may shift based on a wholly external event, for example, "To A, but if the Chicago Cubs win the World Series, to B".

If the conveyance to A is for a limited time, or for the life of A, then the condition triggering the executory interest must occur within that time, or the property will return to the grantor.
- Example: "O grants Blackacre to A for life, but if A ever drinks alcohol, then Blackacre immediately goes to B."
- A has a life estate.
- B has an executory interest, because his interest does not vest unless A's life estate terminates due to the 'unnatural' condition subsequent. The interest is shifting, because if A drinks, then the property "shifts" from one grantee to another. If A never drinks on the property, then A will retain ownership, and on A's death the property will go to O, or the heirs of O.

Springing executory interest

A springing executory interest cuts short the grantor of the property. For example, if O conveys property "To A, if and when he marries"; here, A has a springing executory interest, and O has a fee simple subject to this springing executory interest.

Suppose B is 15 years old.
- Example: "O grants Blackacre to A for life, then to B if B reaches the age of 25 years."
- Analysis (O): O has a *reversion* (see above), since A might die before B reaches 25.
- Analysis (A): A has a life estate.
- Analysis (B): B has an executory interest, because his interest does not vest until he reaches 25, a condition that is unrelated to the expiration of A's interest. If A lives until B is 25, B's interest will vest absolutely. If not, the interest is springing, because when B reaches 25 possession of Blackacre will "spring" from the grantor O, who will have taken possession when A died.

Limitations on the creation

of executory interests

The grantor never retains an ultimate future interest when there is an executory condition present. If the executory condition is never met, the original grantee retains the interest, while if the condition is met, the interest transfers to a third party. However, the grantor may have a future possessory interest.

Executory interests are subject to the rule against perpetuities, which disqualifies any interest that can vest more than twenty-one years after the death of every party who was living at the time the interest was created. However, if all of the potential vesting beneficiaries are named, the rule will never be violated. Thus, a property can *not* be conveyed "to A and her heirs, but if alcohol is consumed on the property, to B and his heirs". Because A's heirs may hew to the condition for generations, causing a violation centuries after the condition was set down and creating chaos in efforts to shift title to the appropriate heirs of B.

Third party beneficiaries of executory interests cannot alienate them, since the interests are contingent upon a condition subsequent, so the interest is not guaranteed to vest.

Source (edited): "http://en.wikipedia.org/wiki/Future_interest"

George Tasker

George Tasker conceived and founded The Society of Trust and Estate Practitioners (STEP) in 1991 and was Chairman for three years, after which he was elected its first worldwide President. STEP was founded with the express aim of uniting together all of the practitioners in the trust and estate field and also to cut across the long established professional boundaries. STEP is now represented in 33 countries around the World and whose full members are the most experienced and senior practitioners in the field of trusts and estates.

For many years he was a Senior Trust Manager with Chartered Accountants Deloitte Haskins + Sells (now PricewaterhouseCoopers), a co-author of their Trust Manual, a member of their National Trust Committee and of their Trust Quality Control Inspectorate.

In 1991, Tasker set up his own practice, George Tasker Inheritance as a Registered Trust Practitioner and Inheritance Consultant drawing on his 40 years experience to provide technical support to firms of accountants, solicitors and independent financial advisers.

He has been lecturing for over 30 years on legal subjects to many of the main professional bodies including Chartered and Certified Accountants, Chartered Institute of Taxation, The Institute of Bankers and the Life Assurance and Securities Institutes. He is accredited by the Law Society and the Institute of Legal Executives as an approved lecturer to their qualified members as part of their Continuing Professional Development (CPD) Schemes.

Additionally, Tasker is an occasional speaker on local radio, a writer in the business press and co-author of various technical publications including the STEP booklet "Why make a trust?"

He has been married for over 40 years and has three grown up children and four grandchildren.

Tasker retired in early 2007 and resigned as President of STEP in late 2006, at which time STEP awarded George the official title of "Founder".

Source (edited): "http://en.wikipedia.org/wiki/George_Tasker"

Grantor Retained Annuity Trust

A **grantor retained annuity trust** (commonly referred to by the acronym **GRAT**), is a financial instrument commonly used in the United States to make large financial gifts to family members without paying a U.S. gift tax.

Basic Mechanism

A donor sets up a GRAT by making a donation into a trust. The trust is set up as an annuity whereby the donor receives an annual payment from the annuity for a fixed period of time. At the end of the term, any remaining value in the trust is passed on to a beneficiary of the trust as a gift. The beneficiary must be a family member of the donor. If the donor dies before the end of the term, then the value of the trust at that time is passed on to the beneficiary.

The United States Internal Revenue Service has a number of regulations governing how the remaining value of the trust at the end of the term (or at the death of the donor) is taxed. When the GRAT is first set up, a "gift value" of the GRAT is calculated. The gift value is set equal to the initial contribution to the GRAT plus a theoretical interest earned on the principal minus the annuity payments that would be made through the end of the term. The theoretical rate of interest is determined by IRS regulations. The rate is set equal to 120% of the federal mid-term rate during the month that the GRAT is established.***

To realize a tax benefit, the sum of the scheduled annuity payments of a GRAT is set to be about equal to the principal plus theoretical interest. Thus, for tax purposes, the initially calculated gift value is zero, since what will be paid back to the donor in annuity payments is anticipated to be about equal to what the donor invested, plus interest. If a GRAT is funded with highly volatile assets, however, it is possible that the actual interest earned on the assets will be substantially higher than the IRS theoretical interest. Thus at the end of the term, the value remaining in the GRAT may still be large, even though the initial IRS calculation suggests that it should have been zero. This remaining value is then passed on to the beneficiary without incurring a gift tax.

Important Legal Cases
- Audrey J. Walton v. Commissioner, 115 T.C. 589 (2000), acq. Notice 2003-72, 2003-44 IRB, 15 October 2003. This case established the current way that the IRS established a gift value for a GRAT.

Patents
The Wealth Transfer Group owns a patent covering different methods for managing SOGRATs. A SOGRAT is a GRAT that is at least partially funded with stock options. The patent number is U.S. Patent 6,567,790, and is entitled "Establishing and managing grantor retained annuity trusts funded by non-qualified stock options". On January 12, 2011, the director of the USPTO initiated a reexamination of US patent 6,567,790. The reexamination serial number is 90/009,868.

Source (edited): "http://en.wikipedia.org/wiki/Grantor_Retained_Annuity_Trust"

Hague Trust Convention

The **Hague Convention on the Law Applicable to Trusts and on their Recognition**, or **Hague Trust Convention** is a multilateral treaty developed by the Hague Conference on Private International Law on the Law Applicable to **Trusts**. It concluded on 1 July 1985, entered into force 1 January 1992, and is as of March 2011 ratified by 12 countries. The Convention aims to harmonise not only the municipal law definitions of a trust, but also the Conflict rules for resolving problems in the choice of the *lex causae*. The key provisions of the Convention are:
- each signatory recognises the existence and validity of trusts. However, the Convention only relates to trusts with a written trust instrument. It would not apply trusts which arise (usually in common law jurisdictions) without a written trust instrument.
- the Convention sets out the characteristics of a trust (even jurisdictions with considerable legal history relating to trusts find this difficult)
- the Convention sets out clear rules for determining the governing law of trusts with a cross border element.

Background
Many states do not have a developed law of trusts, or the principles differ significantly between states. It was therefore necessary for the Hague Convention to define a trust to indicate the range of legal transactions regulated by the Convention and, perhaps more significantly, the range of applications not regulated. The definition offered in Article 2 is:

...the legal relationship created, *inter vivos* or on death, by a person, the settlor, when assets have been placed under the control of a trustee for the benefit of a beneficiary or for a specified purpose.

A trust has the following characteristics:
(a) the assets constitute a separate fund and are not a part of the trustee's own estate;
(b) title to the trust assets stands in the name of the trustee or in the name of another person on behalf of the trustee;
(c) the trustee has the power and the duty, in respect of which he is accountable, to manage, employ or dispose of the assets in accordance with the terms of the trust and the special duties imposed upon him by law. The reservation by the settlor of certain rights and powers, and the fact that the trustee may himself have rights as a beneficiary, are not necessarily inconsistent with the existence of a trust.

Article 3 provides that the Convention only applies to express trusts created voluntarily and evidenced in writing. It will therefore not cover oral trusts, resulting trusts, constructive trusts, statutory trusts or trusts created by judicial order. But signatory states are free to apply the Convention to any form of trust and the Recognition of Trusts Act 1987 has applied the provisions to all trusts arising under English law, no matter when or how they were created, albeit only applying the provisions to transactions affecting those trusts made after 1 August 1987. There are incidental question problems if the trust is testamentary and, under Article 4, if it is alleged that the testator lacked capacity, or that the will is formally or substantively invalid, or that it had been revoked, these issues must be determined first under the *lex fori* Conflict rules on characterisation and choice of law before the Convention rules can apply. This will include, for example, a detailed consideration of any marriage settlement or applicable law containing community property provisions which might prevent the testator alienating property from a spouse or child of the family (see succession (conflict)). Obviously, if the will purporting to create the trust is held invalid, there are no trusts to adjudicate upon.

The applicable law
Article 6 allows the settlor to select the applicable law in the *inter vivos* or testamentary document. Under normal circumstances, the settlor will be acting on professional advice and will make an express selection or it will be implied from the facts of the case. But, under Article 6(2), if the settlor selects a law with no relevant provisions or the provisions in the municipal law selected would be inappropriate, or there is no selection, Article 7 applies to select the law which is most closely connected with the transaction. This is judged by reference to four alternative connecting factors which are to be considered as at the time the putative trust is created:
- the place where the trust is to be administered;
- the place where the assets are to be found (for immovables, there is no problem – the *lex situs* is easily identified; for movables, the most common form is choses in action

such as shares and bonds, and their location does not change (bearer bonds and other instruments where title is determined by mere possession are relatively uncommon), but for tangible assets, this will usually be the place where the assets are located at the time of the hearing given that this represents the place where any Court Order would have to be enforced: see property (conflict));
- the place where the trustee is resident or conducts his or her business;
- the place where the purpose or object of the trust is to be fulfilled.

Despite the identification of these four factors, the court must actually perform a rounded evaluation of all the circumstances. Thus, it would be relevant to consider the distribution of the assets if in separate states, the purpose of the trust (which might be the evasion of taxation or other provisions in some of the states where the assets are located), the *lex domicilii* or *lex patriae* of the settlor and the beneficiaries (particularly if the legal transaction is a marriage settlement or testamentary), the legal form of the document, and the law of the place where the document was executed (this latter factor may either be accidental and so of marginal value, or contrived to take advantage of a favourable law and so highly significant).

The scope of the applicable law

Under Article 8, the law specified by Article 6 or 7 shall govern the validity of the trust, its construction, its effects, and the administration of the trust. In particular that law shall govern:
(a) the appointment, resignation and removal of trustees, the capacity to act as a trustee, and the devolution of the office of trustee;
(b) the rights and duties of trustees among themselves;
(c) the right of trustees to delegate in whole or in part the discharge of their duties or the exercise of their powers;
(d) the power of trustees to administer or to dispose of trust assets, to create security interests in the trust assets, or to acquire new assets;
(e) the powers of investment of trustees;
(f) restrictions upon the duration of the trust, and upon the power to accumulate the income of the trust;
(g) the relationships between the trustees and the beneficiaries including the personal liability of the trustees to the beneficiaries;
(h) the variation of termination of the trust (because variation is expressly within the scope of the Applicable Law, this may be a significant factor in any issue of *forum non conveniens* raised if an application to vary is made to a forum other than a forum of the Applicable Law);
(i) the distribution of the trust assets;
(j) the duty of trustees to account for their administration.

Severance

Articles 9 and 10 allow the Applicable Law by which the validity of the trust has been established, to sever aspects of the trust and its administration so that separate laws shall apply to each component. In fact, the settlor may expressly select an Applicable Law for each component and the forum court should respect his or her wishes. But, in general terms, it is desirable that a single law should be applied to the administration and the fact that there may be assets located in separate states should not, *per se*, justify severing the trust. The relevant *lex situs* can be applied to micromanage the asset(s) by the trustee(s) without having to apply the *situs* law to the administration of the trust in that state. Equally, this is not an argument for a judicial approach which favours the law of the place of administration as the Applicable Law. Although the administration must comply with the municipal laws for general purposes, the duty to honour the intentions of the settlor may make the law of the place where the most significant part of that intention is to be realised the most significant single law.

Recognition

Under Article 11, a trust complying with the Applicable Law shall be recognised as a trust which implies, as a minimum, that the trust property constitutes a separate fund, that the trustee may sue and be sued in his capacity as trustee, and that he or she may appear or act in this capacity before a notary or any person acting in an official capacity. In so far as the law applicable to the trust requires or provides, this recognition implies in particular:
(a) that personal creditors of the trustee shall have no recourse against the trust assets;
(b) that the trust assets shall not form part of the trustee's estate upon his insolvency or bankruptcy;
(c) that the trust assets shall not form part of the matrimonial property of the trustee or his spouse nor part of the trustee's estate upon his death;
(d) that the trust assets may be recovered when the trustee, in breach of trust, has mingled trust assets with his own property or has alienated trust assets.

However, the rights and obligations of any third party holder of the assets shall remain subject to the law determined by the choice of law rules of the *lex fori*. Thus, although the Convention makes provision for the trustee(s) and any third parties, it fails to address the position of the beneficiaries who, for example, might wish to pursue assets intermixed with the trustee's personal property through actions for tracing. One of the problems that beneficiaries might encounter is addressed in Article 12 which considers the problem where the *situs* law does not have a title registration system which reflects ownership registration in a representative capacity. While recognising that the Convention cannot require states to modify their existing registers, it provides that the trustee shall be entitled, in so far as this is not prohibited by or inconsistent with the law of the State where registration is sought, to do so in his capacity as trustee or in such other way that the existence of the trust is disclosed. This implicitly recognises the desirability of all registration systems distinguishing between beneficial and representative titles.

This general difficulty of municipal

laws failure to support trusts is addressed in Article 13, which considers the situation of those who wish to create a trust but can only do so by invoking laws entirely outside their own state. As an application of comity, no forum state is bound to recognise a trust the significant elements of which, except for the choice of the applicable law, the place of administration and the habitual residence of the trustee, are more closely connected with States which do not have the institution of the trust or the category of trust involved. But, because this could be interpreted as an invitation not to validate otherwise perfectly appropriate financial arrangements for deserving beneficiaries, Article 14 provides that the Convention shall not prevent the application of rules of law more favourable to the recognition of trusts. This reflects the positive rules of public policy which require that the validity of a transaction (whether commercial or not) be upheld if at all possible where this will give effect to the reasonable expectations of the parties. The only exceptions shall be where this will produce consequences offending against the mandatory policies of the forum court in which case Article 18 empowers the court to deny the Applicable Law, even if it has been expressly selected by the settlor. But Article 15(2) nevertheless requires the forum court to consider adopting an approach that will preserve the overall validity of the trust insofar as that generality does not offend against the mandatory policy.

States parties

As of March 2012, 12 countries have ratified the convention: Australia, Canada (8 provinces only), China (Hong Kong only), Italy, Luxembourg, Liechtenstein, Malta, Monaco, the Netherlands (European territory only), San Marino, Switzerland and United Kingdom (including 12 dependent territories/crown dependencies).

Source (edited): "http://en.wikipedia.org/wiki/Hague_Trust_Convention"

Henson trust

A **Henson trust** (sometimes called an **absolute discretionary trust**), in Canadian law, is a type of trust designed to benefit disabled persons. Specifically, it protects the assets (typically an inheritance) of the disabled person, as well as the right to collect government benefits and entitlements.

The key provision of a Henson trust is that the trustee has "absolute discretion" in determining whether to use the trust assets to provide assistance to the beneficiary, and in what quantity. This provision means that the assets do not vest with the beneficiary and thus cannot be used to deny means-tested government benefits. An example of such a benefit is the Ontario Disability Support Program.

In addition, the trust may provide income tax relief by being taxed at a lower marginal rate than if the beneficiary's total assets were considered. It can also be used to shield assets from matrimonial division in case of divorce of the beneficiary. In most cases, the trust assets are immune from claims by creditors of the beneficiary.

The Henson trust was first used in Ontario in the late 1980s. It became of wider interest when the Supreme Court of Ontario ruled in 1989 that the trust assets were not vested in the beneficiary and thus could not be used to terminate government benefit programs.

A Henson trust can be established as either a living trust, or a testamentary trust.

The case

Leonard Henson of Guelph, Ontario had set up an absolute discretionary trust for his daughter. The Ontario Ministry of Community and Social Services took his daughter to court, arguing that she had assets. The Supreme Court of Ontario (later the Court of Appeal for Ontario) ruled that she didn't have assets, as they weren't for her to use.

Source (edited): "http://en.wikipedia.org/wiki/Henson_trust"

Holographic will

A **holographic will** is a will and testament that has been entirely handwritten and signed by the testator. Normally, a will must be signed by witnesses attesting to the validity of the testator's signature and intent, but in many jurisdictions, holographic wills that have not been witnessed are treated equally to witnessed wills and need only to meet minimal requirements in order to be probated:

- There must be evidence that the testator actually created the will, which can be proved through the use of witnesses, handwriting experts, or other methods.
- The testator must have had the intellectual capacity to write the will, although there is a presumption that a testator had such capacity unless there is evidence to the contrary.
- The testator must be expressing a wish to direct the distribution of his estate to beneficiaries.

Holographic wills are common and are often created in emergency situations, such as when the testator is alone, trapped and near death. Jurisdictions that do not generally recognize unwitnessed holographic wills will accordingly grant exceptions to members of the armed services who are involved in armed conflicts and sailors at sea, though in both cases the validity of the holographic will expires at a certain time after it is drafted.

Holographic wills often show that the requirements for making a valid will are minimal. The *Guinness Book of World Records* lists the shortest will in the world as "All to wife," written on the bedroom wall of a man who realized his imminent demise and made a swift attempt to distribute his chattels before expiring. It clearly meets the minimum requirements, being his own work and no one else's. On June 8, 1948 in Saskatchewan, Canada, a farmer named Cecil George Harris who had become trapped under his own tractor carved a will into the tractor's fender. It read "In case I die in this mess I leave all to the wife. Cecil Geo. Harris" The fender was probated and stood as his will. The fender is currently on display at the University of Saskatchewan College of Law law library.

Law in various jurisdictions

In the United States, unwitnessed holographic wills are valid in around 19 out of the 50 states. Many states, for example New York, place tight restrictions on who may use a holographic will. Jurisdictions that do not themselves recognize such holographic wills may nonetheless accept them under a "foreign wills act" if drafted in another jurisdiction in which it would be valid.Wisconsin "foreign wills act" Under the Louisiana Civil Code, such a will is known as "olographic" [sic].

In the United Kingdom, unwitnessed holographic wills are valid in Scotland but not in England and Wales or Northern Ireland. Scots law can also accept typed wills annotated by the testator in his own hand with "adopted as holograph" immediately before his signature; the same conditions apply to codicils. When the will is executed three sworn statements are required for it to be accepted as valid.*Wills and Probate: a consumer publication*. London: Consumers' Association; p. 195</ref>

Holographic wills need not be signed, when subscription to the writing appearing on the last page of such sheet is "your loving mother," or words to the effect which designates the family or personal relationship, if it is a material consideration, the signature is sufficient. This is most commonly found in documents written in emergency situations, or those prepared by individuals who have not consulted legal advice.

Utah recognizes a Holographic Will as a valid Will, whether or not it is witnessed, as long as the signature and material provisions of the Will are in the handwriting of the testator. (Section 75-2-503)

Source (edited): "http://en.wikipedia.org/wiki/Holographic_will"

Honorary trust

An **honorary trust**, under the law of trusts, is a device by which a person establishes a trust for which there is neither a charitable purpose, nor a private beneficiary to enforce the trust. While such a trust would normally be void for lack of a beneficiary, many jurisdictions have carved out two specific exceptions to this rule: trusts for the care of that person's pets; and trusts to provide for the maintenance of cemetery plots.

The name of the device derives from the lack of any beneficiary legally capable of enforcing an honorary trust: the trustee is bound by honor, but not by law, to carry out the wishes of the creator of the trust.

Like many states, New York has only recently allowed such trusts by statute.

Source (edited): "http://en.wikipedia.org/wiki/Honorary_trust"

Howe v Earl of Dartmouth

Howe v Earl of Dartmouth (1802) 7 Ves 137 is an English trusts law case. It laid down the rule of equity in relation to the duties of a trustee in relation to a trust fund where there are successive interests in relation to the trust fund, and seeks to strike a fair balance between the rights of the life tenant and the remainderman. It is one of a number of highly technical common law rules which causes considerable angst where wills and trusts have not been professionally prepared.

The general rule in relation to any trust fund is that the life tenant is entitled to all of the income, and the remainderman then takes all of the capital on the death of the life tenant. Under the rule in *Howe v Earl of Dartmouth* there may be duty to convert and reinvest authorised investments in the trust fund to maintain fairness between the life tenant and the remainderman.

There are two limbs to the rule:
- investment; and
- apportionment.

Investment

The first limb of the rule establishes that, subject to any contrary provision in the will, there is a duty to convert where residuary personalty is settled by will in favour of persons who are to enjoy it in succession. The trustees should convert all such parts of the residuary fund which are wasting, or which are future or reversionary in nature or consist of unauthorised securities into a property of a permanent or income bearing character.

So property such as speculative investments, royalties, copyrights, and, in some jurisdictions, leaseholds, should be converted in the interest of the remainderman. These are considered to be non-permanent investments, and may be of significantly reduced or no value by the time of the death of the life tenant. On the other hand "future" property, such as a remainder or a reversionary interest, or other property which at present produces no income, is of no immediate benefit to the life tenant. In the interest of the life tenant, such property should be converted into income bearing properties.

In practical terms, the rule is of relatively limited application. It does not apply to property settled *inter vivos*. It does not apply to specific residuary bequests.

Apportionment

Where there is a duty to convert under the rule in *Howe v Earl of Dartmouth*, there is, in the absence of an intention that the life tenant shall enjoy the income until sale, the second limb of the rule is that the trustee is under a duty also to apportion the property fairly between the life tenant and the remainderman until conversion. The specific rules relating to apportionment are often considered overly technical.

Wasting, hazardous or unauthorised investments

The law assumes that wasting, hazardous or unauthorised investments produce income which exceeds what a life tenant ought reasonably to receive, and that it does so at the expense of the security of the capital. Accordingly, the apportionment is made that:
- the life tenant receives an income which represents the current yield on authorised investments, and
- the excess is added to the capital,

but, subject to the proviso that:
- if the interest received is less than 4 per cent., the balance should be made up out of subsequently accruing income, or from the proceeds of the unauthorised investments when sold.

Future, reversionary or other non-income producing property

The law assumes that future property is of no benefit to the life tenant, and thus must be sold to obtain income producing investments. The proceeds of sale are apportioned between the life tenant and the remainderman by using the formulae set out in *Re Earl of Chesterfield's Trusts* (1883) 24 Ch D 643. This provides that the sum which is reserved for the remainderman is the sum "which, put out at 4 per cent. per annum ... and accumulating at compound interest at that rate with yearly rests, and deducting income tax at the standard rate, would, with accumulation of interest, have produced, at the respective dates of receipt, the amounts actually received; and that the aggregate of the sums so ascertained ought to be treated as principal and be applied accordingly, and the residue should be treated as income." Or, put another way, the principal (which goes to capital for the remainderman) is the sum which, if invested at 4 per cent. at the date of the testator's death, would have produced the sum now received, and the income is assumed to be everything else (which goes to the life tenant).

Contrary intention

All the rules above are subject to any contrary intention being expressed by the testator. The onus is upon the person asserting that the equitable rules are excluded to establish that this is so.

Modern application

The duty to apportion is, in practice, nearly always excluded in any professionally drafted will, both in respect of income from unauthorised securities and in respect of reversionary interests.

In modern times, the rules of conversion and apportionment are generally considered to be out of step with modern investing practice. The problem with speculative and wasting securities is still the same today, but the rule requires that unauthorised investments to be sold in order to "protect" the capital for the benefit of the remainderman, and it deprives the life tenant of the higher income to be earned from such investments. However, as the Law Commission of England and Wales has noted: "At a time when investment in equities may be the only way in which the capital value of the fund can in fact be maintained the traditional theory that re-investment is necessary to protect those interested in the capital no longer holds good."

Reform

Most common law jurisdictions have considered reform of one or both of the limbs of the rule in *Howe v Earl of Dartmouth* but in practice most have not done so. In the United Kingdom the Law Reform Committee recommended replacing the rule (together with other highly technical common law rules, such as the rule in *Re Atkinson* and the rule in *Allhusen v Whittell*) with a general statutory duty to hold a fair balance between the tenant for life and the remainderman, with an express power to convert income into capital and vice versa, and a duty to convert and apportion to the extent necessary to maintain an even hand and in a manner consistent with the whole investment policy of the reversionary trust fund. Such recommendations have not been implemented to date.

Source (edited): "http://en.wikipedia.org/wiki/Howe_v_Earl_of_Dartmouth"

Illustrations of the rule against perpetuities

The **fertile octogenarian** and the **unborn widow** are two legal fictions from the law of real property (and trusts) that can be used either to invoke the rule against perpetuities to make an interest in property void or, alternatively and much more frequently, to demonstrate the seemingly bizarre results that can occur as a result of the rule. The rule itself, simply stated, makes a future interest in property void unless it can be logically proven that the interest must either vest or fail to vest within 21 years after the end of a life in being at the time the interest is created.

The fertile octogenarian

The fertile octogenarian is a fictitious character that comes up when applying the rule against perpetuities. The rule presumes that anyone, even an octogenarian (i.e., someone between 80 and 90 years of age) can parent a child, regardless of gender or health. For instance, suppose that a will devises a piece of land known as Blackacre "to A for her life, and then to the first of A's children to reach 25 years of age." A is, at the time the will is probated, an 85-year-old woman. In applying the rule against perpetuities, an imaginative lawyer will argue (and a court must accept under the common law rule itself) that A could have a child in her 86th year and then in her 87th year all of A's other children could die, then in her 88th year A herself could die. Because the interest will not vest until her new child reaches 25 years of age, which cannot happen until more than 21 years after A and her other children (together who form the "lives in being" to which the rule refers) have all died, the rule against perpetuities makes the entire gift "to the first of A's children to reach 25 years of age" void. A will hold Blackacre for life, and then the property will revert back to the person whose will transferred it to A in the first place. (Actually, it will go to that person's estate, since the will was probated only after his death.)

There is often no statutory maximum age limit to perform an adoption, and adopted children are often treated the same as natural children, so an 86-year old woman who adopts a newborn child is legally in the same position as an 86-year old woman who gives birth.

The legal fiction of the **fertile octogenarian** assumes that a living person, regardless of sex, age, or physical condition, will always be capable of having more children, thus allowing an interest to vest 21 years after all the lives in being at the time of the grant are dead. In certain places this assumption will be limited to a fixed age set by statute. Furthermore, many jurisdictions have discarded old common-law fictions such as the "fertile octogenarian."

A related legal fiction, which assumes that a living person is fertile at birth, is known as the **precocious toddler**.

The unborn widow

The unborn widow poses a similar seemingly silly but logical problem. Suppose that property is left "to A for life, then to his widow for life, then to A's issue." Because the gift to A's widow cannot be resolved until A dies, the law will consider the possibility that, after the property is left to A, he marries a woman who was not born at the time the gift was made. For instance, it is possible that in 1950 the property is left to A, in 1955 a woman B is born, and in 1975 A and B marry each other. Furthermore, it is possible that A will die, say in 1980, and his widow B will outlive him for more than 21 years. Suppose that she dies in 2005. B was not a life in being at the time of the transfer, and the only remaining "validating life" under the rule against perpetuities is A, who has been dead for 25 years by this time. The gift to A's issue does not vest until his widow dies, and since that could theoretically happen more than 21 years after the death of all lives in being at the time of the transfer, the transfer to A's issue is invalid from the start. Note that changing the word "issue" to "children" makes the gift valid, since the class of "A's children" is closed and completely cognizable at the time of A's death (plus a gestation period as allowed by the rule). On the contrary, the class of "A's issue" is subject to expand long after A's death, and thus a gift to A's issue cannot vest in this case until B dies. Because her death is assumed to be more than 21 years after A's death, the result is that the gift to A's issue can vest more than 21 years after the end of all lives in being at the time the gift was created.

The problem of the **unborn widow** is a frequently used illustration of the Rule's complexities. Suppose that a woman, A, wants to devise her estate to her son B and his wife, and then to their children.

A's devise might look something like this:
To B for his life, then to his widow, if any, for life, then to B's children then living.

Though this seems like a reasonable devise, it actually violates the Rule because there is a possibility, however remote, that the interest to "B's children then living" will vest more than 21 years after the deaths of all lives in being.

Suppose B is married without children at the time of the devise. Suppose further that B's wife were to die or B were to divorce. If B were to remarry to someone who was born *after* the devise, the new wife would not be a life in being at the time of the devise. Similarly, any children born to B and his new wife would also not be lives in being at the time of the devise. If B's new wife were to outlive him (making her his widow) and survive him by more than 21 years, then the interest to "B's children then living" would not vest until after the perpetuities period expired (21 years after the death of B, the only relevant life in being at the time of the devise), because only upon the death of the widow can one ascertain who are "B's children then living."

Alternately, if B is not married at the time of the devise and B were to get married afterwards, again the wife could not be a *life in being* since she is not identifiable at the time of the devise. Similarly to the previous case, she could outlive B by more than 21 years, voiding the grant to their children (who also could not be lives in being because they would have been born after the devise was made).

However, if the last interest were simply to *B's children*, rather than to *B's children then living*, it would vest upon B's death because at that time all of B's children would be ascertainable. In this instance, the devise would be valid under the Rule.

Other examples

Other hypothetically relevant possibilities which almost never actually occur but have been invoked by lawyers or courts to invalidate transfers under the rule against perpetuities include the **slothful executor** (a situation where the executor of the estate does not probate the will for many years after the testator's death), the **magical gravel pit** (a transfer to be made as soon as a gravel pit is out of gravel may not vest for hundreds of years), the **war that never ends** (a transfer to be made at the end of a war might never happen), and other similar situations.

Criticism and humor

Because these hypothetical scenarios show how a reasonable gift can be voided based on so unlikely an outcome, they have generated much criticism among legal scholars, resulting in the abrogation of the rule against perpetuities by statute in many jurisdictions. Many U.S. States have adopted laws mollifying the application of the rule by requiring courts to "wait and see" for a period of years, sometimes as long as 360 years (which effectively negates the possibility of litigation ensuing during the life of any person alive at the same time of the author of the will).

Some jurisdictions have ameliorated specific problems of the rule by creating statutory presumptions to counter those problems. Under such statutes, for example, a woman is presumed to no longer be fertile after a particular age (typically 55), and a gift to a person's widow or widower is presumed to vest in whoever was that person's spouse at the time of the gift.

These rules have also long been a target of legal humorists.

Source (edited): "http://en.wikipedia.org/wiki/Illustrations_of_the_rule_against_perpetuities"

Incentive trust

In American estate planning parlance, an **incentive trust** is a trust designed to encourage or discourage certain behaviors by using distributions of trust income or principal as an incentive. A typical incentive trust might encourage a beneficiary to complete a degree, enter a profession, or abstain from harmful conduct such as substance abuse. The beneficiary might be paid a certain amount of money from the trust upon graduating from college, or the trust might pay a dollar of income from the trust for every dollar the beneficiary earns.

Although incentive trusts have apparently become more common in the early 21st century, a 2007 survey found that less than one-third of wealthy Americans attach conditions to the distribution of their estates. According to Joshua Tate, an assistant professor at SMU Dedman School of Law, incentive trusts pose a problem of inflexibility: "because the settlor cannot foresee all potential eventualities or circumstances and take them into account in the trust, the terms of the trust can prove to be a burden for the beneficiaries." Eileen Gallo, a noted psychotherapist, has argued that, although incentive trusts may be effective in changing behavior, they may in fact be damaging to the beneficiaries, in that they rely on external motivation to encourage activities that should be autotelic in nature. The seeming popularity of incentive trusts, however, is reflected in the many websites created by estate planners to market them.

Source (edited): "http://en.wikipedia.org/wiki/Incentive_trust"

Incorporation by reference

Incorporation by reference is the act of including a second document within another document by only mentioning the second document. This act, if properly done, makes the entire second document a part of the main document. Incorporation by reference is often done in creating laws as well as in contract law and trust and estate law.

In law regarding wills, it is a doctrine at common law which allows a testator, or a creator of a will, to dispose of assets in his estate in accordance with a separate document. To be valid, such a document must comply with the following requirements:

- it must have existed at the time the will was executed;
- the will must describe the document with particularity, so that it may be identified; and
- the will must clearly manifest the intent that the document be incorporated.

An exception to the first requirement is made for small gifts of tangible personal property, such as household furniture and items of sentimental value.

Oral instructions can *not* be used as incorporation by reference. For example, if a testator states in the will that he has recited to a third party the intended disposition of testamentary assets, such attempt to circumvent the requirements of a written will is void.

Source (edited): "http://en.wikipedia.org/wiki/Incorporation_by_reference"

Inheritance

William Hogarth's plate 1 from *A Rake's Progress*, "The Young Heir Takes Possession Of The Miser's Effects" as his inheritance.

Inheritance is the practice of passing on property, titles, debts, and obligations upon the death of an individual. It has long played an important role in human societies. The rules of inheritance differ between societies and have changed over time.

Terminology

In jurisdictions, an *heir* is a person who is entitled to receive a share of the decedent's property, via the rules of inheritance in the jurisdiction where the decedent died or owned property at the time of death. Strictly speaking, one becomes an heir only upon the death of the decedent. It is improper to speak of the "heir" of a living person, since the exact identity of the persons entitled to inherit are not determined until the time of death. In a case where an individual has such a position that only her/his own death before that of the decedent would prevent the individual from becoming an heir, the individual is called an heir apparent. There is a further concept of jointly inheriting, pending renunciation by all but one, which is called coparceny.

In modern legal use, the terms *inheritance* and *heir* refer only to succession of property from a decedent who has died intestate. It is a common mistake to refer to the recipients of property through a will as *heirs* when they are properly called *beneficiaries, devisees,* or *legatees*.

Detailed studies have been made in the Anthropological and sociological customs of patrilineal succession, is also known as gavelkind, where only male children can inherit. Some cultures also employ matrilineal succession only passing property along the female line. Other practices include primogeniture, under which all property goes to the eldest child, specifically it is often the eldest son, or ultimogeniture, in which everything is left to the youngest child. Some ancient societies and most modern states employ partible inheritance, under which every child inherits (usually equally).

Historically, there were also mixed systems:

- According to Islamic inheritance jurisprudence, sons inherit twice as much as daughters. The complete laws governing inheritance in Islam are complicated and take into account many kinship relations, but in principle males inherit twice as much as females with some exceptions. However, the Indonesian Minangkabau people (from western Sumatra), despite being Muslim, employ only complete matrilineal succession with property and land passing down from mother to daughter.
- Among ancient Israelites, the inheritance is patrilineal. It comes from the father, who bequeaths only to his male descendants (daughters don't inherit). The eldest son received twice as much as the other sons. The father gives his name to his children; for example: the sons of Israel are called Israelites, because the land belonged to the father, and every one of his twelve sons gave his name to his descendants. Example: the sons of Judah are called Yehudi (which is translated into Latin as Judaeus and into English as Jew.)
- In Galicia (Spain) it was typical that all children (both men and women) had a part of the inheritance, but one son (the one who inherited the house) inherited one-third of all the inheritance. This son was called the *mellorado* (literally, "improved upon"). In some villages the *mellorado* even received two-thirds of all the inheritance. This two-thirds would be all the family's lands, while other children received their part in money.
- In eastern Swedish culture, from the 13th century until the 19th century, sons inherited twice as much as daughters. This rule was introduced by the Regent Birger Jarl, and it was regarded as an improvement in its era, since daughters were previously usually left without.

Employing differing forms of succession can affect many areas of society. Gender roles are profoundly affected by inheritance laws and traditions. Primogeniture has the effect of keeping large estates united and thus perpetuating an elite. With partible inheritance large estates are slowly divided among many descendants and great wealth is thus diluted, leaving higher opportunities to individuals to make a success. (If great wealth is not diluted, the positions in society tend to be much more fixed and opportunities to make an individual success are lower.)

Inheritance can be organized with bbc in a way that its use is restricted by the desires of someone (usually of the decedent). An inheritance may have been organized as a fideicommissum, which usually cannot be sold or diminished, only its profits are disposable. A fideicommissum's succession can also be ordered in a way that determines it long (or eternally) also with regard to persons born long after the original descendant. Royal succession has typically been more or less a fideicommissum, the realm not (easily) to be sold and the rules of succession not to be (easily) altered by a holder (a monarch).

In more archaic days, the possession of inherited land has been much more like a family trust than a property of an individual. Even in recent years, the sale of the whole of or a significant portion of a farm in many European countries required consent from certain heirs, and/or heirs had the intervening right to obtain the land in question with same sales conditions as in the sales agreement in question.

Islamic Laws of Inheritance

The Quran introduced a number of different rights and restrictions on matters of inheritance, including general improvements to the treatment of women and family life compared to pre-Islamic societies. The Quran also presented efforts to fix the laws of inheritance, and thus forming a complete legal system. This development was in contrast to pre-Islamic societies where rules of inheritance varied considerably. Furthermore, the Quran introduced additional heirs that were not entitled inheritance in pre-Islamic times, mentioning nine relatives specifically of which six were female and three were male. In addition to the above changes, the Quran imposed restrictions on testamentary powers of a Muslim in disposing his or her property. In their will, a Muslim can only give out a maximum of one third of their property.

The Quran contains only three verses that give specific details of inheritance and shares, in addition to few other verses dealing with testamentary. But this information was used as a starting point by Muslim jurists who expounded the laws of inheritance even further using Hadith, as well as methods of juristic reasoning like Qiyas. Nowadays, inheritance is considered an integral part of Shariah Law and its application for Muslims is mandatory.

In the Bible

The inheritance is patrilineal. The father—that is, the owner of the land—bequeaths only to his male descendents, so the Promised Land passes from one Jewish father to his sons. The Promised Land is called "The Land of Israel" because it belongs to Israel, and his sons are called Israelites denoting their connection with the land of their father.

There was one exception. In Numbers 27:1-4, the daughters of Zelophehad (Mahlah, Noah, Hoglah, Milcah, and Tirzah) of the tribe of Manasseh come to Moses and ask for their father's inheritance, as they have no brothers. In Numbers 27:7-11, Jehovah grants that if a man has no sons, then his daughters may inherit, and lays down the order of inheritance: a man's sons inherit first, daughters if no sons, brothers if he has no children, and so on.

Later, in Numbers 36, some of the heads of the families of the tribe of Mannasseh come to Moses and point out that, if a daughter inherits and then marries a man not from her paternal tribe, her land will pass from her birth-tribe's inheritance into her marriage-tribe's. So a further rule is laid down: if a daughter inherits land, she must marry someone within her father's tribe. (The daughters of Zelophehad marry the sons' of their father's brothers. There is *no* indication that this was not their choice.)

Inheritance Inequality

The distribution of inherited wealth is unequal in the United States. The majority receive little while only a small number inherit larger amounts.

Arguments for eliminating the disparagement of inheritance inequality include the right to property and the merit of individual allocation of capital over government wealth confiscation and redistribution. In terms of inheritance inequality, some economists and sociologists focus on the inter generational transmission of income or wealth which is said to have a direct impact on one's mobility (or immobility) and class position in society. Nations differ on the political structure and policy options that govern the transfer of wealth.

According to the American federal government statistics compiled by Mark Zandi, currently of "Moody's Economy.com", back in 1985, the average inheritance was $39,000. In subsequent years, the overall amount of total annual inheritance was more than doubled, reaching nearly $200 billion. By 2050, there is an estimated $25 trillion average inheritance transmitted across generations. Some researchers have attributed this rise to the baby boomer generation. Historically, the baby boomers were the largest influx of children conceived after WW2. For this reason, Thomas Shapiro suggests that this generation "is in the midst of benefiting from the greatest inheritance of wealth in history."

Inheritance and Race

Inheritances are transfers of the unconsumed material accumulations of previous generations. Inheritances therefore take on a special meaning with respect to black and white Americans: they directly link the disadvantaged economic position and prospects of today's blacks to the disadvantaged positions of their parents' and grandparents' generations.

Depending on one's race, one inherits an inevitable amount of privilege or disadvantage at the time of their birth. A number of possible explanations for this gap have been suggested, particularly differences in income and various socio-economic characteristics between black and white households. Research reveals that race could be serving as a proxy for other, more fundamental, determinants of differences in inheritance. Among the findings, it was stated that a "father's education and variables indicating the economic conditions of childhood were the most important in predicting the size of inheritances." Based on samples of households in 1976 and 1989, researchers found that white households are at least twice as likely to receive an inheritance (than black households). White households are almost three times as likely to expect to receive an inheritance in the future. Hence, controlling for other factors, these researchers found that race is important in explaining whether or not a household has received an inheritance and the size of the inheritance.

Whites average both better health and inheritance than minority groups in the United States. Blacks and Hispanics are disadvantaged with respect to financial and human capital resources, more specifically, lower educational attainment, income, inheritances, and great concentrations in lower-skilled occupations. Additionally, due to employment discrimination and residential segregation, minority households "have historically been denied the opportunity to accumulate wealth" and thus, acquire inheritance.

Inheritance and Social Stratification

Inheritance inequality has a significant effect on stratification. Inheritance is an integral component of family, economic, and legal institutions, and a basic mechanism of class stratification. It also affects the distribution of wealth at the societal level. The total cumulative effect of inheritance on stratification outcomes takes three forms. The first form of inheritance is the inheritance of cultural capital (i.e. linguistic styles, higher status social circles, and aesthetic preferences). The second form of inheritance is through familial interventions in the form of inter vivos transfers (i.e. gifts between the living), especially at crucial junctures in the life courses. Examples include during a child's milestone stages, such as going to college, getting married, getting a job, and purchasing a home. The third form of inheritance is the transfers of bulk estates at the time of death of the testators, thus resulting in significant economic advantage accruing to children during their adult years. The origin of the stability of inequalities is material (personal possessions one is able to obtain) and is also cultural, rooted either in varying child-rearing practices that are geared to socialization according to social class and economic position. Child-rearing practices among those who inherit wealth may center around favoring some groups at the expense of others at the bottom of the social hierarchy.

Sociological and Economic Effects of Inheritance Inequality

The degree to which economic status and inheritance is transmitted across generations determines one's life chances in society. Although many have linked one's social origins and educational attainment to life chances and opportunities, education cannot serve as the most influential predictor of economic mobility. In fact, children of well-off parents generally receive better schooling and benefit from material, cultural, and genetic inheritances. Likewise, schooling attainment is often persistent across generations and families with higher amounts of inheritance are able to acquire and transmit higher amounts of human capital. Lower amounts of human capital and inheritance can perpetuate inequality in the housing market and higher education. Research reveals that inheritance plays an important role in the accumulation of housing wealth. Those who receive an inheritance are more likely to own a home than those who do not regardless of the size of the inheritance.

Oftentimes, minorities and individuals from socially disadvantaged backgrounds receive less inheritance and wealth. As a result, minorities are more likely to rent homes or live in poorer neighborhoods, as well as achieve lower educational attainment compared whites in America. Individuals with a substantial amount of wealth and inheritance often intermarry with others of the same social class to protect their wealth and ensure the continuous transmission of inheritance across generations; thus perpetuating a cycle of privilege. For this reason, it can even be argued that one's inheritance places them in a specific social class position that requires a level of participation in certain activities that promote the oppression of lower-class individuals in terms of the social hierarchy and system of stratification.

Nations with the highest income and wealth inequalities often have the highest rates of homicide and disease (such as obesity, diabetes, and hypertension). A New York Times article reveals that the U.S. is the world's wealthiest nation, but "ranks 29th in life expectancy, right behind Jordan and Bosnia." This is highly attributed to the significant gap of inheritance inequality in the country. For this reason, it is clear that when social and economic inequalities centered on inheritance are perpetuated by major social institutions such as family, education, religion, etc., these differing life opportunities are transmitted from each generation. As a result, this inequality becomes part of the overall social structure.

Taxation

Many states have inheritance taxes or death duties, under which a portion of any estate goes to the government.
Source (edited): "http://en.wikipedia.org/wiki/Inheritance"

Inquest

An **inquest** is a judicial investigation in common law jurisdictions, conducted by a judge, jury, or government official. The most common kind of inquest is an inquiry including a medical examination by a coroner into the cause of a death that was sudden, violent or suspicious, or occurred in prison. A **coroner's jury** may be convened to assist in this type of proceeding. *Inquest* can also mean such a jury and the result of such an investigation. In general usage, *inquest* is also used to mean any investigation or inquiry.

An inquest uses witnesses, but suspects are not permitted to defend themselves. The verdict can be, for example, natural death, accidental death, misadventure, suicide, or murder. If the verdict is murder or culpable accident, criminal prosecution may follow, and suspects are of course able to defend themselves there.

Since juries are not used in most European civil law systems, these do not have any (jury) procedure similar to an inquest, but medical evidence and professional witnesses have been used in court in continental Europe for centuries.

Larger inquests can be held into disasters, or in some jurisdictions (not England & Wales) into cases of corruption.

History

The **inquest**, as a means of settling a matter of fact, developed in Scandinavia and the Carolingian Empire before the end of the tenth century. It was the method of gathering the survey data for the Domesday Book in England after the Norman conquest.

United Kingdom

In the United Kingdom, all inquests were once conducted with a jury. They acted somewhat like a grand jury, determining whether a person should be committed to trial in connection to a death. Such a jury was made up of up to twenty-three men, and required the votes of twelve to render a decision. Similar to a grand jury, a Coroner's Jury merely accused, it did not convict.

Since 1927, Coroner's Juries have rarely been used in England. Under the *Coroners Act, 1988*, a Jury is only required to be convened in cases where the death occurred in prison, police custody, or in circumstances which may affect public health or safety. The coroner can actually choose to convene a jury in any investigation, but in practice this is rare. The qualifications to sit on a Coroner's Jury are the same as those to sit on a jury in Crown Court, the High Court, and the county courts.

Additionally, a Coroner's Jury only determines cause of death, its ruling does not commit a person to trial. While grand juries, which did have the power to indict, were abolished in the United Kingdom by 1948 (after being effectively stopped in 1933), Coroner's Juries retained those powers until the Criminal Law Act 1977. This change came about after Lord Lucan was charged in 1975 by a Coroner's Jury in the death of Sandra Rivett, his children's nanny.

United States

A coroner's jury deemed Wyatt Earp, Doc Holiday, and their posse guilty in the death of Frank Stilwell in March 1882.
Source (edited): "http://en.wikipedia.org/wiki/Inquest"

Insane delusion

An **insane delusion** is the legal term of art in the common law tradition used to describe a false conception of reality that a testator of a will adheres to against all reason and evidence to the contrary. A will made by a testator suffering from an insane delusion that affects the provisions made in the will may fail in whole or in part. Only the portion of the will caused by the insane delusion fails, including potentially the entire will. Will contests often involve claims that the testator was suffering from an insane delusion.

An insane delusion is distinct from testamentary capacity. A testator might be suffering from an insane delusion but otherwise possess the requisite capacity to make a will. Similarly, an insane delusion is distinct from a mere mistake. If suffering from an insane delusion, a testator is not subject to change his or her mind regarding the delusion if presented with contrary evidence, whereas a mistake is capable of being corrected if the testator is told the truth. Additionally, while an insane delusion may cause portions of a will to fail, most courts will not reform or invalidate a will because of a mistake unless it was the result of fraud.

Origin

The insane delusion concept was created in the 1826 British case *Dew v. Clark*. In that case, a father believed that his daughter was "the devil incarnate" and disinherited her in his will of 1818. After her father's death, evidence presented by the daughter showed that she was well-known for her good disposition and that her father had falsely told others that he lavished his daughter with praise and wealth. The probate court found that the father's mindset when he made the 1818 will was normal in all respects except toward his daughter. The court found that his thoughts about her, "did and could only proceed from, and be founded in, insanity," a "partial insanity" that only extended to his thoughts about his daughter and caused him to disinherit her. The court said that this delusion caused the will to fail.

Examples

In the 1854 case *Addington v. Wilson*, the Supreme Court of Indiana held that a testator who disinherited his daughters because he believed them to be witches was not for that reason alone so insane as to deem him incapable of making a valid will. The court justified its decision by pointing to distinguished jurists and religious figures who affirmed the possibility of witchcraft; if these people's beliefs did not render them insane, neither did the testator's.

In *In re Robertson's Estate* (1948), the Supreme Court of Oklahoma held that a testator who declared that he had "no children" and "no deceased children" in his will, when he actually had two living children, was suffering from an insane delusion, as the testator had "no rational basis whatsoever" to declare that he had no children.
Source (edited): "http://en.wikipedia.org/wiki/Insane_delusion"

Inter vivos

Inter vivos (Latin, *between the living*) is a legal term referring to a transfer or gift made during one's lifetime, as opposed to a testamentary transfer (a gift that takes effect on death).

The term is often used to describe a

trust established during one's lifetime, i.e., an **Inter vivos trust** as opposed to a **Testamentary trust** which is established on one's death, usually as part of a will. An Inter vivos trust is often used synonymously with the more common term Living trust, but an Inter vivos trust, by definition, includes both revocable and irrevocable trust.

The term inter vivos is also used to describe living organ donation, in which one patient donates an organ to another while both are alive. Generally, the organs transplanted are non-vital. A common example of this practice is the inter vivos transplantation of kidneys.

Source (edited): "http://en.wikipedia.org/wiki/Inter_vivos"

Interest in possession trust

An **interest in possession** trust is a form of legal arrangement which gives a person a "present right to the present enjoyment of something". At least one of the beneficiaries of this type of trust will have the right to receive the income generated by the trust (if trust funds are invested) or the right to enjoy the trust assets for the present time in another way, for example by living in a property owned by the trustees. The beneficiary with the right to enjoy the trust property for the time being is said to have an interest in possession and is colloquially described (though not always strictly accurately) as an income beneficiary.

A trust can give the interest in possession to a beneficiary for a fixed period, for an indefinite period or, more usually, for the rest of the beneficiary's life. Such a life interest trust is the most common example of an **interest in possession trust**.

In the example of a life interest trust, the interest in possession ends when the income beneficiary, also called the life tenant, dies. The capital of the trust will then pass to another beneficiary (or more than one). Where a charity has the right to income under a trust, it will also have an interest in possession, but this will clearly not be a life interest trust - an example would be a trust under which an art gallery has the right to display works owned by the trustees for a certain period.

Either the will or trust deed establishing the trust, or the general law, will set out how tax and trustees' expenses will be divided between the income beneficiary and the capital of the trust. Trustee investment policies will also allow emphasis on either present income (which may reduce the real value of the capital) or capital growth (increasing income in the long term and capital remaining when the interest in possession is terminated) or a balance.

Interest in possession trusts are often created as part of a will. Typically, a surviving spouse will be granted a right to the income of the trust by the settlor. When the surviving spouse dies, the rest of the fund (the **remainder**) may pass to the couple's children or other named persons.

Source (edited): "http://en.wikipedia.org/wiki/Interest_in_possession_trust"

Intestacy

Intestacy is the condition of the estate of a person who dies owning property greater than the sum of his enforceable debts and funeral expenses without having made a valid will or other binding declaration; alternatively where such a will or declaration has been made, but only applies to part of the estate, the remaining estate forms the "Intestate Estate."

Intestacy law, also referred to as *the law of descent and distribution* or *intestate succession statutes,* refers to the body of law that determines who is entitled to the property from the estate under the rules of inheritance.

History and the common law

Intestacy has a limited application in those jurisdictions that follow civil law or Roman law because the concept of a will is itself less important; the doctrine of legitime automatically gives a deceased person's relatives title to all or a large part of the estate's property by operation of law, beyond the power of the deceased person to alter by legacy. This share can often only be decreased on account of some very specific misconduct by the heir. When referring to the devolution of estates generally in an international context, the "laws of succession" is the commonplace term covering testate and intestate estates in common law jurisdictions together with forced heirship rules typically applying in civil law and Sharia law jurisdictions. After the Statute of Wills, 32 Henry VIII c. 1, Englishmen (and unmarried or widowed women) could dispose of their lands and property by a will. Their personal property could formerly be disposed of by a "testament," hence the hallowed legal merism "Last Will and Testament."

Common law sharply distinguished between real property and chattels. Real property for which no disposition had been made by will passed by the law of kinship and descent; chattel property for which no disposition had been made by testament was escheat to the Crown, or given to the Church for charitable purposes. This law became obsolete as England moved from being a feudal to a mercantile society, and chattels more valuable than land were being accumulated by townspeople.

Current law

In most contemporary common-law jurisdictions, the law of intestacy is patterned after the common law of descent. Property goes first or in major part to a spouse, then to children and their descendants; if there are no descendants, the rule sends you back up the family tree to the parents, the siblings, the siblings' descendants, the grandparents, the parents' siblings, and the parents' siblings' descendants, and usually so on further to the more remote degrees of kinship. The operation of these laws varies from one jurisdiction to another.

England and Wales

In England and Wales the Intestacy Rules have been uniform since 1925 and strikingly similar rules apply in Northern Ireland, the Republic of Ireland and many Commonwealth countries and Crown dependencies. These rules have been supplemented by the discretionary provisions of the Inheritance (Provision for Family and Dependants) Act 1975 so that fair provision can be made for a dependent spouse or other relative where the strict divisions set down in the intestacy rules would produce an unfair result, for example by providing additional support for a dependent minor or disabled child vis-a-vis an adult child who has a career and no longer depends on their parent.

If a person dies intestate with no identifiable heirs, the person's estate generally escheats (i.e. is legally assigned) to the Crown (via the Bona Vacantia division of the Treasury Solicitor) or to the Duchies of Cornwall or Lancaster when the deceased was a resident of either; in limited cases a discretionary distribution might be made by one of these bodies to persons who would otherwise be without entitlement under strict application of the rules of inheritance.

United States and Canada

In the United States intestacy laws vary from state to state under the American practice of federalism. Likewise, in Canada the laws vary from province to province. As in England, most jurisdictions apply rules of intestate succession to determine next of kin who become legal heirs to the estate. Also, as in England, if no identifiable heirs are discovered, the property may escheat to the government.

Attempts in the United States to make the law with respect to intestate succession uniform from state to state have met with limited success.

The distribution of the property of an intestate decedent is the responsibility of the *administrator* (or *personal representative*) of the estate: typically the administrator is chosen by the court having jurisdiction over the decedent's property, and is frequently (but not always) a person nominated by a majority of the decedent's heirs.

Federal law controls intestacy of Native Americans.

Many states have adopted all or part of the the Uniform Probate Code, but often with local variations, In Ohio, the law of intestate succession has been modified significantly from the common law, and has been essentially codified. The state of Washington also has codified its intestacy law. New York has perhaps the most complicated law of descent of distribution, having been for many years.Florida's intestacy statute permits the heirs of a deceased spouse of the decedent to inherit, in the event that the decedent has no other heirs.

In Alberta, under the current law which gives unmarried couples most of the same rights as married couples, the deceased's family may discover that the surviving husband or wife might receive no part of the estate. Under Alberta's intestacy legislation, the deceased's family may discover that a former or "ex" common-law partner may be given the entire estate; ahead of the deceased's own legally married spouse, parents, or even children.

Rules

Where a person dies without leaving a will, the rules of succession of the person's place of habitual residence or of their domicile apply. In certain jurisdictions such as France, Switzerland and much of the Islamic world, entitlements arise whether or not there was a will. These are known as *forced heirship* rights and are not typically found in common-law jurisdictions, where the rules of succession without a will (intestate succession) play a back-up role where an individual has not (or has not fully) exercised his or her right to dispose of property in a will.

In England and Wales, the rules of succession are the Intestacy Rules set out in the Administration of Estates Act and associated legislation.

The Act sets out the order for distribution of property in the estate of the deceased. For persons with surviving children and a wealth below a certain threshold (£250,000 as from February 2009), the whole of the estate will pass to the deceased's spouse or also, from December 2005, their registered civil partner. For persons with no surviving children but surviving close relatives (such as siblings or parents), the first £450,000 goes to the spouse or civil partner (as from February 2009). Such transfers below the threshold are exempt from UK inheritance tax.

In larger estates, the spouse will not receive the entire estate where the deceased left other blood relatives and left no will. They will receive the following:

- all property passing to them by survivorship (such as the deceased's share in the jointly owned family home);
- all property passing to them under the terms of a trust (such as a life insurance policy);
- a statutory legacy of a fixed sum (being a larger sum where the deceased left no children); and
- a life interest in half of the remaining estate.

The children (or more distant relatives if there are no children) of the deceased will be entitled to half of the estate remaining immediately and the remaining half on the death of the surviving spouse. Where no beneficiaries can be traced, see bona vacantia.

In the United States, each of the separate states uses its own intestacy laws to determine the ownership of its resident's intestate property.

Source (edited): "http://en.wikipedia.org/wiki/Intestacy"

Italian trust law

A trust is a particular juridical instrument by which a settler (disponente) can transfer a property (movable or immovable property) to a "trustee" who has to exercise and manage this right for a "beneficiary" (to whom the full property will be transferred with the termination of the trust) who has the "equitable right". In civil law systems the beneficiary's right is not a "diritto reale" but a "personal right" towards the "trustee". If it is not foreseen by the constitutive contract, the property assets cannot be alienated by neither by the trustee nor by the beneficiary. Trust property cannot be foreclosed by the personal creditors of the trustee, the beneficiary or their heirs.

Current situation

In Italy trusts can be used thanks to the adoption of the Hague Convention (1 July 1985), executive from 1 January 1992. The "trust interno" is a domestic trust but refers to a foreign regulation because as of August 2010 Italy does not have a complete and organic internal regulation on trust. Trusts can be used for various aims : administration, transfer of family business assets, transfer of goods for charity purposes, protection of patrimony, etc. The main advantages are the flexibility of its use and its economic convenience compared to Italian traditional juridical instruments. Nevertheless, they have not had a widespread application in Italy mainly because of the scarce knowledge of its functioning and its potentiality.

Proposed legislation

Italy has proposed its own regulation on trust (fiducia). The Italian Government has been delegated by the community law 2010 (bill/ legge comunitaria) to adopt a specific regulation on trusts (fiducia) within the Italian juridical system (title II art. 11). The "disegno di legge n. 2284/2010" (bill n. 2284/2010) presented by the Ministry of Justice (presented on July 2010 but not yet examined) charges the Government to modify the civil code as concerns "trusts" (fiducia) and the particular security contract.

The proposed Italian regulation on trust (fiducia) is inspired by the French "fiducie" which extended (ordinance n° 2009-112 2009) to individuals and corporations excluded from the payment of company taxes, the capacity to constitute a "trust" (fiducie), and allowed attorneys to become trustees .
Source (edited): "http://en.wikipedia.org/wiki/Italian_trust_law"

Joint wills and mutual wills

Joint wills and **mutual wills** are closely related terms used in the law of wills to describe two types of testamentary writing that may be executed by a married couple to ensure that their property is disposed of identically. Neither should be confused with **mirror wills** which means two separate, identical wills, which may or may not also be mutual wills.

A joint will is a single document executed by more than one person (typically husband and wife), making which has effect in relation to each signatory's property on his or her death (unless he or she revokes (cancels) the will during his or her lifetime). Although a single document, the joint will is a separate distribution of property by each executor (signatory) and will be treated as such on admission to probate. Mutual wills are any two (or more) wills which are mutually binding, such that following the first death the survivor is constrained in his or her ability to dispose of his or her property by the agreement he or she made with the deceased. Historically such wills had an important role in ensuring property passed to children of a marriage rather than a widow or widower's spouse on a remarriage.

The recognition of these forms varies widely from one jurisdiction to the next. Some permit both, some will not recognize joint wills, and many have established a presumption that one or both of these forms creates a will contract.

A joint will differs substantively from a mutual will in that the former is not intended to be irrevocable or to express a mutual intention; it is merely an administrative convenience. A will may be both joint (on one document) and mutual (see below).

Mutual wills have four basic requirements and a strict standard for enforceability:
- The agreement must be made in a particular form.
- The agreement must be contractual in effect. (Contrast *Re Goodchild* 1 WLR and *Lewis v Cotton* 2 NZLR)
- The agreement must be intended to be irrevocable.
- The surviving party must have intended the will to reflect the agreement.

Mutual wills are rare, and often another form of constructive trust is imposed (See *Healey v Browne* 2 WTLR 849). It is also noted (see Carnwath J in *Re Goodchild ibid*) that a mutual will is a technical legal device requiring an intention to form a binding agreement and that this often differs from the "loose moral obligation" presupposed as binding by the layman.

Common law authority

The major common law authority in this area is *Re Oldham* Ch. 75. This discussed the 18th century case of *Dufour v Pereira* which first evinced the doctrine, in which Lord Camden remarked "he, that dies first, does by his death carry the agreement on his part into execution". Astbury J in *Oldham* distinguished mutual wills from mirror wills - that they are made in identical terms "does not go nearly far enough". There must be "an arrangement proved to the satisfaction of the court" and this must be a binding, irrevocable agreement.

In *Re Cleaver* 1 WLR Nourse J took a less strict approach in finding that identical wills went towards proving the existence of an agreement, however this approach was rejected in *Re Goodchild* 1 WLR where Carnwath J stated the importance of having specific evidence as to the testator's mutual intentions at the time of execution of the wills. Carnwath J approved the "floating trust" analogy, first proposed by Dixon J in *Birmingham v Renfrew* CLR, which holds that the law will give effect to the intention (to create a mutually binding will) by imposing a floating trust which becomes irrevocable after the death of the first testator and crystallises after the death of the second.

In the Court of Appeal decision in *Goodchild* Legatt LJ approved the dicta of Carnwath J and added that "for the doctrine to apply there must be a contract". This approach raises problems as will be seen below. However, the contractual requirement has been rejected in other decisions, or at least diluted. Dixon J in *Birmingham*, commenting on *Dufour v Pereira*, noted that it is the trust arising from the course of conduct which is enforced, not the contract itself. This approach has received further credence in the decision of Blanchard J in *Lewis v Cotton*. "A formal legal contract is not needed. A contract made without formality is enough...The crucial factor must be that the terms of the mutual engagement... are sufficiently certain that the Court can see its way to enforce them." The importance of this approach is, as Blanchard J notes, that the focus is on the obligation not to deal with property contrary to the agreement rather than on non-revocation. This therefore covers situations such as that in *Healey v Browne* where there has been an *inter vivos* transfer to avoid the will.

In *Healey v Browne* a husband transferred assets jointly to himself and his son after the death of his wife. Although there was found to be no mutual will (Donaldson QC adopted the contractual requirement), he considered that where there was a valid mutual will the second testator is free to use the assets for his own beneficial interest as long as it is not calculated to defeat the agreement: "Where the fiduciary duty is breached by such a voluntary disposition inter vivos of the property in question, the "crystallisation" of the floating obligation must occur at the moment of that disposition." (Note that Donaldson QC imposed a secret trust in the circumstances which reduced the son's interest to 50%, that being the interest held by the husband)

In *Olins v Walters* 2 WLR 1 C.A. the Court of Appeal has held that although it is a necessary condition for mutual wills that there is clear and satisfactory evidence of a contract between the testators, it is a legally sufficient condition that the contract provide that, in return for one testator agreeing to make a will in a particular form and not to revoke it without notice to the other testator, the latter would also make a will in a particular form and agree not to revoke it without notice to the first testator. Once a contract of that kind is established, equity will impose on the surviving testator a constructive trust not to dispose of the property in any other way. There did not have to be more detailed terms of the contract because the remedy was not founded on specific performance of contractual obligations but upon implementation of the trust, and the intentions of the parties had only to be expressed sufficiently to lay the foundations for that equitable obligation. The case also held that, where established, the equitable obligation under the trust became immediately binding upon the surviving testator upon the death of the first and was not postponed to take effect only after the death of the second or last testator when the property, or what was left of it, came into the hands of his personal representatives.

Revocability

Another issue as regards mutual wills is the question of revocability. In *Re Hobley* Charles Aldous QC held that there could be either unilateral or mutual revocation provided it occurred during the lifetime of both testators. However, the problem with this approach is that unilateral revocation is against the general principle of contract. Several explanations for this could be proffered. Firstly, there could be an implicit term that the agreement is revocable. Secondly, it could be conceptually viewed that the agreement takes on the revocable nature of the will to which it relates. Thirdly, as the doctrine is based on detrimental reliance, the agreement only concretized on the death of the other party. Fourthly, one could apply the unconscionability rationale that unjust enrichment could only be complete when one party takes a benefit under the will of the other party.

Re Hobley adopts the unconscionability rationale such that the imposition of a constructive trust is only justified by unconscionability, therefore there must be detrimental reliance. This would appear to be analogous to the doctrine of estoppel. Another consequence of this approach is that the trust must come into existence before the death of the first testator as otherwise the subject matter of the trust would be uncertain and could possible be avoided by inter vivos dispositions.

Another point of controversy was whether or not the second testator had to benefit from the initial disposition. Commentators had argued that this was the case as if the second testator did not benefit the unjust enrichment argument would be untenable. However, *Re Dale* Ch held that no benefit was necessary. Morritt J reasoned that although the aim of the doctrine was to prevent fraud on the first testator this did not require a corresponding benefit for the second testator. Friel (1996 1 CPLJ) argued against this saying that the trust should not be imposed on the property but rather on the implementation of the contract between the parties. An excellent rebuke to this approach and support for the view in *Re Dale* is to be found in the judgment of Rowles JA in the Court of Appeal (British Columbia) decision in *University of Manitoba v Sanderson*. Rowles contended that the doctrine imposes a constructive trust on the survivor because the first to die is considered to have carried out the agreement by her death in reliance on the survivor's promise to act in accordance with the agreement. It is also important to note that these cases do not use the fraud rationale in the conventional sense of deceptive receipt of property. Instead an estoppel argument based on representation, reliance, detriment and irrevocability is utilised.

Re Hagger 2 Ch held that the constructive trust comes into existence on the death of the first testator, however this approach was revised in *Re Hobley* which decided that it must come into existence before the death of the first testator to satisfy the requirement of certainty of subject matter.

In the case of *Ottaway v Norman* Ch., Brightman J held that a floating obligation attaches to secret trusts: "A valid trust is created in favour of the secondary donee which is in suspense during the lifetime of the donee, but attaches to the estate of the primary donee at the moment of the latter's death." Edward Nugee QC sitting as deputy High Court judge in *Re Basham* 1 WLR applied a comparable test in relation to proprietary estoppel. He held that the belief, for detrimental reliance, need not relate to a clearly identified piece of property. Following *Cleaver* and *Birmingham*, if it is established by cogent evidence that the intention was to leave the entire estate, proprietary estoppel will enforce that intention. (It is interesting to recall that Edward Nugee was counsel in *Ottaway v Norman* and that Brightman J adopted his floating obligation theory)

Source (edited): "http://en.wikipedia.org/wiki/Joint_wills_and_mutual_wills"

Knowing receipt

Knowing receipt, or **unconscionable receipt** in more recent times, is a type of third party liability under trust law. To be liable for knowing receipt, the plaintiff must show, first, a disposal of his trust assets in breach of fiduciary duty; second, the beneficial receipt by the defendant of assets which are traceable as representing the assets of the plaintiff; and third, knowledge on the part of the defendant that the assets he received are traceable to a breach of fiduciary duty.

Underlying principle

The underlying principle of knowing receipt is beneficial receipt of D is unjust enrichment at the expense of the rightful owner. In Royal Brunei Airlines Sdn Bhd v Tan, knowing receipt is characterized as restitution-based liability (as opposed to accessory liability).

Degree of knowledge required

Under knowing receipt, the onus is on the claimant beneficiary to establish recipient's knowledge.

The degree of knowledge required has been a controversial issue and there are numerous lines of authority on it. For example in some cases it was held that Baden category 1 to 3 knowledge, i.e. dishonesty is needed, or in some cases it was held that all 5 categories would suffice, i.e. either dishonesty or negligence.

In Belmont Finance Corp Ltd v Williams Furniture (No 2) it was held that fraud/dishonesty not required, i.e. negligence would suffice. In El Ajou v Dollar Land Holdings plc 3 All ER 717, it was held that constructive knowledge was sufficient; Though in Polly Peck Int'l plc v Nadir (No 2) 4 All ER 769, Scott LJ agreed that courts are always reluctant to extend constructive notice doctrine to circumstances when money is paid in ordinary course of business.

At last, in BCCI (Overseas) Ltd v Akindele Ch 437, it was held that the degree of knowledge for for knowing receipt is knowledge that makes it unconscionable for recipient to retain benefit of receipt. It was also held that the five categories of knowledge in Baden is not useful.

Source (edited): "http://en.wikipedia.org/wiki/Knowing_receipt"

Labour Leader's Office Fund

The **Labour Leader's Office Fund** was a blind trust established and run by Lord Levy to finance Tony Blair's work in opposition before the 1997 General Election. Contributors to it included the millionaires Sir Trevor Chinn, Sir Emmanuel Kaye, Alex Bernstein and Bob Gavron, the latter two of whom later received peerages.

Quotes about the fund

- "While it does not necessarily follow that the scheme was anything other than the model of probity, there is at least an argument that Lloyd George knew its father." -- David Osler, author of *Labour Party PLC: New Labour as a Party of Business*. (Lloyd George was infamous for selling honours in the early 20th century.)

Source (edited): "http://en.wikipedia.org/wiki/Labour_Leader%27s_Office_Fund"

Lapse and anti-lapse

Lapse and **anti-lapse** are complementary concepts under the law of wills, which address the disposition of property that is willed to someone who dies before the testator (the writer of the will).

Lapse

At common law, lapse occurs when the beneficiary or the devisee under the will predeceases the testator, invalidating the gift. The gift would instead revert to the residuary estate or be granted under the law of intestate succession.

If the deceased beneficiary was intended to inherit part or all of the residuary estate, then that portion of the estate would pass by intestate succession, as though the testator had left no will. This rule is referred to as the doctrine of no residue of a residue, because the portion of the residuary estate that did not itself pass under the will could not be considered part of the residuary estate at all.

Under section 2-604(b) of the uniform probate code, "if the residue is devised to two or more persons, the share of a residuary devisee that fails for any reason passes to the other residuary devisee, or to other residuary devisees in proportion to the interest of each in the remaining part of the residue." Simply put, if there are two parties in the remainder and one has not survived, the entirety of the remainder goes to the surviving residuary devisee.

In jurisdictions which have adopted the Uniform Simultaneous Death Act, or the 1991 version of the Uniform Probate Code (but not the previous Uniform Probate Code), any devisee who dies within 120 hours *after* the testator is legally considered to have died *before* the testator. In such jurisdictions, only a devisee who survives more than 120 hours after the testator is considered to have met this "statutory survival test."

Anti-lapse statutes

Most common-law jurisdictions have enacted an **anti-lapse statute** to address this situation. The anti-lapse statute "saves" the bequest if it has been made to parties specified in the statute, usually members of the testator's immediate family, if those family members had descendants. If this is the case, then the descendants of the deceased beneficiary will inherit whatever was willed to that beneficiary. The testator can prevent the operation of an anti-lapse statute by providing that the gift will only go to the named beneficiary *if* that beneficiary survives the testator, or by simply stating in the will that the anti-lapse statute does not apply.

Another modification to the common law of lapse is the elimination of the "no residue of a residue" rule where multiple beneficiaries are named to inherit the residue. The modern view is that where a beneficiary was intended to inherit part of the residuary estate who predeceases the testator, and that beneficiary is not covered by the anti-lapse statute, then that beneficiary's inheritance will return to the residuary estate, to be inherited by the other beneficiaries to whom the residue has been willed.

Source (edited): "http://en.wikipedia.org/wiki/Lapse_and_anti-lapse"

Last will and testament of Adolf Hitler

The **last will and testament of Adolf Hitler** was dictated by Hitler to his secretary Traudl Junge in his Berlin Führerbunker on April 29, 1945, the day he and Eva Braun married. They committed suicide the next day (April 30), two days before the surrender of Berlin to the Soviets on May 2, and just over a week before the end of World War II in Europe on May 8. It consisted of two separate documents, a will and a political testament.

The last will was a short document signed on 29 April 1945 at 4:00 am.

- It acknowledged his marriage—but does not name Eva Braun—and that they choose death over disgrace of deposition or capitulation; and that their bodies were to be cremated.
- His art collection is left to "a gallery in my home town of Linz on Donau".
- Objects of "sentimental value or is necessary for the maintenance of a modest simple life" went to his relatives and his "faithful co-workers" such as secretary Mrs. Winter.
- Whatever else of value he possessed went to the National Socialist German Workers Party.
- Martin Bormann was nominated as the will's executor.

The will was witnessed by Dr. Joseph Goebbels, Martin Bormann and Colonel Nicholaus von Below.

The last political testament was signed at the same time as Hitler's last will, 4:00 am on April 29, 1945. The first part of the testament is a restatement of the political position and justifications which he had stated many times before. His intention to commit suicide soon after writing the testament and the imminent destruction of the Third Reich did not alter his political position. The second part lays out Hitler's intentions for the government of Germany and the Nazi Party after his death. Also included in the testament are several statements that he did not want to instigate war with other nations and blamed Jews for the war.

The second part dealt with the question of who was to succeed him. Hitler had designated Reichsmarschall Hermann Göring as his successor in the event of his death, but expelled him from the party and canceled his succession rights for asking permission to take over a few days earlier. Instead, Hitler named Großadmiral Karl Dönitz as President of the Reich and Supreme Commander of the Armed Forces. Reichsführer-SS and Interior Minister Heinrich Himmler was also expelled from the party for attempting to negotiate a peace deal with the Allies without Hitler's permission. Hitler accused Göring and Himmler of betraying him and bringing "irreparable shame on the whole nation" by negotiating with the Allies.

Hitler appointed the following as the new Cabinet and as "leaders of the nation":

- President of the Reich (*Reichspräsident*), Minister of War (*Kriegsminis-*

ter) and Commander-in-Chief of the Navy (*Oberbefehlshaber der Kriegsmarine*): Grand Admiral Karl Dönitz
- Chancellor of the Reich (*Reichskanzler*): Dr. Joseph Goebbels
- Party Minister (*Parteiminister*): Martin Bormann
- Foreign Minister (*Aussenminister*): Arthur Seyss-Inquart
- Interior Minister (*Innenminister*): Gauleiter Paul Giesler
- Commander-in-Chief of the Army (*Oberbefehlshaber des Heeres*): Field Marshal Ferdinand Schörner
- Commander-in-Chief of the Air Force (*Oberbefehlshaber der Luftwaffe*): Field Marshal Robert Ritter von Greim
- Reichsführer-SS and Chief of Police (*Reichsführer-SS und Chef der Deutschen Polizei*): Gauleiter Karl Hanke
- Minister of Economy (*Wirtschaft*): Walter Funk
- Minister of Agriculture (*Landwirtschaft*): Herbert Backe
- Minister of Justice (*Justiz*): Otto Thierack
- Minister of Culture (*Kultus*): Dr. Gustav Adolf Scheel
- Minister of Propaganda (*Propaganda*): Dr. Werner Naumann
- Minister of Finance (*Finanzen*): Johann Ludwig Graf Schwerin von Krosigk
- Minister of Labour (*Arbeit*): Dr. Theo Hupfauer
- Minister of Munitions (*Rüstung*): Karl-Otto Saur
- Director of the German Labour Front and member of the Cabinet (*Leiter der Deutschen Arbeitsfront und Mitglied des Reichskabinetts: Reichsminister*) Dr. Robert Ley

Witnessed by Dr. Joseph Goebbels, General Wilhelm Burgdorf, Martin Bormann, and General Hans Krebs.

On the afternoon of 30 April, about a day and a half after he signed his last will and testament, Hitler committed suicide.

Authorship

In his book *The Bunker*, James O'Donnell, after comparing the wording of Hitler's last testament to the writings and statements of both Hitler and Joseph Goebbels, concluded that Goebbels was at least partly responsible for helping Hitler to write it. Junge claimed Hitler was reading from notes when he dictated the testament; since Hitler could barely write by this stage.

Death of the witnesses

All four witnesses to the political testament died shortly afterwards. Goebbels and his wife committed suicide. Burgdorf and Krebs committed suicide together on the night of 1/2 May in the bunker. Bormann's exact time and place of death remain uncertain; his remains were discovered near the site of the bunker in 1972 and identified by DNA analysis in 1998. Therefore, he was most likely killed the same night trying to escape from the Führerbunker.

Source (edited): "http://en.wikipedia.org/wiki/Last_will_and_testament_of_Adolf_Hitler"

Last will and testament of Frederica Evelyn Stilwell Cook

The last will and testament of **Frederica Evelyn Stilwell Cook**, who died 9 January 1925, age 68, is thought to be the longest will ever filed for probate.

The will

The will was 1066 pages (95,940 words) and occupied four gilt-edged, leather-bound volumes. It was entered into probate at Somerset House, the then home of the probate registry in London, on 2 November 1925.

Of the four volumes in which the will was bound, two contain 702 pages each, and the other two 406 pages each. The paper is gilt-edged and the bindings are of leather with heavy corners and canvas covers.

Aside from the pages containing the introductory clauses, the pages are ruled with a single column and contain a priced inventory of laces, jewelry, furs, embroideries, dressing bags and objects of art. A large number of the articles are explained in footnotes. A large part of the will is in Mrs. Cook's own handwriting. It is dated 17 October 1919, but there is a codicil dated 2 March 1924.

Probate of the will was granted to Mrs. Cook's brother and son, both of them Londoners, the latter a racing motorist. Practically all of her bequests were to her children, and her two executors were directed to burn her diaries, to bury her wedding ring with her, and to see that her age is not inscribed on her tombstone. She is buried in Richmond Cemetery in Richmond, England; section J, grave 1289.

Frederica Evelyn Stilwell Cook

Frederica Evelyn Stilwell Cook was the daughter or F. J. Freeland, and married Wyndham Francis Cook, son of Sir Francis Cook, 1st Bt. and Emily Martha Lucas, on 22 November 1887. Her children were:
- Humphrey Wyndham Cook b. Mar 1893, d. 1978
- Cecil Emily Freda Wyndham Cook b. 1 Jul 1896
- Ursula Maud Wyndham Cook b. 20 Nov 1900

Source (edited): "http://en.wikipedia.org/wiki/Last_will_and_testament_of_Frederica_Evelyn_Stilwell_Cook"

Laughing heir

A **laughing heir** in the law of inheritance, is an heir who is legally entitled to inherit the property of a person who has died, even though that heir is only distantly related to the deceased, and therefore has no personal connection or reason to feel bereaved over the death. In most jurisdictions, the law of intestacy requires that the property of a person who died without leaving a will must first go to that person's immediate family, such as a spouse, descendants, ascendants, or persons descended from the same parents or grandparents. Under the common law, if no such persons exist, the property passes to the nearest living person who can demonstrate some degree of kinship with the deceased, no matter how distant the relation.

Some jurisdictions have a **laughing heir statute**, which cuts off the right of inheritance when the remaining relatives become too remote. In such jurisdictions, if no relative falls within the limitation set by the statute, then the property escheats to the state. §2-103 of the Uniform Probate Code, which has been adopted by a number of states, sets the outer limits of the right to inheritance with grandparents, aunts and uncles, and first cousins. Under the code, heirs that are farther removed from the deceased are left with no claim to the estate at all.

By contrast, some states (such as Florida and Virginia) have extended the principle to cover the family of a predeceased *spouse*. In those states, if the decedent had been married, and their spouse had died before the decedent, and if the decedent had no blood relatives at all, then the decedent's property would pass to any living relatives of the *spouse*, no matter how remote.

Jurisdictions with no "laughing heir" statute

Africa
- South Africa

North America
- Florida (also extends inheritance rights to relatives of a predeceased spouse)
- Texas
- Virginia (also extends inheritance rights to relatives of a predeceased spouse)

Jurisdictions with a "laughing heir" statute

North America
- Alabama (cuts off inheritance with descendants of the grandparents of the deceased)

Source (edited): "http://en.wikipedia.org/wiki/Laughing_heir"

Legal history of wills

Wills have a lengthy history.

In the ancient world

The development of Roman law furthered the modern understanding of wills. and led to the development of the law of estates in many European states, greatly aided later by ecclesiastics versed in Roman law.

In India, the will was unknown before English conquest. In Christian tradition, Eusebius and others have related of Noah's testament, made in writing, and witnessed under his seal, by which he disposed of the whole world. Additionally, wills are spoken of in the Old Testament (in Genesis 48), where Jacob bequeaths to his son Joseph, a portion of his inheritance, double to that of his brethren.

The Ancient Greek practice concerning wills was not the same in all places; some states permitted men to dispose of their estates, others wholly deprived them of that privilege. We are told by Plutarch, that Solon "is much commended for his law concerning wills; for before his time no man was allowed to make any, but all the wealth of deceased persons belonged to their families; but he permitted them to bestow it on whom they pleased, esteeming friendship a stronger tie than kindred, and affection than necessity, and thus put every man's estate in the disposal of the possessor; yet he allowed not all sorts of wills, but required the following conditions in all persons that made them:

- That they must be citizens of Athens, not slaves, or foreigners, for then their estates were confiscated for the public use.
- That they must be men who have arrived to twenty years of age, for women and men under that age were not permitted to dispose by will of more than one medimn of barley.
- That they must not be adopted; for when adopted persons died without issue, the estates they received by adoption returned to the relations of the men who adopted them.
- That they should have no male children of their own, for then their estate belonged to these. If they had only daughters, the persons to whom the inheritance was bequeathed were obliged to marry them. Yet men were allowed to appoint heirs to succeed their children, in case these happened to die under twenty years of age.
- That they should be in their right minds, because testaments extorted through the phrenzy of a disease, or dotage of old age, were not in reality the wills of the persons that made them.
- That they should not be under imprisonment, or other constraint, their consent being then only forced, nor in justice to be reputed voluntary.
- That they should not be induced to it by the charms and insinuations of a wife; for (says Plutarch) the wise lawgiver with good reason thought that no difference was to be put between deceit and necessity, flattery and compulsion, since both are equally powerful to persuade a man from reason.

Wills were usually signed before several witnesses, who put seals to them for confirmation, then placed them in the hands of trustees, who were obliged to see them performed. At Athens, some of the magistrates were very often present at the making of wills. Sometimes the *archons* were also present. Sometimes the testator declared his will before sufficient witnesses, without committing it to writing. Thus Callias, fearing to be cut off by a wicked conspiracy, is said to have made an open declaration of his will before the popular assembly at Athens. There were several copies of wills in Diogenes Laertius, as those of Aristotle, Lyco of Troas, and Theophrastus; whence it appears they had a common form, beginning with a wish for life and health."

In the *Leges barbarorum*, where they are unaffected by Roman law, the will, if it existed at all, was of a very rudimentary character. The will is, on the other hand, recognized by Rabbinical and Islamic law.

The early Roman will differed from the modern will in important respects. It was effectual during the lifetime of the person who made it; it was made in public *vivâ voce*; all knew of the legator's intentions, the testator declaring his will in the presence of seven witnesses; and it could not be changed – these they called *nuncupative* testaments; but the danger of trusting the will of the dead to the memory of the living soon abolished these; and all testaments were ordered to be in writing.

The objective, as in adoption, was to secure the perpetuation of the family. This was done by securing the due vesting of the breed in a person who could be relied upon to keep up the family rites. There is much probability in the conjecture that a will was only allowed to be made when the testator had no known gentile relatives, unless they had waived their rights. The Romans were wont to set aside testaments, as being *inofficiosa*, deficient in natural duty, if they disinherited or totally passed by (without assigning a true and sufficient reason) any of the children of the testator. But if the child had any legacy, though ever so small, it was a proof that the testator had not lost his memory nor his reason, which otherwise the law presumed. Hence probably has arisen that groundless, vulgar error of the necessity of leaving the heir a shilling, or some other express legacy, in order to effectually disinherit him; whereas the modern law, though the heir, or next of kin, be totally omitted, admits no *querela inofficiosa*, to set aside such testament.

It is certain from the text of Gaius that the earliest forms of will were those made in the *comitia calata* and those made in *procinctu*, or on the eve of battle. The former were published before the *comitia*, as representative of the patrician genies, and were originally a legislative act. These wills were the peculiar privilege of patricians. At a later time the form of plebeian will developed (*irs/amentum per aes ci libram*), and the law of succession under testament was further modified by the influence of *tile practor*, especially in the direction of recognition of *fideicommissa* similar in some respects to testamentary trusts. *Codicilli* or informal wills, also came into use, and were sufficient for almost every purpose but the appointment of an heir.

In the time of Justinian a will founded partly on the *jus civile*, partly on the edict of the *praetor*, partly on imperial constitutions and so called *testamentum tripertitum*, was generally in use. The main points essential to its validity were that the testator should possess testamentary capacity, and that the will should be signed or acknowledged by the testator in the presence of seven witnesses, or published orally in open court. The witnesses must be *idonei*, or free from legal disability. For instance, women and slaves were not good witnesses.

The whole property of the testator could not be alienated. The rights of heirs and descendants were protected by enactments which secured to them a legal minimum, the querela inofficiosi testamenhi being the remedy of those passed over. The age at which testamentary capacity began was fourteen in the case of males, twelve in the case of females. Up to 439 A.D. a will must have been in Latin; after that date Greek was allowed.

Certain persons, especially soldiers, were privileged from observing the ordinary forms. The liability of the heir to the debts of the testator varied during different periods. At first it was practically unlimited. The law was then gradually modified in favour of the heir, until in the time of Justinian the heir who duly made an inventory of the property of the deceased was liable only for the assets to which he had succeeded. This limitation of liability is generally termed by the civilians *beneficium inventarii*.

Something like the English probate is to be found in the rules for breaking the seals of a will in presence of the praetor. Closely connected with the will was the donatio mortis causa, the rules of which have been as a whole adopted in England (see below). An immense space in the Corpus juris is occupied with testamentary law. The whole of part v. of the Digest (books xxviii.-xxxvi.) deals with the subject, and so do a large number of constitutions in the Code and Novels.

The effect of Christianity upon the will was very marked. For instance, the duty of bequeathing to the Church was inculcated as early as Constantine, and heretics and monks were placed under a disability to make a will or take gifts left by will. A will was often deposited in a church. The Canon law follows the Roman law with a still greater leaning to the advantage of the Church. No Church property could be bequeathed. Manifest usurers were added to the list of those under disability. For the validity of a will it was generally necessary that it should be made in the presence of a priest and two witnesses, unless where it was made in pias causes. The witnesses, as in Roman law, must be done. Gifts to the Church were not subject to the deductions in favour of the heir and the children necessary in ordinary cases. In England, the Church succeeded in holding in its own hands for centuries jurisdiction in testamentary matters.

This is practically in accordance with the definition of Modestinus in *Digest* xxviu. I, 1, *voluntatis nostrae justa sen*-

tentia de eo quod quis post mortem suam fieri velit. Ancient Law, chap. vi. dii. ioi.

The Roman law of wills has had considerable effect upon English law. In the words of Sir Henry Maine, "The English law of testamentary succession to personalty has become a modified English form of the dispensation under which the inheritances of law. Roman citizens were administered." At the same time there are some broad and striking differences which should be borne in mind. The following among others (as of 1911) may be noticed:

- A Roman testator could not, unless a soldier, die partly testate, and partly intestate. The will must stand or fall as a whole. This is not the case in England.
- There is no one in English law to whom the *unirersitas furis* of the testator descends as it did to the Roman heirs, whose appointment was essential to the validity of a formal will, and who partook of the nature of the English heir, executor, administrator, devisee and legatee.
- The disabilities of testators differed in the two systems. The disability of a slave or a heretic is peculiar to Roman law, of a youth between fourteen and twenty-one to English law.
- The whole property may he disposed of in England; but it was not so at Rome, where, except by the wills of soldiers, children could not be disinherited unless for specified acts of misconduct. During the greater part of the period of Roman law the heir must also have had his Falcidian fourth in order to induce him to accept the inheritance.
- In English law all wills must conform to certain statutory requirements; the Romans recognized from the time of Augustus an informal will called *codicilli*. The English codicil has little in common with this but the name. It is not an informal will, but an addition to a will, read as a part of it, and needing the same formalities of execution.
- The Roman testatum applied to both movables and immovables; in England a legacy or bequest is a gift of personalty only, a gift of real estate being called a devise.
- The Roman will spoke from the time of making; the English speaks from the time of death. This difference becomes very important in case of alteration in the position of the testator between the making of the will and his death, As a rule the Roman will could not, the English can, pass after-acquired property.

Development of the Law of Wills in England

Liberty of alienation by will is found at an early period in England. To judge from the words of a law of Canute, intestacy appears to have been the exception at that time. How far the liberty extended is uncertain; it is the opinion of some authorities that complete disposition of land and goods was allowed, of others that limited rights of wife and children were recognized. However this may be, after the Conquest a distinction, the result of feudalism, to use a convenient if inaccurate term, arose between real and personal property. It will be convenient to treat the history of the two kinds of will separately.

Land

It became the law after the Conquest, according to Sir Edward Coke, that an estate greater than for a term of years could be disposed of by will, unless in Kent, where the custom of gavelkind prevailed, and in some manors and boroughs (especially the City of London), where the pre-Conquest law was preserved by special indulgence. The reason why devise of land was not acknowledged by law was, no doubt, partly to discourage deathbed gifts in mortmain, a view supported by Glanvill, partly because the testator could not give the devisee that seisin which was the principal element in a feudal conveyance. By means of the doctrine to uses, however, the devise of land was secured by a circuitous method, generally by conveyance to feoffees to uses in the lifetime of he feoffor to such uses as he should appoint by his will. Up to comparatively recent times a will of lands still bore traces of its origin in the conveyance to uses *inter vivos*. On the passing of the Statute of Uses lands again became non-devisable, with a saving in the statute for the validity of wills made before 1 May 1536. The inconvenience of this state of things soon began to be felt, and was probably aggravated by the large amount of land thrown into the market after the dissolution of the monasteries. As a remedy an act was passed in 1540 (which came to be known as the Statute of Wills), and a further explanatory act in 1542-1543.

The effect of these acts was to make lands held in fee simple devisable by will in writing, to the extent of two-thirds where the tenure was by knight service, and the whole where it was in socage. Corporations were incapacitated to receive, and married women, infants, idiots and lunatics to devise. An act of 1660, by abolishing tenure by knight service, made all lands devisable, in the same vein the Statute of Frauds (1677) dealt with the formalities of execution. Up to this time simple notes, even in the handwriting of another person, constituted a sufficient will, if published by the testator as such. The Statute of Frauds required, *inter alia*, that all devises should be in writing, signed by the testator or by some person for him in his presence and by his direction, and should also be subscribed by three or four credible witnesses. The strict interpretation by the courts of the credibility of witnesses led to the passing of an act in 1751-1752, making interested witnesses sufficient for the due execution of the will, but declaring gifts to them void. The will of a man was revoked by marriage and the birth of a child, of a woman by marriage only. A will was also revoked by an alteration in circumstances, and even by a void conveyance *inter vivos* of land devised by the will made subsequently to the date of the will, which was presumed to be an attempt by the grantor to give legal effect to a change of intention. As in Roman law, a will spoke from the time of the making, so that it could not avail to pass after-acquired property without republication, which was equivalent to making a new will, Copyholds were not devisable before 1815, but were usually surrendered to the use of the will of the copyhold tenant; an act of 1815 made them devisable simply. Devises of lands have gradually been made liable to the claims of creditors by a series of statutes beginning with the year 1691.

Personal property

The history of wills of personalty was considerably different, but to some extent followed parallel lines. In both cases partial preceded complete power of disposition. The general opinion of the best authorities is that by the common law of England a man could only dispose of his whole personal property if he left no wife or children; if he left either wife or children he could only dispose of one-half, and one-third if he left both wife and children. The shares of wife and children were called their *pars rationabilis*. This *pars rationabilis* is expressly recognized in Magna Carta and was sued for by the writ *de rationabili parte*. At what period the right of disposition of the whole personalty superseded the old law is uncertain. That it did so is certain, and the places where the old rule still existed—the province of York, Wales and the City of London--were regarded as exceptions. The right of bequest in these places was not assimilated to the general law until comparatively recent times by acts passed between 1693 and 1726. A will of personalty could be made by a male at fourteen, by a female at twelve. The formalities in the case of wills of personalty were not as numerous as in the case of wills of land. Up to 1838 a nuncupative or oral will was sufficient, subject, where the gift was of £30 or more, to the restrictions contained in the Statute of Frauds. The witnesses to a written will need not be "credible," and it was specially enacted by an act of 1705 that any one who could give evidence in a court of law was a good witness to a will of personalty. A will entirely in tile testator's handwriting, called a holograph will, was valid without signature. At one time the executor was entitled to the residue in default of a residuary legatee, but the Executors Act 1830 made him in such an event trustee for the next of kin.

Jurisdiction over wills of personalty was until 1858 in the ecclesiastical courts, probate being granted by the diocesan court if the goods of the deceased lay in the same diocese, in the provincial court of Canterbury (the prerogative court) or York (the chancery court) if the deceased had *bona notabilia*, that is, goods to the value of £5 in two dioceses. The ecclesiastical jurisdiction was of a very ancient origin. It was fully established under Henry II, as it is mentioned by Glanvill. In the city of London wills were enrolled in the Court of Hustings from 1258 to 1688 after having been proved before the ordinary. Contested cases before 1858 were tried in the provincial court with an appeal originally to the Court of Delegates, later to the Judicial Committee of the Privy Council. There were also a few special local jurisdictions, courts baron, the university courts, and others, probably for the most part survivals of the pre-Conquest period, when wills seem to have been published in the county court. The ecclesiastical courts had no jurisdiction over wills of land, and the common law courts were careful to keep the ecclesiastical courts within their limits by means of prohibition. No probate of a will of land was necessary, and title to real estate by will might be made by production of the will as a document of title. The liability of the executor and legatee for the debts of the testator has been gradually established by legislation. In general it is limited to the amount of the succession. Personal liability of the executor beyond this can by the Statute of Frauds only be established by contract in writing.

Legislation

Such were the principal stages in the history of the law as it affected wills made before 1838 or proved before 1858. The principal acts in force in the early twentieth century were the Wills Act 1837, the amending act of 1852, the Court of Probate Act 1857, the Judicature Acts 1873 and 1875, and the Land Transfer Act 1897. All but the acts of 1837 and 1852 deal mainly with what happens to the will after death, whether under the voluntary or contentious jurisdiction of the Probate Division.

The earliest on the statute roll is an act of Henry III (1236), enabling a widow to bequeath the crops of her lands. Before the Wills Act uniformity in the law had been urgently recommended by the Real Property Commissioners in 1833. It appears from their report that at the time of its appearance there were ten different ways in which a will might be made under different circumstances.

The act of 1837 affected both the making and the interpretation of wills. Excluding the latter for the present, its main provisions were these.

- All property, real and personal, and of whatever tenure, may be disposed of by will.
- If customary freeholds or copyholds be devised, the will must be entered on the court rolls.
- No will made by any person under the age of twenty-one is valid.
- Every will is to be in writing, signed at the foot or end thereof by the testator or by some person in his presence and by his direction, and such signature is to be made or acknowledged by the testator in the presence of two or more witnesses present at the same time, who are to subscribe the will in the presence of the testator. It is usual for the testator and the witnesses to sign every sheet.
- Gifts to a witness or the husband or wife of a witness are void.
- A will is revoked by a later will or by destruction with the intention of revoking, but not by presumption arising from an alteration in circumstances.
- Alterations in a will must be executed and attested as a will.
- A will speaks from the death of the testator, unless a contrary intention appear.
- An unattested document may be, if properly identified, incorporated in a will.

Rules of interpretation or construction

depend chiefly on decisions of the courts, to a smaller extent on statutory enactment. The law was gradually brought into its present condition through precedents extending back for centuries, especially decisions of the court of chancery, the court par excellence of construction, as distinguished from the court of probate. The court of probate did not deal unless incidentally with the meaning of the will; its jurisdiction was confined to seeing that it was duly executed. The present state of the law of interpretation is highly technical. Some phrases have obtained a conventional meaning which the testators who used them probably did not dream of. Many of the judicial doctrines which had gradually become established were altered by the Wills Act.

Rules of interpretation founded on principles of equity independent of statute are very numerous. Some of the more important, stated in as general a form as possible, are these:

- The intention of the testator is to be observed. This rule is called by Sir E Coke the pole star to guide the judges.
- There is a presumption against intestacy, against, double portions, against constructing merely precatory words to import a trust, etc.
- One part of the will is to he expounded by another.
- Interlineations and alterations are presumed to have been made after, not as in deeds before, execution.
- Words are supposed to be used in their strict and primary sense. Many words and phrases, however, such as "money," "residue" and "issue" and other words of relationship, have become invested with a technical meaning, but there has been a recent tendency to include illegitimate children in a gift to "children."
- Evidence is admissible in certain cases to explain latent ambiguity, and parol evidence of the terms of a lost will may be given as in the famous case of Sugden v. Lord St Leonards (1876), 1 Prob. Div. 154.

A will may be void, in whole or in part, for many reasons, which may be divided into two great classes, those arising from external circumstances and those arising from the will itself. The main examples of the former class are revocation by burning, tearing, etc., by a later will, or by marriage of the testator (except as below), incapacity of the testator from insanity, infancy or legal disability (such as being a convict), undue influence and fraud, any one of which is ground for the court to refuse or revoke probate of a will, A will being ambulatory is always revocable, unless in one or two exceptional instances. Undue influence is a ground upon which frequent attempts are made to set aside wills. Its nature is well explained in a judgment of Lord Penzance's: "Pressure of whatever character, whether acting on the fears or the hopes, if so exerted as to overpower the volition without convincing the judgment, is a species of restraint under which no valid will can be made. There is nothing corresponding to the *querela inofficiosi testamenti*, but unnatural provisions may be evidence of mental defect.

The circumstances appearing on the face of the will which make it open to objection may either avoid it altogether or create a partial intestacy, the will remaining good as a whole. Where the will is not duly executed, e.g. if it is a forgery or if it is not signed by the testator or the proper number of witnesses, the will is not admitted to probate at all. Where it contains devises or bequests bad in law, as in general restraint of marriage, or tending to create perpetuities, or contrary to public policy, or to some particular enactment, only the illegal part is void. A remarkable instance is a well-known case in which a condition subsequent in a devise was held void as against public policy, being a gift over of the estate devised in case the first devisee, the eldest son of an earl, did not before his death obtain the lapsed title of Duke of Bridgewater.

At common law there could be no larceny of a will of lands. But by the Larceny Act of 1861 stealing, injuring or concealing a will, whether of real or personal estate, was punishable with penal servitude for life. Forgery of a will (at one time a capital crime) rendered the offender liable to the same penalty. Fraudulent concealment of a will material to the title by a vendor or mortgagor of land or chattels is, by the Law of Property Amendment Act 1859, a misdemeanour punishable by fine or imprisonment or both.

History of Wills in other jurisdictions

United States

In the 21st century, eighteen is the typical age of testamentary capacity. Full liberty of disposition is not universal. In particular, many states normally grant spouses the right to at least half the estate regardless of what the will says (or if no will can be found). Some require that children cannot be disinherited without good cause. In many case, children omitted in a will may still take their share. Louisiana followed French law, by which the testator can under no circumstances alienate by will more than half his property if he leave issue or ascendants. In 1911, the husband's consent was sometimes required for a married woman's will to be valid, but this is no longer the case. Nuncupative and holographic wills are valid in some states, but are forbidden in others. The former are confined to personality and must generally be reduced to writing within a short time after the words are spoken. In Louisiana the mystic or sealed will still existed in 1911. The number of witnesses necessary for the validity of a will of any kind is usually two, but Vermont requires three. To be valid, witnesses must not be heirs under the will. In 1911, wills of soldiers and sailors were privileged, as in England.

In modern U.S. law, wills are not required to be registered prior to death in most states, but are registered and put in the public record after the person making the will dies and the estate is probated. However, it is often still a good idea to have the signing and witnessing of a will notarized, to reduce the risk of disputes over the will's validity after death. Wills can be used to nominate guardians for minor children, but because children are not property, the will cannot have the final word on the question. Guardianship is decided by courts, though the usual outcome is that guardianship is awarded to the other surviving parent, or, if no parents survive, to the guardian nominated in the last surviving parent's will.

Scotland (as of 1911)

Up to 1868 wills of immovables were not allowed under Scots law. The usual means of obtaining disposition of heritage after death was a trust disposition and settlement by deed *depraesenti*, under which the truster disposed the property to trustees according to the trusts of the settlement, reserving a life interest. Thus something very similar to a testamentary disposition was secured by means resembling those employed in England before the Wills Act of Henry VIII. The main disadvantage of the trust disposition was that it was liable to be overthrown by the heir, who could reduce *ex capite lecti* all voluntary deeds made to his prejudice within sixty days of the death of his ancestor. In 1868 the Titles to Land Consolidation Act made it competent to any owner of lands to settle the succession to the same in the event of death by testamentary or mortis causa deeds or writings. In 1871 reduction ex capite lecti was abolished. A will of immovables must be executed with the formalities of a deed and registered to give title. The disability of a woman as a witness was removed by the Titles to Land Consolidation Act. As to wills of movables, there are several important points in which they differ from corresponding wills in England, the influence of Roman law being more marked. Males may make a will at fourteen, females at twelve. A nuncupative legacy is good to the amount of £100 Scots (£8, 6s. 8d.), and a holograph testament is good without witnesses, but it must be signed by the testator, differing in this from the old English holograph. By the Conveyancing Act 1874 such a will is presumed to have been executed on the date which it bears. Not all movables can be left, as in England. The movable property of the deceased is subject to *jus relictae* and *legitime*. See McLaren, *Wills and Succession*, for the law, and *Judicial Styles* for styles.

France (as of 1911)

The law is mainly contained in ss. 967–1074 of the Code Napoleon. Wills in France may be of three kinds:
- holograph, which must be wholly written, dated and signed by the testator;
- made as a public instrument, i.e. received by two notaries before two witnesses or by one notary before four witnesses; this form of will must be dictated by the testator and written by the notary, must be read over to the testator in the presence of the witnesses and must be signed by testator and witnesses;
- mystic, which are signed by the testator, then closed and sealed and delivered by him to a notary before six witnesses; the notary then draws up an account of the proceedings on the instrument which is signed by the testator, notary and witnesses.

Legatees and their blood relations to the fourth degree may not be witnesses. Nuncupative wills are not recognized. Soldiers' and sailors' wills are subject to special rules as in most other countries. Full liberty of disposition only exists where the testator has no ascendants or descendants, in other cases his quantile disponible is subject to reserve; if the testator has one child he may only dispose of half his estate, if two only one-third, if three or more only one-fourth; if he has no descendants but ascendants in both lines he may dispose of half, if ascendants in one line only he may dispose of three-fourths. The full age of testamentary capacity is twenty-one years, but minors over the age of sixteen may dispose by will of half of the estate of which they could dispose had they been of full age. There is no restriction against married women making wills. A contract to dispose of the succession is invalid, s. 791.

The civil codes of southern Continental Europe are in general accordance with the French law.

Germany (as of 1911)

Most of the law will be found in the *Bürgerliches Gesetzbuch*, ss. 2064–2273. A holograph will, either single or joint, is allowed. Other wills must be declared before a judge or notary or (outside Germany) a consul. Two witnesses are required, unless the witness be a notary or the registrar of the court, who is sufficient alone. The formalities may be relaxed in certain cases, such as imminent death, a state of siege, a prevailing epidemic, etc. Descendants, ascendants and the husband and wife, are entitled to compulsory portions (*pflicht-teilsberechtigt*). But those *prima facie* entitled may be deprived of their share for certain specified kinds of misconduct. A contract to make any specified testamentary disposition is inoperative. But a contract of inheritance (*Erbvertrag*) made inter mvos by direct disposition is valid in certain cases and will operate on the death of the contractor. The modes of revocation are much the same as in England (except marriage). But there is one peculiar to Germany, the inconsistency of a will with an *Erbvertrag*; in such an event the will is wholly or *pro tanto* revoked.

International Law

There are three main directions which the opinion of jurists and the practice of courts have taken, as of 1911:
- The whole property of the testator may be subjected to the law of his domicil. To this effect is the opinion of Savigny and the German practice. Certain modifications have been made by modern law, especially by the *Einführungsgesetz* of 1896.
- The property may be subjected to the law of the place where it happens to be at the time of the testator's death.
- The movable property may be subjected to the law of the domicil. The immovable (including leaseholds) to the law of the place where it is situated, the *lex loci rei sitae*. England and the United States follow this rule.

Testamentary capacity is generally governed by the law of the testator's domicil at the time of his death, the form of the instrument in most countries either by the law of his domicil or the law of the place where the will was made, at his option. The old rule of English law was to allow the former alternative only. The law was altered for the United Kingdom in 1861 by the Wills Act 1861 (known as Lord Kingsdown's Act), by which a will made out of the United Kingdom by a British subject is, as far as regards personal estate, good if made according to the forms required by the law of the place where it was made, or by the law of the testator's domicil at the time of making it, or by the law of the place of his domicil of origin. Subsequent change of domicile does not avoid such a will. Another act passed on the same day, the Domicile Act 1861, enacted that by convention with any foreign government foreign domicil with regard to wills could not be acquired by a testator without a year's residence and a written declaration of intention to become domiciled. By the same act foreign consuls may by convention have certain authority over the wills and property of subjects of foreign states dying in England.

In the United States some states have adopted the narrow policy of enacting by statute the old common law rule, and providing that no will is valid unless made in the form required by the law of the state of the testator's domicile. The capacity of the testator, revocation and construction of a will, are governed by the law of the domicile of the testator at the time of his death-except in cases affected by Lord Kingsdown's Act, as he must be supposed to have used language in consonance with that law, unless indeed he express himself in technical language of another country. A good instance is Groos' Case (1904), Prob. 269, where it was held that the will of a Dutch woman (at the time of her death domiciled in England) duly made in Holland was not revoked by her marriage, that being no ground of revocation by the law of Holland.

The persons who are to take under a will are decided by different rules according as the property is movable or immovable, the former being governed by the law of the domicile, the latter by the Lex loci rei sitae. It was held, however, in 1881 by the court of appeal in England that, under the will of an Englishman domiciled in Holland, leaving personal property to children, children legitimated per subsegitens matrimonium could take, as they were legitimate by the law of Holland, though not by the law of England (re Goodman's Trusts, 17 Ch. D. 266). This principle was carried further in re Grey's Trusts (1892), 3 Ch. 88, where it was held that a legitimated child was entitled to share in a devise of English realty. But it is to be noted that a person born out of lawful wedlock, though legitimated, could not succeed as heir to real estate in England as of 1911 (Birtwhistle v. Vardill, 2 Cl. and F. 895). A will duly executed abroad is generally required to be clothed with the authority of a court of the country where any property affected by the will is situate.

This article incorporates text from a publication now in the public domain: Chisholm, Hugh, ed (1911). *Encyclopædia Britannica* (Eleventh ed.). Cambridge University Press.
Source (edited): "http://en.wikipedia.org/wiki/Legal_history_of_wills"

Legatee

A **legatee**, in the law of wills, is any individual or organization bequeathed any portion of a testator's estate.

Usage
Depending upon local custom, legatees may be called "devisees." Traditionally, "legatees" took personal property under will and "devisees" took land under will. Brooker v. Brooker, (Tex. Civ.App., 76 S.W.2d 180, 183) asserts that "devisee" may refer to "those who take under will without any distinction between realty and personalty...though commonly it refers to one who takes *personal property* under a will."
Source (edited): "http://en.wikipedia.org/wiki/Legatee"

Letter of wishes

A **letter of wishes** is a non-binding indication by the settlor of the manner in which he wishes the trustees to exercise their discretion in relation to a discretionary trust.

Letters of wishes are normally used in testamentary trusts, although theoretically there is no reason why they should not be used in an *inter vivos* trust.

Letters of wishes are useful where a trust instrument gives the trustees very wide powers and discretions. The letter of wishes principally sets out the manner in which the settlor wishes the trustees to exercise their powers and discretions, but is not binding on the trustees. All binding requirements must be contained in the trust instrument itself. It is also quite common for letters of wishes to make posthumous expressions of thanks or love to the objects of the trust.
Source (edited): "http://en.wikipedia.org/wiki/Letter_of_wishes"

Letters of Administration

Letters of Administration are granted by a Surrogate Court or probate registry to appoint appropriate people to deal with a deceased person's estate where property will pass under Intestacy Rules or where there are no executors living (and willing and able to act) having been validly appointed under the deceased's will. Traditionally, letters of administration granted to a representative of a testate estate are called "letters of administration with the will annexed" or "letters of administration *cum testamentio annexio*" or "c.t.a.".

Source (edited): "http://en.wikipedia.org/wiki/Letters_of_Administration"

Massachusetts business trust

A **Massachusetts business trust** (**MBT**) is a legal trust set up for the purposes of business, but not necessarily one that is operated in The Commonwealth of Massachusetts. They may also be referred to as an **unincorporated business organization** or **UBO**. Business trusts may be established under the laws of other U.S. states.

Many businesses are formed as MBTs to mitigate taxation; mutual funds in the U.S. are often structured as MBTs, though sometimes they are organized as Maryland corporations (or other states such as Minnesota). More recently, a **Delaware statutory trust** or *DST* has become a popular form of organization, and many new funds have been organizing as DSTs and exiting funds converting to DSTs. Since mutual funds are investment companies and not operating companies, many traditional corporation rules and requirements don't fit them well.

During the last century and through the mid years of this century the tax laws and State regulations strongly favored corporate structures, tightening of these laws in the past 10–15 years have resulted in the resurgence of the use of the UBO. For example, in 1985 the Scudder Capital Growth Fund, Inc. and Kemper Money Market Fund, Inc. changed their forms of organization from a corporation to a business trust.

History

The business trust made its debut in Massachusetts in 1827. As a result, a U.S. business trust today is often called a "Massachusetts trust" in legal circles. The U.S. Supreme Court defined the Massachusetts trust as a form of business organization, common in Massachusetts consisting essentially of an arrangement whereby property is conveyed to trustees: in accordance with terms of the trust. The business is to be held and managed for the benefit of persons who hold transferable certificates issued by the trustees showing the shares into which the beneficial interest in the property is divided.

This method of transacting business in commercial enterprises originated in Massachusetts as a result of negative laws prohibiting the development of real estate without a special act of the legislature or in other words, without "permission" of the State . So, the Business Trust was created under Common-law right to contract to obtain legislatively constructed business organizations advantages but without having to gain "permission" to enter into a business activity and suffer under the burdens and restrictions that are placed on "statutorily constructed organizations".

It states on page 1681 of Black's Law Dictionary 4Ed., 1957, under the term "Massachusetts or Business Trust"; See "Trust Estate as Business Company." This particular definition is found on page 1684 and it states this:

TRUST ESTATE AS BUSINESS COMPANIES. A practice originating in Massachusetts of vesting a business or certain real estate in a group of trustees, who manage it for the benefit of the beneficial owners; the ownership of the latter is evidenced by negotiable (or transferable) shares. The trustees are elected by the shareholders, or in case of a vacancy, by the board of trustees. Provision is made in the agreement and declaration of the trust to the effect that when new trustees are elected, the trust estate shall vest in them without further conveyance. The declaration of the trust specifies the power of the trustees. They have a common seal; the board is organized with the usual officers of a board of trustees; it is governed by by-laws; the officers have the usual powers of like corporation officers; so far as practicable, the trustees in their collective capacity, are to carry on the business under a specified name. The trustees may also hold shares as beneficiaries. Provision may be made for the alteration or specified manner. In *Eliot v. Freeman*, 31 Sup. Ct. 360, 220 U.S. 178, 55 L. Ed. 424, it was held that such a trust was not within the corporation tax provisions of the tariff act of Aug. 5 1909 See also *Zonne v. Minneapolis Syndicate*, 31 S. Ct. 361, 220 U.S. 187, 55 L. Ed. 428 (Black's Law Dictionary 1957, 4Ed., page 1684)

Taxation

The terms "business trust", "Massachusetts trust", and "unincorporated business organization" are not used in the Internal Revenue Code. (The terms "business trust" and "Massachusetts trust" are used in other Federal laws to clarify that they are to be treated as corporations under those laws.) The regulations require that trusts operating a trade or business be treated as a corporation, partnership, or sole proprietorship, if the grantor (also known as a "settlor" or "trustor"), beneficiary or fiduciary (also known as a "trustee") materially participates in the operations or daily management of the business. If the grantor maintains control of the trust, then grantor trust rules will apply. Otherwise, the trust would be treated as a simple or complex trust, depending on the trust instrument. (Source: www.irs.gov)

Federal income tax implications

For federal income tax purposes in the United States, there are several kinds of trusts: **grantor trusts** whose tax consequences flow directly to the settlor's Form 1040 (U.S. Individual Income Tax Return) and state return, **simple** trusts in which all the income created must be distributed to one of more beneficiaries and is therefore taxed to the non-settlor beneficiary (e.g. the widow of a trust created by the late husband), whether or not the income is actually distributed (which can occur), and complex trusts, which are, in general, all trusts that aren't grantor trusts or simple trusts. Some trusts may alternate between simple and complex under certain conditions. Many but not all trust organizations do their own tax work. This can be highly specialized work.

All simple and complex trusts are irrevocable and in both cases any capital gains realized in the portfolios are taxed to the trust corpus or principal.
Source (edited): "http://en.wikipedia.org/wiki/Massachusetts_business_trust"

Merger doctrine (trust law)

In the law of trusts the term "doctrine of merger" refers to the fusing of legal and equitable title in the event the same person becomes both the sole trustee and the sole beneficiary of a trust. In such a case, the trust is sometimes deemed to have terminated (with the result that the beneficiary owns the trust property outright).
Source (edited): "http://en.wikipedia.org/wiki/Merger_doctrine_(trust_law)"

National Collegiate Trust

See Student loans in the United States
National Collegiate Trust generically refers to a series of individual Delaware business trusts registered with the U.S. Securities and Exchange Commission under the respective trust title as according to the date of issue. The trusts are the product of the securitization of pools of education loans made under education loan programs by program lenders.

Source (edited): "http://en.wikipedia.org/wiki/National_Collegiate_Trust"

No-contest clause

A **no-contest clause**, also called an *in terrorem* clause, is a clause in a legal document, such as a contract or a will, that is designed to threaten someone, usually with litigation or criminal prosecution, into acting, refraining from action, or ceasing to act. The phrase is typically used to refer to a clause in a will that threatens to disinherit a beneficiary of the will if that beneficiary challenges the terms of the will in court. Many states allow for a Will to have a no contest clause, so long as the person challenging the will doesn't have probable cause to do so.

No-contest clause in wills

The Uniform Probate Code (UPC) §§ 2-517 and 3-905 allow for no contest clauses so long as the person challenging the will doesn't have probable cause to do so. The full wording is:
A provision in a will purporting to penalize an interested person for contesting the will or instituting other proceedings relating to the estate is unenforceable if probable cause exists for instituting proceedings.

—UPC §§ 2-517 and 3-905
The UPC has been adopted in several smaller states, including Alaska, Idaho, Montana, and New Mexico, but also by Florida, one of the larger states in population.
Some states allow for "living probate" and "ante mortem" probate, which are statutory provisions which authorize testators to institute an adversary proceeding during their life to declare the validity of the will, in order to avoid later will contests.

No-contest clauses by state

California
In California, no-contest clauses are completely effective, and will divest any party that unsuccessfully contests a will containing such a clause. California's statutory scheme governing the enforceability of no-contest clauses was revised, effective January 1, 2010, with the enactment of new Prob.C. §§ 21310–21315. As of that date, the predecessor statutes are repealed.

Florida
In Florida no-contest clauses in wills are specifically unenforceable, irrespective of probable cause, pursuant to statute. See Fla. Stat. 733.517 (2009) which states:
A provision in a will purporting to penalize any interested person for contesting the will or instituting other proceedings relating to the estate is unenforceable.

Nevada
Nevada law specifically directs the court to enforce no-contest clauses. These statutes recognize that a beneficiary may, without penalty, seek enforcement of the will or trust, seek a judicial ruling as to the meaning of the will or trust. The statutes also recognize an exception where legal action challenging the validity of the document is *"instituted in good faith and based on probable cause that would have led a reasonable person, properly informed and advised, to conclude that there was a substantial likelihood that the trust or other trust-related instrument was invalid."*

New York

New York has rejected the "probable cause" defense to enforcement of such clauses. Such clauses are given full effect upon challenge. Some exceptions apply, *e.g.* election against the will by a minor, contest on ground of forgery or revocation by later Will.

N.Y. EPTL specifically states:
A condition, designed to prevent a disposition from taking effect in case the will is contested by the beneficiary, is operative despite the presence or absence of probable cause for such contest, subject to [exceptions]
—N.Y. EPTL § 3-3.5

Virginia

Virginia has generally rejected the "probable cause" defense.
Source (edited): "http://en.wikipedia.org/wiki/No-contest_clause"

Offshore trust

An **offshore trust** is simply a conventional trust that is formed under the laws of an offshore jurisdiction.

Generally offshore trusts are similar in nature and effect to their onshore counterparts; they involve a settlor transferring (or 'settling') assets (the 'trust property') on the trustees to manage for the benefit of a person or class or persons (the 'beneficiaries').

However, a number of offshore jurisdictions have modified their laws to make their jurisdictions more attractive to settlors forming offshore structures as trusts.

Also, two civil jurisdictions, who are sometimes considered to be offshore, Switzerland and Liechtenstein have artificially imported the trust concept from common law jurisdictions by statute.

Rule against perpetuities

Trusts in general are subject to the rule against perpetuities which, in practical terms, puts limits on the length of time within which all trust property must be distributed. Because of the strictures of the rule, a number of trusts have been struck down in wildly hypothetical circumstances because of possible infringement of the rule (see, e.g. the *fertile octogenarian*).

Most offshore jurisdictions which have sophisticated trust laws have modified their laws relating to perpetuity to allow settlor to select lengthy, fixed, perpetuity periods, to avoid the use of "Royal lives" clauses. Many have also adopted "wait and see" laws, which mean that trusts which might potentially infringe the rule against perpetuities are no longer automatically invalid, but instead the trust remains valid unless and until the perpetuity period is breached.

No recognised offshore jurisdiction has yet gone as far as some U.S. states and abolished the rule against perpetuities entirely in relation to trusts.

Management of underlying companies

Trusts in general are subject to the rule in *Bartlett v Barclays Bank* which provides (briefly) that where trust property includes the shares of a company, then the trustees must take a positive role in the affairs on the company. The rule has been criticised, but remains part of trust law in many common law jurisdictions.

A number of offshore jurisdictions (notably the Cayman Islands, with STAR trusts, and the British Virgin Islands, with VISTA trusts) have created special forms of trust that may be expressly settled without imposing an obligation of the trustees to interfere in management in this way.

Paradoxically, these specialised forms of trusts seem to infrequently be used in relation to their original intended uses. STAR trusts seem to be used more frequently by hedge funds forming mutual funds as unit trusts (where the fund managers wish to eliminate any obligation to attend meetings of the companies in whose securities they invest) and VISTA trusts are frequently used as a part of orphan structures in bond issues where the trustees wish to divorce themselves from supervising the issuing vehicle.

Critics in onshore jurisdictions have suggested that these specialised trusts have provisions that so fundamentally undermine the nature of a trust that they should not be recognised in an onshore jurisdiction, but whatever the view of onshore tax authorities and regulators, it seems unlikely that the courts in onshore jurisdictions would be prepared to derogate from the Hague Convention on the Law Applicable to Trusts and on their Recognition.

Asset protection

Certain jurisdictions (notably the Cook Islands, but the Bahamas also has a species of asset protection trust) have provided special trusts which are styled as asset protection trusts. Whilst all trusts, to a degree, have an asset protection element to them some jurisdictions have enacted laws trying to make life difficult for creditors to press claims against the trust (for example, by providing for particularly short limitation periods). In practice the effectiveness of such trusts is limited as the bankruptcy and/or divorce laws in the settlor's home jurisdiction will usually operate to set aside transfers to the trusts, and most jurisdictions (including offshore jurisdictions) set aside transactions entered into defraud creditors.

Powers of investment

Most traditional jurisdictions only permit trustees to make very conservative financial investments. Most offshore jurisdictions permit (or allow the settlor to specify in the trust instrument that they are permitted) a wider range of investments, including higher risk investments such as derivatives and futures contracts.

Purpose trusts

Whilst in most common law jurisdictions, trusts must either be formed for the benefit of persons, or charitable purposes, many offshore jurisdictions have also amended their laws to permit trusts to be formed for non-charitable purposes. Such trusts need to enforce a "protector" to be able to enforce the terms of the trust, but doubt remains as to who should be treated as the beneficial owner of the trust funds for tax purposes prior to its distribution.

Interestingly, no offshore jurisdiction yet appears to have made a serious effort to expand upon the flexibility of discretionary trusts in relation to certainty of objects, as expounded in *McPhail v Doulton*. This may be because the common law rules are now considered to be sufficiently flexible to make no widening necessary to attract trust business.

Anachronistic common law rules

Many offshore jurisdictions have also legislated to abolish certain anachronistic common law rules which sometimes cause difficulty for trust planning. These include:

- Rule in *Howe v Earl of Dartmouth*
- Rule in *Maloney v Alveranga*
- Rule in *Re Atkinson*

Use of offshore trusts

Official statistics on trusts are difficult to come by as in most offshore jurisdictions (and in most onshore jurisdictions), trusts are not required to be registered.

There is a common perception that offshore trusts are predominantly used by wealthy individuals and families as part of their tax planning. This may be true, however there are also other purposes that offshore trusts are used for.

- Offshore trusts are also sometimes formed as unit trusts to operate as a mutual fund.
- Offshore trusts are often used as part of an orphan structure in capital markets or trade finance transactions.
- Pan-national non-governmental bodies are sometimes established as offshore trusts. For example, the International Cricket Council is formed in the British Virgin Islands.

Swiss trust companies

One of the most commonly used forms of offshore corporations are the so-called seasoned or vintage Swiss trust companies. These are typically corporations that were established in the second half of the 20th century and therefore meet the minimum time since incorporation requirement to be awarded trust status. Typically, Swiss trust companies were incorporated but subsequently became dormant for a variety of reasons. Such dormant companies are then identified and acquired by agencies specializing in vintage Swiss companies with the intention of selling them to end clients, usually for offshore asset management, asset holding or investment flagship purposes.

Source (edited): "http://en.wikipedia.org/wiki/Offshore_trust"

Oldland Mill, Keymer

Oldland Mill is an 18th century post mill situated in the village of Keymer, West Sussex.

History

Oldland Mill was built c.1700 (the earliest record of a windmill in the area dates from 1703). It was originally an open trestle mill, with the roundhouse being added later. Records show that a mill stood in Keymer in 1755, and the mill was marked on a map dated 1783, but it is not shown on one dated 1795. The 1801 National Defence Schedule records the mill but the 1813 Ordnance Survey and Greenwood's 1829 map omit the mill. Records show that the mill was standing in 1828. Oldland Mill was working by wind until 1912. The mill began to fall into disrepair in the early part of the 20th century and continued to deteriorate.

The Sussex Archaeological Society acquired the mill in 1927 and repairs were carried out by E Hole and Sons of Burgess Hill in 1934. In 1976, at the Annual General Meeting of the Hassocks Amenity Association, there was a talk was given on the work of Weald and Downland Open Air Museum. The question of how to preserve Oldland Mill was raised. The mill was then in the ownership of the Sussex Archaeological Society. The mill was surveyed in 1977 by millwrights Vincent Pargeter and Edwin Hole and found to be close to collapse. Following negotiations with the Sussex Archaeological Society in 1979 the Hassocks Amenity Association leased the mill in 1980 and began a period of volunteer led restoration.

Since then the mill has benefited from a DEFRA grant and substantial work has been completed. The mill was stripped to her bare essentials and many new parts completely and accurately built from scratch to replace rotten parts. The whole mill has been reclad and as of 18 October 2007 the four sails had been lifted into position. The mill ground its first batch of corn for many decades in October 2008. Today the mill is looked after by The Oldland Mill Trust, a registered charity.

As of mid 2010 the mill restoration is largely completed.

Restoration

The first working party on 2 August 1980 cleared rubbish around the mill and made a temporary repair to the roof of the roundhouse. In 1981, the two remaining sails and stock were removed with the assistance of sailors from HMS *Daedalus*. In 1983, an "A" frame was constructed to support the windshaft. The mill was restored over the next ten years, with much of the framing being replaced, including the trestle, crown tree, breast, tail and side frames. A new 8-foot-8-inch (2.64 m) diameter clasp arm head wheel and brake was constructed in 2006. The head wheel is of elm with hornbeam cogs and oak arms.

Description

Oldland Mill is a post mill on a single storey octagonal roundhouse. It has four spring sails and is winded by a tailpole. The windshaft is cast iron and was cast by Boaz Medhurst, the Lewes millwright in 1873. There are two pairs of millstones, arranged head and tail.

Millers

- Josh Beard 1828
- Joseph Winchester 1839 - 1854
- William Winchester 1839 - 1854
- J Turner - 1899
- John White 1899 - 1904
- David Driver 1904 - 1912

Reference for above:-
Source (edited): "http://en.wikipedia.org/wiki/Oldland_Mill,_Keymer"

Oral will

An **oral will** (or **nuncupative will**) is a will that has been delivered orally (that is, in speech) to witnesses, as opposed to the usual form of wills, which is written and according to a proper format.

A minority of U.S. states (approximately 20 as of 2009), permit nuncupative wills under certain circumstances. Under most statutes, such wills can only be made during a person's "last sickness," must be witnessed by at least three persons, and reduced to writing by the witnesses within a specified amount of time after the testator's death. Some states also place limits on the types and value of property that can be bequeathed in this manner. A few U.S. states permit nuncupative wills made by military personnel on active duty. Under the law in England and Wales oral wills are permitted to military personnel and merchant seamen on duty (see law report below) and it is common practice for in Commonwealth countries.

An analogy can be drawn to the concept of last donations (*donatio mortis causa*) established by Roman law and still in effect in England and Wales.
Source (edited): "http://en.wikipedia.org/wiki/Oral_will"

Percy Sladen Memorial Trust

The **Percy Sladen Memorial Trust** is a trust fund administered by the Linnean Society of London for the support of scientific research. It was endowed by the wife of marine biologist Percy Sladen (1849–1900) in his memory.

The Trust has in general been devoted to the support of field work. Major scientific expeditions that have been funded under the Trust include:
- the Percy Sladen Trust Expedition to the Indian Ocean (1905);
- the Percy Sladen Trust Expedition to Melanesia;
- the Percy Sladen Trust Expedition to West Africa;
- the Percy Sladen Trust Expeditions to the Abrolhos Islands (1913,1915);
- the Percy Sladen Trust Expedition to Lake Titicaca (1937)

Other uses of the fun include a grant to the Royal Albert Memorial Museum in Exeter, towards curation of the Sladen Collection of echinoderms.
Source (edited): "http://en.wikipedia.org/wiki/Percy_Sladen_Memorial_Trust"

Personal injury trust

The expression **personal injury trust** is a legal *term of art* found in the context of the modern English law of trusts (also applicable, where relevant, to Wales, Scotland and Northern Ireland).

A personal injury trust is a form of trust, a legally binding arrangement, where funds are held by persons called trustees for the benefit of another or others upon the terms of a document called a trust deed.

"A trust does not need to have a specific generic title or be one sort of trust or another at law to be a personal injury trust. It is the source of the trust fund which determines the trust's nature ... needs ... relevant circumstances and the relevant law should dictate the type of trust. But whatever legal type of trust it is, if it is funded by an award of compensation for a personal injury then it will be a personal injury trust."

Special characteristics

A personal injury trust has several special characteristics:
- It is constituted exclusively by funds derived from a payment (or payments) made in consequence of a personal injury e.g. compensation for a road traffic accident.
- The person founding the trust (called the settlor) will be the injured party (that is except in limited circumstances involving an official compensatory body such as the Criminal Injuries Compensation Authority).
- The person founding the trust from their payment must also be the sole beneficiary or at least one of the potential beneficiaries of the trust.

These are important because it means that a trust does not need to have a generic title or label or be one particular type of trust or another at English law to be considered a personal injury trust. It is or is not a personal injury trust on account of its source and the involvement of the injured settlor.

Types of trust

A personal injury trust can be:
- a bare trust where the money involved, the trust fund, is held for the injured party outright with administrative powers being given to the trustees. Upon the death of that person it forms part of their estate and passes under their will or under

the law of intestacy which operates when there is no will.
- a life interest trust where the trust fund is held by the trustees for the life of the injured party for their benefit and then after their death it passes to others under the terms of the trust.
- a discretionary trust where the trust fund is held by the trustees for the benefit of the injured party and potentially others at the discretion of the trustees. The trust may continue or be wound up when the injured party dies.
- a hybrid trust such as a *flexible life interest* combining features of the life and discretionary trust as desired.

The needs of the settlor, their family circumstances and tax or other relevant law should dictate the type of trust used. But whatever the legal type of the trust, if it is funded by an award of compensation for a personal injury then it will be a personal injury trust.

Personal injury trusts are sometimes referred to as *special needs trusts* but that expression is more general and can create confusion with certain trusts in other jurisdictions. A more accurate and informative alternative description might be *compensation protection trust* as that alludes to its actual purpose under English law.

Role and practice

The role and practice of personal injury trusts under English law.

(1) Basic advantages

The existence of a personal injury trust can enable the injured party to obtain certain means-tested State benefits entitlements and to make the best use of the award under English law but there are also other potential advantages.

(2) When advice should be given/sought.

Advice on personal injury trusts is usually given by lawyers involved in all injury related cases concerning:
- Accidental injuries
- Criminal injuries
- Clinical and other medical negligence causing injury
- Compensation given for any disease or injury caused as a result of a disease

That is irrespective of whether or not the harm caused was physical or mental. It is irrespective of where the injury occurred. It may have occurred in the UK or abroad. It is also irrespective of the size of the payment made.

(3) Means-tested benefits advantages.

A personal injury trust is also considered relevant even if a person is not currently in receipt of means-tested benefits. That is because they might potentially have access to them in the future if their "assessable capital" for means-testing purposes is low enough. Long term care provision in England and Wales, either at home or in a care home, is a means-tested benefit provided by or through local authorities.

(4) Other practical advantages of a personal injury trust.

There are also other potential advantages of personal injury trusts apart from the retention of means-tested benefits. That is particularly in the case of older, very young, mentally incapable or other vulnerable persons:
- They may have no experience of handling a large sum of money.
- They may want the protection which trustees can offer against grasping relatives.
- They may have unstable mental conditions which renders the use of trustees helpful.
- They may just want to get on with their lives without having to concern themselves with financial administration.
- They may fear the impact of divorce and separation on their finances and want to try and *ring-fence* their resources in some way.

(5) Further points of note.
Under English law:
- The award placed in the personal injury trust may be negotiated or mediated and no court order making an award is required to facilitate a personal injury trust unless the compensated person is either a minor or mentally incapable of managing their own affairs.
- Cases involving minors will involve the High Court agreeing to the foundation of a personal injury trust.
- Cases involving mentally incapable persons will involve the Court of Protection agreeing to the foundation of a personal injury trust.

(6) Tax issues.

Personal injury trusts usually carry no UK tax advantages. Compensated people need access to their award via their chosen trustees. Thus it is essential that they retain an interest as a named beneficiary in the award which they settle to form the trust fund.

The UK taxation anti-avoidance rules prevent tax advantages being given to such *settlor interested* trusts. They apply to settlor interested personal injury trusts in the same way as they apply to trusts founded from non-personal injury related funds.

Personal injury trusts can create adverse tax consequences under UK tax law if the wrong sort is chosen. For example if an award of more than the *nil rate band* for inheritance tax is placed in a discretionary trust or (since March 21, 2006) an ordinary life interest trust, an inheritance tax charge on the surplus becomes due immediately. The limit is £325,000 for the 2009-10 tax year. Above that a 20% charge at the inheritance tax lifetime rate will apply to the surplus.

Importantly the above adverse tax consequences do not apply to bare trusts and certain other highly specialised types of trust arrangement.

(7) Investment of personal injury awards. UK trustees will wish to comply with the Trustee Act 2000 and the general law on trustee investment. This is a complex technical field.

Source (edited): "http://en.wikipedia.org/wiki/Personal_injury_trust"

Pet trust

A **pet trust** is a legal arrangement to provide care for a pet after its owner dies. A pet trust falls under trust law and is one option for pet owners. Options include honorary trusts, provisions in a will and traditional legal trusts.

Pet trusts stipulate that in the event of a grantor's disability or death a trustee will hold property (cash, for example) "in trust" for the benefit of the grantor's pets. The "grantor" (also called a settlor or trustor in some states) is the person who creates the trust, which may take effect during a person's lifetime or at death. Payments to a designated caregiver(s) will is made on a regular basis.

Depending upon the state law, trusts usually continue for the life of the pet or 21 years, whichever occurs first. Some states allow a pet trust to continue for the life of the pet, without regard to a maximum duration of 21 years. This is particularly advantageous for companion animals who have longer life expectancies than cats and dogs, such as horses and parrots.

History

The development of pet trusts is part of the animal rights movement.

Source (edited): "http://en.wikipedia.org/wiki/Pet_trust"

Pour-over will

A **pour-over will** is a testamentary device wherein the writer of a will creates a trust, and decrees in the will that the property in his or her estate at the time of his or her death shall be distributed to the Trustee of the trust. Such device was always void at English common law, because it was not deemed as a binding trust, in that the testator can change the disposition of the trust at any time and therefore essentially execute changes to the will without meeting the formalities required for the change.

More recently, however, a number of jurisdictions have recognized the validity of a pour-over will. In the jurisdictions in the U.S. which allows a pour-over will, testators do not usually put all of their assets into trusts for the reasons of liquidity, convenience, or simply because they did not get around to do so before they died. A pour-over clause in a will gives probate property to a trustee of the testator's separate trust and must be validated either under incorporation by reference by identifying the previously existing trust which the property will be poured into, or under the doctrine of acts of independent significance by referring to some act that has significance apart from disposing of probate assets, namely, the revocable living trust (*inter vivos* trust). The testator's property is subject to probate until such time as the pour-over clause is applied, and the estate assets "pour" into the trust. Although the trust instrument must be in existence at the time when the will with the pour-over clause is executed, the trust need not be funded *inter vivos*. The pour-over clause protects property not previously placed in a trust by pouring it into the previously established trust through the vehicle of the will.

Source (edited): "http://en.wikipedia.org/wiki/Pour-over_will"

Power of appointment

A **power of appointment** is a term most frequently used in the law of wills to describe the ability of the testator (the person writing the will) to select a person who will be given the authority to dispose of certain property under the will. Although any person can exercise this power at any time during their life, its use is rare outside of a will. The power is divided into two broad categories: **general powers of appointment** and **special powers of appointment**. The holder of a power of appointment differs from the trustee of a trust in that the former has no obligation to manage the property for the generation of income, but need only distribute it.

General power of appointment

Example: "I leave my video game collection to be distributed as my son Andrew sees fit."

In the United States, a general power of appointment is defined for federal estate tax purposes in the Internal Revenue Code §2041. A general power of appointment is one which allows the holder of the power to appoint to himself, his estate, his creditors, or the creditors of his or her estate. The holder of a general power of appointment is treated for estate tax purposes as if he or she is the owner of the property subject to the power, whether or not the power is exercised. Thus, the property which is subject to the power is includable in the power holder's estate for estate tax purposes.

A general power of appointment is a key element of a type of marital deduction trust as prescribed in Internal Revenue Code §2056(b)(5). It is a trust that qualifies for the marital deduction, provided that the surviving spouse is given the income at least annually and the surviving spouse has a general power of appointment over the trust property remaining at his death.

Most general powers of appointment are exercisable under a will. The holder of the power refers to the document creating the power in his or her will and designates who among the permissible objects of the power should receive the property. The power could be exercised by creating further trusts.

If the power of appointment is not exercised, the default provision of the document that created the power takes over.

Special power of appointment

Example: "I leave my cactus collection to my children, my wife Pat to choose who receives which cactus."

A special power of appointment allows the recipient to distribute the designated property among a specified group or class of people, not including donee, donee's estate, creditors of donee, or creditors of donee's estate. For example, a testator might grant his brother the special power to distribute property among the testator's three children. The brother would then have the authority to choose which of the testator's children gets which property. Unlike a general power of appointment, the refusal of the appointed party to exercise a specific power of appointment causes the designated property to revert as a gift to the members of a group or a class.

A special power of appointment may be exclusive or nonexclusive. If exclusive, the donee can appoint all the property to one or more members of the class of permissible appointees to the exclusion of the other members of the class. If nonexclusive, the donee must appoint some property to each object.

Testamentary power and power presently exercisable

In addition to general and special powers, donors may limit when the power may be exercised by the donees. Testamentary powers are usually indicated by the inclusion of limiting language in the granting instrument such as "to B for life, remainder to persons as B shall 'by will' appoint". General powers presently exercisable do not contain such limitations on power. Wording such as "to B for life, and upon B's death to those that B shall appoint" indicates a power presently exercisable, not a testamentary power.

In some jurisdictions, the donee's creditors cannot reach the appointive property when the donee has a presently exercisable power of appointment as long as the power is unexercised.

Source (edited): "http://en.wikipedia.org/wiki/Power_of_appointment"

Pretermitted heir

A **pretermitted heir** is a term used in the law of property to describe a person who would likely stand to inherit under a will, except that the *testator* (the person who wrote the will) did not know, or did not know of, the party at the time the will was written. The most common category of pretermitted heir is the **pretermitted child**, born after the execution of the will.

Rights of a pretermitted child

Many jurisdictions have enacted statutes that permit a pretermitted child to demand an inheritance under the will. Some allow the child to claim their intestate share, while others limit the inheritance to an amount that is comparable to devises made in the will for the children who were alive when the will was written. This may be accomplished by proportionally reducing the gift under the will to the other children, or by reducing gifts under the will to non-family members. An exception common to many jurisdictions prohibits a pretermitted child from claiming an inheritance if the will devised substantially all of the testator's estate to the surviving spouse, and the surviving spouse is the other parent of the pretermitted child.

Some jurisidictions provide the same rights for a child who was pretermitted because, although born *before* the will was executed, he was not *known* of at the time the will was made. This may be because the child was incorrectly believed to be dead, or was later adopted by the testator.

A will may contain a clause, however, which explicitly disinherits any heirs unknown at the time that the will is executed, or any heirs not named in the will. A pretermitted heir may also be denied the right to take under the will if they received an *advancement* against their inheritance - an *inter vivos* gift from the testator of an amount equivalent to what the pretermitted child might take under the will.

Pretermitted spouse

Another party for whom the state might provide is the **pretermitted spouse**, whom the testator does not marry until after the execution of the will. Many jurisdictions provide that a pretermitted spouse will receive either her intestate share (what she would have received had the testator died with no will), or the elective share (a set amount or formula provided by law for spouses who are disinherited in the will).

Like a pretermitted child, a pretermitted spouse may be explicitly disinherited in the will, or may be excluded from taking under the will if they received an advancement on their inheritance in anticipation of the marriage. A pretermitted spouse may also disclaim any interest in the testator's estate through an antenuptial or prenuptial agreement.

Source (edited): "http://en.wikipedia.org/wiki/Pretermitted_heir"

Private annuity trust

A **private annuity trust** (PAT) enables the value of highly appreciated assets, such as real estate, collectables or an investment portfolio, to be realized without directly selling them and incurring substantial taxes from their sale.

A PAT can defer 100% of the United States federal capital gains tax due on the sale of an asset, provide a stream of income, and effectively remove the asset from the owner's estate, thus reducing or eliminating estate taxes. With these advantages, a PAT provides an alternative to other methods of deferring capital gains taxes, such as the charitable remainder trust (CRT), installment sale, or tax-deferred 1031 exchange.

As of October 2006 the IRS ruled that the PAT is no longer a valid capital gains tax deferral method. Those who utilized the PAT before the IRS ruling are grandfathered in and will continue to recognize its tax deferral benefits.

Prior to October 2006, PAT's were very attractive to sellers of highly appreciated real estate. A PAT will allow the owner of investment property to defer up to 100% of the taxes without ever having to buy another property. This is very important because good quality investment properties are difficult to locate. The PAT will also allow the seller of a highly appreciated primary residence to defer up to 100% of the taxes as well. This is important because all gains on primary residences over $250,000 for a single person, and $500,000 for a married couple will be taxed if a PAT is not used.

A properly structured PAT involves first transferring the asset to the PAT in return for a lifetime income stream in the form of an annuity. The transfer of the asset is not a taxable transaction. It is important to understand that a PAT is not issued by a commercial insurance company. Anytime after the asset is placed into the PAT the asset can be sold without taxation to the trust. There is no tax on the sale to the PAT because the PAT has actually purchased the asset from the owner for the fair market value of the asset. The PAT pays the owner for the asset with a lifetime income stream. The PAT has a basis equal to the fair market value so the PAT can sell the asset for fair market value and not be subject to taxation. The original owner of the asset pays taxes only on the PAT payments received, not on the transfer of the asset to the PAT.

PAT payment amounts are based on IRS Life expectancy tables for a single individual or for the joint lives of the asset owner and his or her spouse. The lifetime annuity payments are then made from the PAT assets and/or investment earnings from asset or, alternately, the asset is sold and the proceeds are reinvested by the trustee to fund the payments. PAT payments are calculated using an IRS formula based on the age of the asset owner(s), the value of the asset, and the current IRS interest rate called the Applicable Federal Rate - AFR. PAT payments can be made monthly, quarterly, or annually.

Neither the transfer of the asset to the trust nor its later sale is subject to income taxes if, as is usually the case, the annuity payment is established at a level that gives the annuity a present value equal to the value of the asset sold. However, each annuity payment when received will be partially taxable on the share of capital gains, depreciation recapture and ordinary income included in the payment. The portion representing recovery of original tax basis is not taxable.

To preserve the benefits of a PAT, the trustee must be independent, the annuity cannot be secured in any way, and the annuitants cannot have any control over the trust or its investments. Informal suggestions and advice, however, are not prohibited.

The primary benefit of a PAT is that it allows the full appreciated value of the asset to be invested and to earn income before capital gains and recapture taxes are paid. This means that the taxes due can be stretched out over the owner's entire lifetime. The IRS does not charge any interest or penalties for this form of tax deferral. If the trust's earnings are greater than the annuity amounts paid, the excess value will accrue or can be paid out to the ultimate beneficiaries. The owner's heirs who will also receive any remaining investments in the PAT completely free of estate taxes after the owner has died. If the owner dies before living out his or her life expectancy, the trust might be required to pay a portion of the deferred capital gains taxes. On the other hand, in most cases if the owner lives at least 2/3 of his or her life expectancy, the trust will receive additional tax benefits.

The investment of the pre-tax proceeds potentially gives private annuity trusts the ability to generate substantially more money over the long run than a direct and taxed sale. However, partially offsetting this advantage are the compressed income tax brackets for trusts that cause the investment earnings to reach the maximum income tax bracket when income exceeds $9,000–$10,000 annually. Also, the PAT is not allowed to deduct the amount of imputed interest built into the annuity payments that it makes. Sometimes the PAT will invest in a deferred annuity in an effort to minimize trust income taxes, but at the expense of sizable commissions, fees, and taxes. Investing PAT assets in a deferred annuity issued by a commercial insurance company should be avoided at ALL costs.

Thus, potential benefits from a private annuity trust include lifetime income, deferral of capital gains and depreciation recapture, investment flexibility and diversification, enhancement of retirement income, and tax-free inheritance of the remaining trust funds by the designated beneficiaries. These benefits in many cases will enable a PAT to provide superior results as compared to a charitable remainder trust (CRT), installment sale, or tax-deferred 1031 exchange.

After October 2006 the PAT is no longer a method to defer capital gains taxes. Allstate Insurance developed the Structured Sale which utilizes a structured annuity. The Structured Sale (Ensured Installment Sale) has generally considered to be a much superior tax deferral method to the PAT. However, this is heavily debated by E. Anthony Reguero, who contends that if used properly, the Private Annuity Trust is superior to the Structured Sale both in terms of the tax benefits to the beneficiary or client AS WELL AS the number of ways the IRS can benefit by taxing the trust.

Source (edited): "http://en.wikipedia.

org/wiki/Private_annuity_trust"

Private trustee

In the United States a **Private Trustee** is a position set up through a Trust Indenture. It is a private agreement, between the Settlor of a Trust and the Trustee.

Even though this position was established long before 1634, no records can be found, by this author, of it existence prior to this date. This makes both the Trust and the Trustee private. This arrangement differs from a bank Trustee or a corporate Trustee, both mainly focus on legalities and accounting in the public arena.

A Private Trustee works for and with the family and Beneficiaries becoming familiar with their needs and wishes. Thus, the Private Trustee is more likely to move the Trust group forward keeping these priorities in mind. Usually the Settlor and the Trustee work closely together establishing investments for the trust.

Source (edited): "http://en.wikipedia.org/wiki/Private_trustee"

Probate

Probate is the legal process of administering the estate of a deceased person by resolving all claims and distributing the deceased person's property under the valid will. A surrogate court decides the validity of a testator's will. A probate interprets the instructions of the deceased, decides the executor as the personal representative of the estate, and adjudicates the interests of heirs and other parties who may have claims against the estate.

Probate Administration

Probate is a process by which a will of a deceased person is proved to be valid, such that their property can in due course be retitled (US terminology) or transferred to beneficiaries of the will. As with any legal proceeding, there are technical aspects to probate administration:
- Creditors need to be notified and legal notices published.
- Executors of the Will need to be guided in how and when to distribute assets and how to take creditors' rights into account.
- A Petition to appoint a personal representative may need to be filed and Letters of Administration obtained.
- Homestead property, which follows its own set of unique rules in states like Florida, must be dealt with separately from other assets. In many common law jurisdictions such as Canada, parts of the US, the UK, Australia and India, jointly owned property will pass automatically to the surviving joint owner separately from any will, unless the equitable title is held as tenants in common.
- There are time factors involved in filing and objecting to claims against the estate.
- There may be a lawsuit pending over the decedent's death or there may have been pending suits that are now continuing. There may be separate procedures required in contentious probate cases.
- Real estate or other property may need to be sold to effect correct distribution of assets pursuant to the will or merely to pay debts.
- Estate taxes, gift taxes or inheritance taxes must be considered if the estate exceeds certain thresholds.
- Costs of the administration including ordinary taxation such as income tax on interest and property taxation will be deducted from assets in the estate before distribution by the executors of the will.
- Other assets may simply need to be transferred from the deceased to his or her beneficiaries.

Etymology

The etymology of "probate" stems from Latin, old French, and old English words with somewhat different meanings. The earliest definition, dated to 1463, means the "official proving of a will," and originates from the Classical Latin word *probatus*, meaning "proven" or "a thing proven." This is the past participle of *probāre*, which means "to try, test, prove" or "prove to be worthy". It also traces its roots to the old French word *prouwe*, dated circa 1175, or *prover*, and is related to the English word "prove", and the Welsh word "profi" (to test). The term "probative," used in the law of evidence, comes from the same Latin root but has a different English usage.

Commonwealth

In England and Wales, Northern Ireland, Commonwealth countries (common law jurisdictions), Ireland and in the U.S., probate ("official proving of a will") is obtained by executors of a will while Letters of Administration are granted where there are no executors.

In any jurisdictions in the U.S. that recognize a married couple's property as tenancy by the entireties, if a person dies intestate, the portion of his/her estate so titled passes to a surviving spouse without a probate.

If the estate is not automatically devised to the surviving spouse in this manner or through a joint tenancy, and is not held within a trust, it is necessary to "probate the estate", whether or not the decedent had a valid will. A court having jurisdiction of the decedent's estate (a probate court) supervises probate, to administer the disposition of the decedent's property according to the law of the jurisdiction and the decedent's intent as manifested in his testamentary instrument. There are exceptions for smaller estates.

If the decedent died without a will, known as intestacy, the estate will be distributed according to the laws of the state where the decedent resided or held by the court. If the decedent died with a will, the will usually names an executor (personal representative), a person tasked with carrying out the instructions laid out in the will. The executor marshals the decedent's assets. If there is no will, or if the will does not name an executor, the probate court can appoint one. Traditionally, the representative of an intestate estate is called an *administrator*. If the decedent died with a will, but only a copy of the will can be located, many states will allow the copy to be probated, subject to the rebuttable presumption that the testator destroyed the will before death.

In some cases, where the person named as executor cannot administer the probate, or wishes to have someone else do so, another person will be named as administrator. An executor or an administrator may receive compensation for his service.

The probate court may require that the executor provide a fidelity bond, an insurance policy in favor of the estate to protect against possible abuse by the executor.

The representative of a testate estate who is someone other than the executor named in the will is an *administrator with the will annexed*, or administrator c.t.a. (from the Latin *cum testamento annexo*.) The generic term for executors or administrators is personal representative.

Steps of probate

Some of the decedent's property may never enter probate because it passes to another person contractually, such as the death proceeds of an insurance policy insuring the decedent or bank or retirement account that names a beneficiary or is owned as "payable on death", and property (sometimes a bank or brokerage account) legally held as "jointly owned with right of survivorship".

Property held in a revocable or irrevocable trust created during the grantor's lifetime also avoids probate. In these cases in the U.S. no court action is involved and the property is distributed privately, subject to estate taxes.

After opening the probate case with the court, the personal representative inventories and collects the decedent's property. Next, he pays any debts and taxes, including estate tax in the United States, if the estate is taxable at the federal or state level, or the Pennsylvania inheritance tax. Finally, he distributes the remaining property to the beneficiaries, either as instructed in the will, or under the intestacy laws of the state.

A party may challenge any aspect of the probate administration, such as a direct challenge to the validity of the will, known as a will contest, a challenge to the status of the person serving as personal representative, a challenge as to the identity of the heirs, and a challenge to whether the personal representative is properly administering the estate. Issues of paternity can be disputed among the potential heirs in intestate estates, especially with the advent of inexpensive DNA profiling techniques. In some situations, however, even biological heirs can be denied their inheritance rights, while non-biological heirs can be granted inheritance rights.

The personal representative must understand and abide by the fiduciary duties, such as a duty to keep money in interest bearing account and to treat all beneficiaries equally. Not complying with the fiduciary duties may allow interested persons to petition for the removal of the personal representative and hold the personal representative liable for any harm to the estate.

Avoiding probate

Probate generally lasts several months, and often over a year before all the property is distributed, and can incur substantial court and attorney costs in large estates. One of the many ways used in the US to avoid probate is to execute a living trust. Alternatively property can be passed outside probate by setting up P.O.D (paid on death) designations on bank accounts and T.O.D (transfer on death) on brokerage accounts, 401ks and IRAs that pass automatically to designated beneficiaries, or placing property in joint tenancies with the right of survivorship. As for real estate, a testator may add a named beneficiary to a deed by executing a life estate deed. The property can be passed several generations. The cost of such measures to avoid probate should be weighed against probate court fees, as the administration of a living trust or other arrangement will also incur legal and administrative charges, and as with all trusts is ultimately subject to the supervision of the court.

Avoiding probate does not eliminate estate taxes. Under the federal estate tax law as modified, included in the definition of a taxable estate are property held in a living trust, life insurance, payable on death or transfer on death financial instruments, and other property a party receives upon decease of the decedent.

England and Wales

When someone dies, the term "Probate" usually refers to the legal process whereby the deceased's assets are collected together and, following various legal and fiscal steps and processes, eventually distributed to the beneficiaries of the estate. Technically the term "Probate" has a particular legal meaning but it is generally used within the English legal profession as a term to cover all procedures concerned with the administration of a deceased person's estate. As a legal discipline the subject is vast and it is only possible in an article such as this to cover the most common situations, but even that only scratches the surface.

All legal procedures concerned with Probate (as defined above) come within the jurisdiction of the Family Division of the High Court of Justice by virtue of Section 25 of the Senior Courts Act 1981. The High Court is therefore the only body that is able to issue the documents which give persons the ability to actually deal with a deceased person's estate, such as to enable them to close bank accounts or sell property or shares. It is the production and issuing of these documents, known collectively as

"Grants of Representation" that is the primary function of the Probate Registries, which are part of the High Court, and are to whom the general public and probate professionals alike apply to for the Grants of Representation. To find your local Probate Registry see

There are many different types of Grants of Representation, each one designed to cover a particular circumstance. The most common ones are those which cover the two most common situations - either the deceased died leaving a valid Will or they did not. If someone left a valid Will then it is more than likely that the Grant will be a "Grant of Probate". If there was no Will then the Grant required is likely to be a "Grant of Administration". There are many other Grants which can be required in certain circumstances and many have strange Latin names but the general public is most likely to encounter these two - the Grant of Probate and the Grant of Administration.

The general public can apply to a local probate registry for a Grant themselves but most people use a probate practitioner such as a solicitor. If an estate is small some banks and building societies will allow accounts to be closed by the deceased's immediate family without a Grant, but there usually needs to be less than about £15,000 in the account for them to allow this.

The persons who are actually given the job of dealing with the deceased's assets are called "personal representatives" or "PR's". If the deceased left a valid Will then the PR's will be the "Executors" who are appointed by the Will - "I appoint X and Y to be my Executors etc." If there is no Will or if the Will does not contain a valid appointment of Executors (for example if they are all dead) then the PR's are called "Administrators". So, Executors obtain a Grant of Probate which enables them to deal with the estate and Administrators obtain a Grant of Administration which enables them to do the same. Apart from that distinction the function of Executors and Administrators is exactly the same.

For an explanation of the intestacy probate process in England and Wales, see Administration of an estate on death.

Source (edited): "http://en.wikipedia.org/wiki/Probate"

Probate court

A **probate court** (also called a **surrogate court**) is a specialized court that deals with matters of probate and the administration of estates.

Probate courts administer proper distribution of the assets of a decedent (one who has died), adjudicates the validity of wills, enforces the provisions of a valid will (by issuing the grant of probate), prevents malfeasance by executors and administrators of estates, and provides for the equitable distribution of the assets of persons who die intestate (without a valid will), such as by granting a grant of administration giving judicial approval to the personal representative to administer matters of the estate).

In contested matters, a probate court examines the authenticity of a will and decides who is to receive the deceased person's property. In a case of an intestacy, the court determines who is to receive the deceased's property under the law of its jurisdiction. The probate court will then oversee the process of distributing the deceased's assets to the proper beneficiaries. In some jurisdictions, such courts are also referred to as **orphans courts**, or **courts of ordinary**. Not all jurisdictions have probate courts, in many places, probate functions are performed by a chancery court or another court of equity.

Probate courts may also deal with other matters, including conservatorships, guardianships, name changes, marriages, and adoptions; although in some jurisdictions these issues are dealt with by family courts.

The surrogate court can be petitioned by interested parties in an estate, such as when a beneficiary feels that an estate is being mishandled. The court has the authority to compel the executor to give an account of his actions.

The Orphan's Court

The **orphan's court** was an organization established in the Chesapeake Bay colonies during colonization. The major goal of the organization was to protect orphaned children and their right to their deceased family's estate from against claims and abuses by stepparents and others.

Modern-day orphan's courts are surrogate courts, hearing matters involving wills of decedents' estates which are contested and supervising estates which are probated judicially.

List of probate courts

- England and Wales
  - Prerogative court - former
  - Court of Probate - former
  - High Court of Justice Family Division - current
- United States (state courts)
  - California Superior Court
  - Connecticut - Connecticut Probate Courts (a system of 54 probate court districts)
  - District of Columbia - Superior Court of the District of Columbia, Probate Division
  - Georgia - Court of Ordinary (judge known as *ordinary*) (former)
  - Missouri - conducted by Circuit Courts, some of which have separate probate divisions
  - New Hampshire - New Hampshire Probate Court
  - New Jersey - New Jersey Superior Court, Chancery Division, Probate Part
  - New York - New York Surrogate's Court (judges known as *surrogates*)
  - Ohio - conducted by Courts of Common Pleas, Family and Probate Divisions
  - Vermont - Probate Courts (one in each of Vermont's 14 counties)

Source (edited): "http://en.wikipedia.

org/wiki/Probate_court"

Probate research

Probate research deals with finding heirs and proving their right to an inheritance. In some estates there may be no known heirs, or there may be missing heirs whose names are known but their contact information is not. There may be also be known heirs from one part of the family, but another part of the family may be unknown. In all these instances, professional probate researchers work to trace the next-of-kin.

Probate researchers are also called heir hunters, heir searchers, and forensic genealogists.

Intestacy laws vary enormously from one country to another, and in the US, they also vary from state to state. Thus probate researchers must have extensive knowledge of the law to know which family members are legally entitled to inherit. They also employ specialized genealogical and investigative techniques to search public records and databases to identify the extended family of the descendent, often starting with no more than a name and date of death and in some cases looking for relatives as distant as second cousins. In many cases the heirs that are finally identified have little or no knowledge of the person from whom they are inheriting.

Probate researchers are hired by solicitors in the United Kingdom, or Estate Attorneys in the United States. It is also common for them to independently review many cases to find a single case with missing or unknown heirs.

Fees Charged

Many probate researchers work primarily on a contingent fee or "no win no fee" basis which involves the potential heir signing an agreement to pay a percentage of their inheritance to the probate research company if they actually inherit something. Legitimate firms *never* request out of pocket or up front fees from potential beneficiaries. However, there are many email scams that ask for money for information about false inheritances.

The industry remains unregulated, and there is some public concern over the fees charged by probate researchers. Typically these range from 10-40% of the inheritance as each case varies in its complexity, size, number of heirs, and firms involved. However, these fees are in the same range as the 20-50% charged by attorneys for contingent work. Contingent fees must be large enough for the companies to be profitable despite the large amount of work that is done when no fee is received (due to insolvency of estates, failure of the heirs' claims, and the large number of cases that must be reviewed to find a single case with missing heirs).

Some probate research is done on an hourly basis billed to the estate and deducted from the available funds that will be distributed to all the heirs regardless of whether additional heirs are found or not.

Popular Culture

The BBC has made five series (105 programmes)Heir Hunters shown on UK BBC TV about Fraser and Fraser and a number of other companies. Episodes have also been screened in South Africa, Australia and New Zealand. However, it should be noted that any involvement in Heir Hunters is by no means an endorsement by the BBC.

The Future of Probate Research

As the population lives longer due to improved health, and is more mobile the problem of tracing missing heirs potentially becomes more difficult despite the growth of more web based research tools.

Many people are still reluctant to draft a proper will, or make bad ones which later prove invalid, or can easily be contested. As a consequence billions pass to the state, after a qualify period in trust waiting for claims from entitled beneficiaries, or being found by probate researchers or Heir Hunters.

Source (edited): "http://en.wikipedia.org/wiki/Probate_research"

Probate sale

Probate sale is the term used to describe the process executed at a county court in the USA where the executor for the estate of a deceased person sells property from the estate (typically real estate) in order to divide the property among the beneficiaries.

Source (edited): "http://en.wikipedia.org/wiki/Probate_sale"

Protective trust

The **Protective Trust** is a form of settlement found in England and Wales and several Commonwealth countries. It has marked similarities to asset-protection trusts found in several offshore jurisdictions and US Spendthrift trusts.

In such a trust assets are ordinarily held to pay an income to the beneficiary. The beneficiary may also have access to capital of the trust with the trustee's permission. The right to receive income from a trust would ordinarily be an asset in the hands of the beneficiary and could be sold, thwarting the intention of the donor to spread the gift over the recipient's lifetime. Additionally on a bankruptcy the right to the income would be sold by the beneficiary's trustee in bankruptcy.

To give protection to beneficiaries, a protective trust automatically converts into a discretionary trust, under which the beneficiary has no right to the income, if he or she does anything which breaches a condition specified in the document creating the trust.

The establishment of this discretionary trust is ordinarily exempt from the charge to UK inheritance tax on the establishment of discretionary trusts.

Such protective trusts have a long-standing history. To reduce the verbose definitions that had previously to be recited in the establishing documents of a protective trust, in England and Wales s33 of the Trustee Act 1925 (and equivalent legislation in other jurisdictions) provides that this protection will arise in any trust described as a "protective trust" in its trust deed.

Protective trusts are subject to challenge under creditor protection legislation as are any other forms of asset-protection. However many jurisdictions do not permit a trust to be broken where a debtor who remains a discretionary beneficiary only under a trust and cannot access the fund without the exercise of the trustees' discretion in his favour.

Source (edited): "http://en.wikipedia.org/wiki/Protective_trust"

Protector (trust)

In trust law, a **protector** is a person appointed under the trust instrument to direct or restrain the trustees in relation to their administration of the trust.

Historically, the concept of a protector developed in offshore jurisdictions where settlors were (perhaps understandably) concerned about appointing a trust company in a small, distant country as sole trustee of an offshore trust which is to hold a great deal of the settlor's wealth. However, protectors now form a part of mainstream tax planning in most jurisdictions which recognise trusts.

There are a number of reasons that a settlor may wish to appoint a protector in relation to a trust:
- protectors allow a great degree of flexibility when dealing with changes in circumstances, including both factual circumstances (death, premature divorce, previously unknown children) and legal changes (any legal changes, but most frequently changes to applicable revenue laws);
- the settlor may be concerned that the trustee may not pay sufficient attention to his wishes;
- the settlor wishes certain powers to be withheld from the trustees; or
- the settlor wishes a third party to act as a main point of contact, between the beneficiaries and the trustees.

The powers vested in the protector vary both according to the proper law of the trust and the terms of the trust instrument. The powers may include:
- power to remove and appoint trustees;
- power to approve a change of proper law;
- power to approve the addition or removal of beneficiaries;
- power to approve proposed trust distributions;
- power to approve the appointment of an agent or adviser either generally or in relation to specific matters;
- power to approve investment recommendations;
- power to appoint replacement protectors; and
- power to terminate the trust or approve the termination of the trust.

Conceptually many commentators have difficulty with the idea of a protector, as this undermines the role which in law has historically been fulfilled by the trustees. As protectors are a relatively recent innovation in trust law, case law is scant. Is it not even clear if as a matter a law a protector would owe fiduciary duties to the beneficiaries (although in practice, many trust instruments expressly state that they shall).

It is sometimes suggested that where the protector is too close to the beneficial interest in the trust (for example, if the protectors have power to confer benefits upon themselves, directly or indirectly) this may destroy the essential nature of the trust. If the protector has power to grant beneficial interests in the trust fund to the settlor, this may have disastrous tax consequences in some jurisdictions.

Source (edited): "http://en.wikipedia.org/wiki/Protector_(trust)"

Prudent man rule

The **Prudent Man Rule** is based on common law stemming from the 1830 Massachusetts court decision, *Harvard College v. Armory* 9 Pick (26 Mass) 446, 461 (1830). The prudent man rule directs trustees "to observe how men of prudence, discretion and intelligence manage their own affairs, not in regard to speculation, but in regard to the permanent disposition of their funds, considering the probable income, as well as the probable safety of the capital to be invested." A copy of the Prudent Man Rule is also known as the Restatement of Trusts 2d.

Description

Under the **Prudent Man Rule**, when the governing trust instrument, state law is silent concerning the types of investments permitted. The fiduciary is required to invest trust assets as a "prudent man" would invest his own property with the following factors in mind: the needs of beneficiaries, the need to preserve the estate (or corpus of the trust) and the amount and regularity of income. The application of these general principles depends on the type of account administered. The **Prudent Man Rule** continues to be the prevailing statute in a small number of states.

Investment Choices

The **Prudent Man Rule** requires that each investment be judged on its own merits. Isolated investments in a portfolio may have been imprudent at the time of acquisition. However, as a part of a portfolio designed under a strategy, e.g. a hedge fund, the investment could be prudent. Thus, a fiduciary may not be held liable for a loss in one investment.

Under the **Prudent Man Rule**, speculative or risky investments must be avoided. Certain types of investments, such as second mortgages or new business ventures, are viewed as intrinsically speculative and therefore prohibited as fiduciary investments. As with any fiduciary relationship, margin accounts and short selling of uncovered securities are also prohibited.

Since the **Prudent Man Rule** was last revised in 1959, numerous investment products have been introduced or have come into the mainstream. For example, in 1959, there were 155 mutual funds with nearly $16 billion in assets. By year-end 2000, mutual funds had grown to 10,725, with $6.9 trillion in assets (as reported by CDA/Wiesenberger). In addition, investors have become more sophisticated and are more attuned to investments since the last revision of the Rule. As these two concepts converged, the **Prudent Man Rule** became less relevant. This discounting of the relevance of the prudent man rule is more the result of market forces than it is of the needs of individuals for "safety of capital". The 10,000+ mutual funds of 2000 have grown to over 15,000 mutual funds in 2006. Does any advisor claim to be expert on all of these funds? Does any one of the rating agencies promise that the funds they rate highly will perform better than those they don't? The Prudent Man Rule is even more important today than it was in 1830 if for no other reason than that the market has become so complex and no individual advisor or advisory firm can claim to be fully informed about the investments they recommend.

The Prudent Man Rule in its broader interpretations implies that the fiduciary should perform enough due diligence to insure that the company meets the investment needs of the investors. Typical due diligence includes discussions with management, vendors and customers, as well as proper evaluation of any risk factors that might affect the performance of the company or its' securities.

The modern interpretation of the "Prudent Man Rule" goes beyond the assessment of each asset individually to include the concept of due diligence and diversification. This is sometimes referred to as the "**Prudent Investor Rule**". The logic is this: an asset may be too risky to put all your money in (thus failing the Prudent Man Rule) but may still be very diversifying and therefore beneficial in a small proportion of the total portfolio.

Source (edited): "http://en.wikipedia.org/wiki/Prudent_man_rule"

Purpose trust

A **purpose trust** is a type of trust which has no beneficiaries, but instead exists for advancing some non-charitable purpose of some kind. In most jurisdictions, such trusts are not enforceable outside of certain limited and anomalous exceptions, but some countries have enacted legislation specifically to promote the use of non-charitable purpose trusts. Trusts for charitable purposes are also technically purpose trusts, but they are usually referred to simply as charitable trusts. People referring to purpose trusts are usually taken to be referring to non-charitable purpose trusts.

Trusts which fail the test of charitable status usually fail as non-charitable purpose trusts, although there are certain historical exceptions to this, and some countries have modified the law in this regard by statute. The court will not usually validate non-charitable purpose trusts which fail by treating them as a power. In *IRC v Broadway Cottages Trust* Ch 20 the English Court of Appeal held: "I am not at liberty to validate this trust by treating it as a power. A valid power is not to be spelled out of an invalid trust."

Conceptual objections

The basis for the general prohibition against non-charitable purpose trusts is usually phrased on one or more of several specific grounds.

The beneficiary principle

A trust is, at its root, an obligation. And accordingly, "every [non-charitable] trust must have a definite object. There must be someone in whose favour the court can decree performance." With a charitable trust, this power of enforcement is usually vested in the Attorney General. However, such conceptual objections seem less strong since the decision of the House of Lords in *McPhail v Doulton* AC 424 where Lord Wilberforce rode roughshod over objections to widening the class of valid discretionary trusts on the basis that there would be difficulty ascertaining beneficiaries for the court to enforce the trust in favour of.

Uncertainty

Where the objects of a trust are a purpose rather than an individual or individuals, there is much greater risk that a trust would not be enforceable due to lack of certainty. Cases such as *Morice v Bishop of Durham* (1804) 9 Ves Jr 399 and *Re Astor* Ch 534 re-affirm the court's disinclination to enforce trusts that are not specific and detailed. It is noteworthy that the common law exceptions to the general prohibition on purposes trusts tend to relate to specific and detailed matters, such as maintenance of a specific tomb, or caring for a particular animal.

Excessive delegation of testamentary power

Purpose trusts have been attacked conceptually on the basis that it would amount to the delegation of a testamentary power, although subsequent cases have cast doubt on the correctness of that reasoning.

Perpetuity

Charitable purpose trusts are exempt from the rule against perpetuities. Private trusts are not. Accordingly, all non-charitable purposes trusts, to be valid, need to comply with the perpetuity rules in the relevant jurisdiction.

Common law exceptions

There are, nonetheless, several well recognised exceptions at common law where non-charitable purposes trusts will be upheld.

Tombs and monuments

Provisions for the building or maintenance of tombs or monuments have been upheld as a matter of grave concern in common law, although solely on the basis of ancient precedent. In *Re Hooper* 1 Ch 38 a trust for the maintenance of graves was upheld, but the court indicated that it would not have done so had it not been bound by *Pirbright v Salwey* WN 86. Such trusts still need to comply with the requirement of certainty. Hence a bequest to a Parish council for "the purpose of providing some useful memorial to myself" was struck down.

Animals

Trusts for the care of specific animals have been upheld. In *Re Dean* (1889) 41 Ch D 552, North J upheld a trust for maintenance of horses and hounds for 50 years relying upon upon much older authorities and the monument cases.

Quistclose trusts

Historically, *Quistclose* trusts have sometimes been considered to be purpose trusts, but the modern view is that they are resulting trusts to the settlor subject to a power to dispose of the assets in a predetermined fashion.

Others

In most academic textbooks, there are usually a swath of "other" purpose trusts or purported purpose trusts that are held up as a residual anomalous category. The most commonly cited example is *Re Thompson* 342 where a gift to Trinity Hall, Cambridge for the promotion and furtherance of fox hunting was upheld. It has been suggested academically that the case has "been elevated to a position of importance which it does not merit".

In *Re Endacott* Ch 232 it was made clear that the existing exceptions at common law would not be extended; they were described as "troublesome, anomalous and aberrant".

Mistakes about the Common Law

Paul Baxendale-Walker has argued in the book "Purpose Trusts" (Butterworths 1999)Paul BW Chaplin#Biography that the courts took a wrong turn in the mid 20th century and ignored hundreds of previous years of judicial precedents in which purpose trusts of all kinds had been upheld as valid. He contends that the "beneficiary principle" has been misunderstood. His view have received support from Professor Jill Martin and others.

Statutory exceptions

A number of offshore jurisdictions have enacted statutes which expressly validate non-charitable purpose trusts outside of the small group of specific exceptions recognised at common law. Some of the jurisdictions which have done so include the Bahamas, Bermuda, the British Virgin Islands and the Cayman Islands.

Characteristically, in those jurisdictions a non-charitable purpose trust requires a written trust instrument and the trust instrument must specify a **protector** or **enforcer** who will have *locus standi* to enforce the terms of the trust against the trustees. This role is created to address the concerns expressed by the courts as to how the courts would have power to control the trustees.

However, no real steps have been taken in any of those jurisdictions to address the fundamental conceptual issues of where the beneficial title to the trust assets should be regarded as residing whilst they form part of the trust fund. Arguably, if no other person is regarded as having a beneficial claim to the assets, they would be regarded as being owned solely by the trustees, which could have disastrous tax implications for the trustees.

Unincorporated associations

Special problems arise in connection with the holding of property by unincorporated associations of persons. Whereas a company has separate legal personality and can hold property, with certain statutory exceptions, unincorporated associations of persons cannot. Accordingly, where an unincorporated association is formed for a non-charitable purpose (which is most often the case), a gift to an unincorporated association can fail as an invalid purpose trust. However, the courts have usually tried to avoid such a result by construing the gift as a gift to the *members* of the unincorporated association. The difficulty is that such a gift would then have to be construed as a distributive gift to the individual members, rather than a purposive gift for the objects of the unincorporated association. In *Re Recher's Will Trust* Ch 526 a more purposive approach was taken, and Brightman J held that a gift to The London and Provincial Anti-Vivisection Society was to be construed as a beneficial gift in favour of the members, not so as to entitle them to an immediate distributive share, but as an accretion to the funds of the society subject to the contract of the members as set out in the rules. Further, it was held that such a construction would be possible whether the society was inward looking (ie. existed to promote the interests of its members) or outward looking (ie. existed to promote some external cause or purpose).

Source (edited): "http://en.wikipedia.org/wiki/Purpose_trust"

Rabbi trust

In the United States a **Rabbi trust** is a type of trust used by businesses or other entities to defer the taxability to the person or entity receiving (the payee) such payments as employee compensation or purchase payments in the acquisition of another business.

History

The first such trust set up was for the benefit of a rabbi, resulting in the name. Revenue Procedure 92-64 further clarified the acceptable rules for Rabbi trusts along with a model trust document and the required features to avoid constructive receipt of income to the employee.

Applications

An example of a Rabbi trust applying where an employee receives compensation the taxation of which is deferrable is a nonqualified deferred compensation plan.

The Rabbi trust is likewise applicable when one business purchases another business but wants to set aside part of the purchase price and defer its payment as well as taxability to the payee upon the satisfaction of conditions to which both parties agree.

Non-qualified deferred compensation plans

A non-qualified deferred compensation plan is where current income of an employee is deferred but not taxable to the employee. The employer, however, sets aside the assets in a separate trust for the employee's future. Ordinarily, this would cause current inclusion into gross income even though the employer has yet to reduce the money to income because of the economic benefit theory doctrine. So the IRS allowed by private letter ruling that the trust would not result in income, according to Section 83(a) of the Code, if the assets of the trust were available to the reach of the employer's general creditors. This is because until the employee is vested, he is under a substantial risk of forfeiture and under Section 83(a) and accompanying regulations 1.83-1 and as such is not subject to current inclusion into gross income.

All non-qualified deferred-compensation plans must involve substantial risk of forfeiture or other methods of avoiding constructive receipt, such as conditioning payment upon performance of future conditions or service. The unique feature of the Rabbi trust is that the money placed in it is protected from changes of heart of the employer. Once placed in the trust the money cannot be revoked by decisions of the employer. So as long as the employer's financial position is sound, the money is relatively protected. If, however, the employer goes into bankruptcy proceedings, the money may be subjected to the claims of the employer's general unsecured creditors.

Acquisition of a business

When one business purchases another business, the purchasing business may want to set aside part of the purchase price and defer its payment to the payee upon the satisfaction of conditions to which both parties agree. A Rabbi trust may be used in this situation to defer the taxability to the payee of the deferred payments of the purchase price.

For the Rabbi trust to be successfully applied, there must be a real risk of forfeiture upon the failure by the payee to fulfill the agreed upon conditions. If the condition is impossible to fail, then constructive receipt may overcome the successful application of the Rabbi trust. The Rabbi trust allows the deferment of compensation whether employment income or the purchase price of a business acquisition, and the absence of this would result in the taxability to the payee of the compensation not yet received by the payee. This would serve as a disincentive for deferring such payments.
Source (edited): "http://en.wikipedia.org/wiki/Rabbi_trust"

Real estate investment trust

A **real estate investment trust** or **REIT** (/ˈriːt/) is a tax designation for a corporate entity investing in real estate that reduces or eliminates corporate income taxes. In return, REITs are required to distribute 90% of their income, which may be taxable, into the hands of the investors. The REIT structure was designed to provide a similar structure for investment in real estate as mutual funds provide for investment in stocks.

Like other corporations, REITs can be publicly or privately held. Public REITs may be listed on public stock exchanges like shares of common stock in other firms.

REITs can be classified as equity, mortgage, or hybrid.

The key statistics to look at in a REIT are its net asset value (*NAV*), adjusted funds from operations (*AFFO*) and cash available for distribution (*CAD*). REITs face challenges from both a slowing U.S. economy and the global financial crisis, depressing share values by 40 to 70 percent in some cases.

REITs originated in the 1880s at a time when investors could avoid "double tax" or a tax at corporate and individual level. In the 1930s this tax benefit was changed, making investors pay "double tax". President Eisenhower signed the REIT tax provision contained in the Cigar Tac Excise Tax Extension in 1960.

By region

Australia

The REIT concept was launched in Australia in 1971. General Property Trust was the first Australian real estate investment trust (LPT) on the Australian stock exchanges (now the Australian Securities Exchange). REITs which are listed on an exchange were known as Listed Property Trusts (LPTs) until March 2008, distinguishing them from private REITs which are known in Australia as Unlisted Property Trusts. They have since been renamed Australian Real Estate Investment Trusts (A-REITs) in line with international practice.

There are now more than 70 A-REITs listed on the ASX, with market capitalization in excess of A$100bn.

Australia is also receiving growing recognition as having the world's largest REITs market outside the United States. More than 12 percent of global listed property trusts can be found on the ASX.

Brazil

REITs were introduced in Brazil in 1993 by the law 8668/93 and initially ruled by the instruction 205/94 and, nowadays, by instruction 472/08 from CVM (Comissao de Valores Mobiliários - which is the Brazilian equivalent of SEC). Locally they are denominated FIIs or "Fundos de Investimento Imobiliário". FII's dividends are free of taxes for personal investors (not companies) since 2006, but only for the funds which have at least 50 investors and that are publicly negotiated in the stock market. FIIs, referred to as "REIT" as the similar investment vehicle in the US, have been used either to own and operate independent property investments and associated with a single property or a portion thereof, or owning several real properties (multiple properties) and funding them through the public capital markets.

Bulgaria

REITs were introduced in Bulgaria in 2004 with the so called "Special Purpose Investment Companies Act". They are pass-through entities for corporate income tax purposes (i.e. they are not subject to corporate income tax), but are subject to numerous restrictions.

Canada

Canadian REITs were established in 1993. They are required to be configured as trusts and are not taxed if they distribute their net taxable income to shareholders. REITs have been excluded from the income trust tax legislation passed in the 2007 budget by the Conservative government. Many Canadian REITs have limited liability. On December 16, 2010, the Department of Finance proposed amendments to the rules defining "Qualifying REITs" for Canadian tax purposes. As a result, "Qualifying REITs" are exempt from the new entity-level, "specified investment flow-through" (SIFT) tax that all publicly traded income trusts and partnerships are paying as of January 1, 2011.

Finland

Finnish REITs were established in 2010, when 'the tax exemption law' (Laki eräiden asuntojen vuokraustoimintaa harjoittavien osakeyhtiöiden verohuojennuksesta, 299/2009) was passed by the Finnish parliament. Together with the 'Law on Real Estate Funds' (Kiinteistörahastolaki, 1173/1997) it enables the existence of tax efficient residential REITs.

Qualification
- REITs will have to be established as a public listed company (julkinen osakeyhtiö, Oyj) for this specific purpose. When the REIT is established the minimum equity is 5M€ and it has to be distributed over 5 separate investors.
- Minimum holding period: 5 years.
- At least 80% of its assets have to be invested in residential real-estate.
- At least 80% of the REIT's gross revenues must come from residential rental income.
- At least 90% of the REIT's taxable income, excluding unrealised capital gains, has to be distributed to its shareholders through dividends.
- The corporation is income-tax-exempt, but the shareholders will have to pay individual income tax on the dividends.
- Largest individual shareholder may own less than 10% of company shares (max. 30% till the end of 2013).

Germany

Germany is also planning to introduce German REITs (short, G-REITs) in order to create a new type of real estate investment vehicle. Government fears that failing to introduce REITs in Germany would result in a significant loss of investment capital to other countries. Nonetheless there still is political resistance to these plans, especially by the social democratic party ('SPD'). As of June 2006 the ministry of finance has announced that they still plan to introduce G-REITs in 2007. The legal details seem to adopt much of UK-REITs regulations (taxation, public listing, etc.), as far as it is possible to tell yet.

A law concerning G-REITs was enacted 1 June 2007, and is retroactive to 1 January 2007.

Qualification

- REITs will have to be established as a corporation "REIT-AG" or "REIT-Aktiengesellschaft".
- At least 75% of its assets have to be invested in real-estate.
- At least 75% of the G-REIT's gross revenues must be real-estate related.
- At least 90% of the REIT's taxable income has to be distributed to its shareholders through dividends.
- The corporation is income-tax-exempt, but the shareholders will have to pay individual income tax on the dividends.
- Some restrictions apply on establishing residential REIT's

Ghana

REITs have been in existence in Ghana since 1994. The Home Finance Company, now HFC BANK, established the first REIT in Ghana in August 1994. HFC Bank has been at the forefront of mortgage financing in Ghana since 1993. It has used various collective investment schemes as well as corporate bonds to finance its mortgage lending activities. Collective Investment Schemes, of which REIT's are a part, are currently regulated by the Securities and Exchange Commission of Ghana.

Hong Kong

REITs have been in existence in Hong Kong since 2005, when The Link REIT was launched by the Hong Kong Housing Authority on behalf of the Government. Since 2005, there have been 7 REIT listings as at July 2007, most of which, including Sunlight REIT have not enjoyed success due to low yield. Except for The Link and Regal Real Estate Investment Trust, share prices of all but one are significantly below IPO price. Hong Kong issuers' use of financial engineering (interest rate swaps) to improve initial yields has also been cited as having deterred investors' interest

India

As of January 2010, India was formulating legislation for REITs in the Indian real estate market. Once introduced these Indian REITs (country specific/generic version I-REITs) will help individual investors enjoy the benefits of owning an interest in the securitised real estate market. The best benefit being that of fast and easy liquidation of investments in the real estate market unlike the traditional way of disposing real estate. The government and Securities and Exchange Board of India SEBI through various notifications is in the process of easing the norms of investing in real estate in India directly and indirectly through foreign direct investment, through listed real estate companies, mutual funds etc. With the current real estate boom and the market being flooded with Initial Public Offer of various listed real estate companies in India it will be the best time for investors to own a share of the profiting market economy. Legislative framework, revised investment norms, a favourable investment opportunity, and a clear taxation policy will provide the right kind of investing opportunity in India in the time to come.

Japan

Japan is one of a handful of countries in Asia with REIT legislation (other countries/markets include Hong Kong, Singapore, Malaysia, Taiwan and Korea), which permitted their establishment in December 2001. J-REIT securities are traded on the Tokyo Stock Exchange, and most service providers of the J-REITs are Japanese real estate companies, Japanese conglomerates and foreign investment banks.

Since the burst of the real estate bubble in 1990, property prices in Japan have seen steady drops through 2004, with some signs of price stabilization and possibly price increase in 2005 and 2006. Some see J-REITs as a way to increase investment in the real estate market, although notable increases in asset values has not yet been realized.

A J-REIT (a listed real estate investment trust) is strictly regulated under the Law concerning Investment Trust and Investment Company (the "LITIC") and established as an investment company under the LITIC.

In addition to REITs, Japanese law also provides for a parallel system of special purpose companies which can be used for the securitization of particular properties on the private placement basis.

Pakistan

The Securities and Exchange Commission of Pakistan is in process of implementing REIT regulatory framework that will allow full foreign ownership, free movement of capital and unrestricted repatriation of profits. It will curb speculation in Pakistani real estate markets and gives access to small investors diversifying into real estate as well. The Securities and Exchange Commission of Pakistan following regulatory framework similar to Singapore and Hong Kong REITs.

The Securities and Exchange Commission of Pakistan expects that about six REITs will be licensed within the first year, mainly large assets management companies applying for it. Pakistan is recently seeing an outflux of investments by foreign real estate development mostly Malaysian and Dubai based companies.

Philippines

REITs in the Philippines will soon be available to the public after the Real Estate Investment Trust of 2009 (RA 9856) lapsed into law on December 17, 2009 and its Implementing Rules and Regulations approved by the Securities and Exchange Commission on May 2010.

Singapore

Commonly referred to as S-REITs. There are currently 20 REITs listed on the SGX, starting with CapitaMall Trust in July 2002. They represent a range of property sectors including retail, office, industrial, hospitality and residential. S-REITs hold a variety of properties in countries including Japan, China, Indonesia and Hong Kong, in addition to local properties.

S-REITs are regulated as Collective Investment Schemes under the Monetary Authority of Singapore's Code on Collective Investment Schemes, or alternatively as Business Trusts.

S-REITs benefit from tax advantaged status.

United Arab Emirates

The REIT legislation was introduced by Dubai International Financial Centre (DIFC) to promote the development of REIT's in the UAE by passing The Investment Trust Law No.5 that went into effect of August 6, 2006. This restricts all 'true' REIT structures to be domiciled within the DIFC. The first REIT license to be issued will be backed by Dubai Islamic Bank with a REIT named 'Emirates REIT.'

United Kingdom

The legislation laying out the rules for REITs in the United Kingdom was enacted in the Finance Act 2006 and came into effect in January 2007 when nine UK property companies converted to REIT status, including the five that were FTSE 100 members at that time: British Land, Hammerson, Land Securities, Liberty International and Slough Estates (now known as "SEGRO"). The other four were: Brixton, Great Portland Estates, Primary Health Properties and Workspace Group.

British REITs have to distribute 90% of their income. They must be a close-ended investment trust and be UK resident and publicly listed on a stock exchange recognised by the Financial Services Authority.

To support the introduction of REITs in the UK, the REITs and Quoted Property Group was created by several commercial property and financial services companies. Other key bodies involved are the London Stock Exchange, the British Property Federation and Reita. The Reita campaign was launched on 16 August 2006 by the REITs and Quoted Property Group, in order to provide a source of information on REITs, quoted property and related investments funds. Reita's aim is to raise awareness and understanding of REITs and investment in quoted property companies. It does this primarily through its portal www.reita.org, providing knowledge, education and tools for financial advisers and investors.

Doug Naismith, managing director of European Personal Investments for Fidelity International, said: "As existing markets expand and REIT like structures are introduced in more countries, we expect to see the overall market grow by some ten percent per annum over the next five years, taking the market to $1 trillion by 2010."

Nigeria

REITs recently took centre stage in Nigeria when the N50billion Union Homes Hybrid Real Estate Investment Trust was launched in September 2008. In 2007, the Securities and Exchange Commission (SEC) issued the first set of guidelines for the registration and issuance of requirements for the operation of REITs in Nigeria is detailed in the Investment and Securities Act (ISA).

United States

In the United States a REIT is a company that owns, and in most cases operates, income-producing real estate. Some REITs finance real estate. To be a REIT, a company must distribute at least 90 percent of its taxable income to shareholders annually in the form of dividends.

Qualification

In order to qualify for the advantages of being a pass-through entity for U.S. corporate income tax, a REIT must:
- Be structured as corporation, trust, or association
- Be managed by a board of directors or trustees
- Have transferable shares or transferable certificates of interest
- Otherwise be taxable as a domestic corporation
- Not be a financial institution or an insurance company
- Be jointly owned by 100 persons or more
- Have 95 percent of its income derived from dividends, interest, and property income
- Pay dividends of at least 90% of the REIT's taxable income
- No more than 50% of the shares can be held by five or fewer individuals during the last half of each taxable year (5/50 rule)
- At least 75% of total investment assets must be in real estate
- Derive at least 75% of gross income from rents or mortgage interest
- No more than 20% of its assets may consist of stocks in taxable REIT subsidiaries.

Source (edited): "http://en.wikipedia.org/wiki/Real_estate_investment_trust"

Residuary estate

A **residuary estate**, in the law of wills, is any portion of the testator's estate that is not specifically devised to someone in the will, or any property that is part of such a specific devise that fails. It is also known as a **residual estate** or simply **residue**. The will may identify the taker of the residuary estate through a *residuary clause* or *residuary bequest*. The person identified in such a clause is called the *residuary taker*, *residuary beneficiary*, or *residuary legatee*. If no such clause is present, however, the residuary estate will pass to the testator's heirs by intestacy.

At common law, if the residuary estate was divided between two or more beneficiaries, and one of those beneficiaries was unable to take, the share that would have gone to that beneficiary would instead pass by intestacy, under the doctrine that there was *no residuary of a residuary*. The modern rule, however, is that the failure of a residuary gift to one beneficiary causes that beneficiary's share to be divided among the remaining residuary takers.

Source (edited): "http://en.wikipedia.org/wiki/Residuary_estate"

Resulting trust

A **resulting trust** (from the Latin 'resultare' meaning 'to jump back') is the creation of an implied trust by operation of law, as where property gets transferred to one who pays nothing for it; and then is implied to have held the property for benefit of another person. The trust property is said to "result" back to the transferor (implied settlor).

In this instance, the word 'result' means "in the result, remains with", or something similar to "revert" except that **in the result** the beneficial interest is held on trust for the settlor. Not all trusts whose beneficiary is also its settlor can be called a resulting trust. In common law, the resulting trust refers to a subset of trusts which have such outcome; express trusts which stipulate that the settlor is to be the beneficiary are not normally considered resulting trusts. (or he might not be in the existence,Re Vandervall case)Presumption is Constructive Trust

The beneficial interest **results** in the settlor, or if the settlor has died the property forms part of the settlor's estate (intestacy). And the distinguishment of beneficiary interest should be noted(Beneficial interest only will move but the beneficiary interest will not move)s53(1)(c).it remains with the person and Re Vandervall case has proven that only the Beneficial interest disappears but not the beneficiary interest.

Some jurisdictions may establish a rebuttable presumption of gift for property transfers between relatives. Said presumption may operate as an affirmative defense to a petition to establish a resulting trust implied by operation of law.

The law presumes that it is legitimate to transfer property to a family member, particularly for a relative's support. But an unrelated transferee who receives substantial value without consideration is ordinarily presumed to hold the property in trust for benefit of the transferor. The rebuttable presumption of gift affects transfers between siblings, uncles, aunts, children, and grandchildren.

A notable exception to the presumption of gift is for property transfers between husband and wife (transmutations)(refer to changes in intestacy). The marital exception to presumption of gift arises from the fiduciary duty that spouses owe to one another. Spouses have a special trusted relationship that imputes an obligation of utmost good faith and fair dealing. Accordingly, spouses are deemed incapable of transmutation except under specified circumstances, such as when making an EXPRESS DECLARATION of transmutation as by clear statement in a deed or other writing of substantial dignity.

Unlawful Purposes

Resulting trust laws arise in equity rather than common law because equity gives clean hand. Accordingly, some jurisdictions might impose equitable defenses such as laches, unclean hands, and the responsibility to do equity. Where a transferor has transferred property for an unlawful purpose, and gained the benefit, then a court might hold that he has waived his right to claim a resulting trust(i.e.:settlor)(inter vivos). In such situations, a court balances the transferee's unjust enrichment with the enablement of cheating by the transferor. Enabling a cheater at gaining from his transaction would erode the legitimacy of the court.

Other jurisdictions may elect to disregard an unlawful purpose.

In situations involving illegality, it can become difficult to distinguish implementation of a resulting trust theory (implied by operation of law) from an oral express trust (one implied by the facts). A transferor failing upon one theory might still prevail upon the other.

Resulting trusts in English law
Classification

One attempt to classify resulting trusts was made by Megarry J in Re Vandervell's Trusts (no.2) Ch 269. According to Megarry J there are two sorts of resulting trusts in English law.

Presumptive resulting trusts

These are transfers made by A to B, where the law creates a rebuttable presumption of a resulting trust applying if the intention is not made clear by A.(written evidence produced)

For example, when A transfers property to B, unless the transfer was made by father to child or by husband to wife, in the absence of any other evidence the law presumes that a resulting trust has been created for A.(Y this category excluded:i.e.:A evidence cannot stand in Course of testimony & remains Hearsay)(A will not get the property if H&W/F&C can adduce evidence it is their property and resulting trust will not arise.

The main categories of fact situations giving rise to a presumption of a resulting trust are: - Where A makes a voluntary conveyance of property to B - Where A has made a monetary contribution to the purchase of property for B (The Venture, P 218,(1907) 77 L.J.P. 105.)

The presumptions are, however, easily rebutted. In Fowkes v Pascoe (1875) LR 10 Ch App 343, evidence was shown that a woman had purchased stock in the names of herself and her grandson; evidence by the grandson and granddaughter-in-law that this had been done as a gift was admissible. On the other hand, the presumption is solely concerned with evidence of an intent to create a trust; ulterior motives to create a trust are not taken into account. In Tinsley v Milligan 1 AC 340, a woman transferred property to her lover on trust in order to fraudulently claim social security payments; it was held that this did not defeat the presumption of a resulting trust.

The fact that is being proved by the presumption of a resulting trust is the intention to create a trust for the settlor. This view of presumed resulting trusts has been endorsed by Lord Browne-Wilkinson in *Westdeutsche Landesbank v Council of London Borough of Islington* AC 669);

"...the presumption of resulting trust is rebutted by evidence of any intention inconsistent with such a trust, not only by evidence of an intention to make a gift."

Some have argued that this presumption arises as a result of a lack of intention to transfer any beneficial interest,. This view has generally not received judicial endorsement.(obiter dicta)

Automatic resulting trusts

In these trusts " there is no mention of any expression of intention in any instrument, or of any presumption of a resulting trust: the resulting trust takes effect by operation of law,(by law:implied that property will revert back to u) and so appears to be automatic." (per Megarry J, *Re Vandervell's Trusts (No 2)*)

Automatic resulting trusts can arise when the settlor tries to set up a trust for a third party, but there is an initial failure for want of objects; for example, by naming beneficiaries which cannot be defined, as in Morice v Bishop of Durham 1805 10 Ves 522, or when the objectives of the trust no longer become possible or relevant by the time of the transfer to the trustee, as in Re Gillingham Bus Disaster Fund Ch 300.

Settlor's intention in automatic resulting trusts

In relation to automatic resulting trusts, there is some difference in expressing the nature of the settlor's intention:

- In **Westdeutsche** Lord Browne-Wilkinson stated that a resulting trust arises due to a legal "presumed intention to create a trust in favour of the donor"
- It has also been suggested that it is the fact of a "lack of intention to benefit the recipient" that creates the trust. The settlor intends to retain the beneficial interest in the property, but transfers the legal title to someone else (for example, to let an active child manage the assets). The trust is **implied** by the settlor's lack of intention to transfer any beneficial interest

Although in many cases the outcome would be the same, the difference is significant. It is often difficult to prove intention, but easier to prove the circumstances when a legal presumption will arise. It may be more or less easy to rebut a presumption than to disprove an intention.

Lord Browne-Wilkinson was afraid that this would create a "floodgates" problem, by giving every claimant a proprietary right in bankruptcy - making many more claimants secured creditors, and thus making the position of a secured creditor much less valuable.

Resulting Trusts in South Africa

In South Africa there is no doctrine of resulting trusts. The main remedy if any of the trust purposes should fail would be through Unjust enrichment. **(Westdeutsche Landesbank v Council of London Borough of Islington)**
Source (edited): "http://en.wikipedia.org/wiki/Resulting_trust"

Royal lives clause

A **Royal lives clause** is a contract clause which provides that a certain right must be exercised within (usually) the lifetime plus 21 years of the last living descendant of a British Monarch who happens to be alive at the time when the contract is made.

A sample clause would read:

" The option must be exercised before the end of the period ending at the expiry of 21 years from the death of the last survivor of all the lineal descendants of [his late Majesty King George V or some other British monarch] who have been born on the date of this agreement. "

Rationale

The clause became part of contractual drafting in response to common law rule developed by the courts known as the **rule against perpetuities**. That rule provided that any future disposition of property must vest within "a life in being plus 21 years". The rule generally affects two types of transactions: trusts and options to acquire property. Generally speaking, such transfers must vest before the end of the maximum period, or the grant will be void. Under the old common law, a transaction would be void even if the property *might possibly* vest after the end of the maximum period, but now most jurisdictions have, by statute, adopted "wait and see" laws.

In an attempt to mitigate the perceived harshness of the common law rule, and to maximise the possible length of time for which trusts in particular could subsist, lawyers began to draft so-called Royal lives clauses. Royal lives were chosen because (a) it was assumed that being affluent, at least one or two members of the family could be assumed to live a reasonably long period of time, and (b) being Royalty, it would be reasonably easy to calculate the lives of the descendants. In practice, a dead monarch was usually chosen so as to maximise the possibility of a grandchild or great-grandchild who would be outside of the immediate Royal family having recently been born.

Despite the purported ease of finding out the descendants of British Monarchs, attempts to choose much older Monarchs to widen the pool of descendants have periodically been known to cause trouble.

In the United States, **President's lives clauses** are used for similar reasons; well-documented political and industrial families (such as the Kennedys and Rockefellers) are also used. In the Commonwealth, use of Royal lives tends to persist. In Ireland, the descendants of Éamon de Valera are frequently used.
Source (edited): "http://en.wikipedia.org/wiki/Royal_lives_clause"

Rule against perpetuities

The common law **rule against perpetuities** forbids some future interests (traditionally contingent remainders and executory interests) that may not vest within the time permitted; the rule "limit[s] the testator's power to earmark gifts for remote descendants". In essence, the rule prevents a person from putting qualifications and criteria in his will that will continue to control or affect the distribution of assets long after he or she has died, a concept often referred to as control by the "dead hand" or "mortmain". "No interest is good unless it must vest, if at all, not later than twenty-one years after the death of some life in being at the creation of the interest." For the purposes of the rule, a life is "in being" at conception. Although most discussions and analysis relating to the rule revolve around wills and trusts, the rule applies to any future dispositions of property, including options. When a part of a grant or will violates the rule, only that portion of the grant or devise is removed. All other parts that do not violate the rule are still valid. The perpetuities period under the common law rule is not a fixed term of years. By its terms, the rule limits the period to at the latest 21 years after the death of the last identifiable individual living at the time the interest was created ("life in being"). This "measuring" or "validating" life need not have been a purchaser or taker in the conveyance or devise. The measuring life could be the grantor, a life tenant, a tenant for a term of years, or in the case of a contingent remainder or executory devise to a class of unascertained individuals, the person capable of producing members of that class.

The rule against perpetuities at common law has been amended by statutes. In England, the Statute of Uses (1536) and the Statute of Wills (1540) and the consequent rise of flexible future interests made the rule a significant judicial tool in defeating the intent of landowners in grants and devises. Major alterations to the common law rule in the United Kingdom came into effect under the Perpetuities and Accumulations Act 1964, including the application of traditional 21-year limitation on options.

In the United States it has been abolished by statute in Alaska, Idaho, New Jersey, Pennsylvania and South Dakota. Twenty-eight other U.S. states have adopted the Uniform Statutory Rule Against Perpetuities, which validates non-vested interests that would otherwise be void under the common law rule if that interest actually vests within 90 years of its creation. Other jurisdictions apply the "wait and see" or "cy-près doctrine" that validate contingent remainders and executory interests void under the traditional rule in certain circumstances. These doctrines have also been codified in the United Kingdom by the 1964 statute.

The rule has its origin in the Duke of Norfolk's Case of 1682. That case concerned Henry, 22nd Earl of Arundel (later the Duke of Norfolk), who had tried to create a shifting executory limitation so that one of his titles would pass to his eldest son (who was mentally deficient) and then to his second son, and another title would pass to his second son, but then to his fourth son. The estate plan also included provisions for shifting the titles many generations later, if certain conditions should occur.

When his second son, Henry, succeeded to one title, he did not want to pass the other to his younger brother, Charles. Charles sued to enforce his interest, and the court (in this instance the House of Lords) held that such a shifting condition could not exist indefinitely. The judges believed that tying up property too long beyond the lives of people living at the time was wrong, although the exact period was not determined until another case, *Cadell v. Palmer*, 150 years later.

The rule against perpetuities is closely related to another doctrine in the common law of property, the rule against unreasonable restraints on alienation. Both stem from an underlying principle or reference in the common law against restraints on property rights. However, while a violation of the rule against perpetuities is also a violation of the rule against unreasonable restraints on alienation, the reciprocal is not true. As one has stated, "The rule against perpetuities is an ancient, but still vital, rule of property law intended to enhance marketability of property interests by limiting remoteness of vesting." For this reason, another court has declared that the provisions of the rule are predicated upon "public policy" and thus "constitute non-waivable, legal prohibitions."

Common law

Black's Law Dictionary defines the rule against perpetuities as "[t]he common-law rule prohibiting a grant of an estate unless the interest must vest, if at all, no later than 21 years (plus a period of gestation to cover a posthumous birth) after the death of some person alive when the interest was created."

At common law, the length of time was fixed at 21 years after the death of an identifiable person alive at the time the interest was created. This is often expressed as "lives in being plus twenty-one years." Under the common-law rule, one does not look to whether an interest actually will vest more than 21 years after the lives in being. Instead, if there exists any possibility at the time of the grant, however unlikely or remote, that an interest will vest outside of the perpetuities period, the interest is void and is stricken from the grant.

The rule does not apply to interests in the grantor himself. For example, the grant "For A so long as alcohol is not sold on the premises, then to B" would violate the rule as to B. However, the conveyance to B would be stricken, leaving "To A so long as alcohol is not sold on the premises." This would create a *fee simple determinable* in A, with a possibility of *reverter* in the grantor (or the grantor's heirs). The grant to B would be void as it is possible alcohol would be sold on the premises more than 21 years after the deaths of A, B, and the grantor. However, as the rule does not apply to grantors, the possibility of reverter in the grantor (or his heirs) would be valid.

Statutory modification

Many jurisdictions have statutes that either cancel out the rule entirely or change it to make clearer as to the period of time and persons who are affected by it.

- In the **United Kingdom**, dispositions of property subject to the rule before 14 July 1964 remain subject to the rule. The Perpetuities and Accumulations Act 1964 provides for the effect of the rule of interests created thereafter. This act codifies the "wait and see" doctrine developed by courts.
- In the **Republic of Ireland**, the rule is abolished as of 1 December 2009.
- The states of the **United States** have differing approaches.
  - Some states follow the "wait-and-see approach," or "second look doctrine," and/or apply the "cy pres doctrine". Under the wait and see approach, the validity of a suspect future interest is determined on the basis of facts as they now exist at the end of the measuring life, and not at the time the interest was created. Under the cy pres doctrine, if the interest does violate the rule against perpetuities, the court may

reform the grant in a way that does not violate the rule, and will reduce any offensive age contingency to 21 years.
- Other states have adopted the **Uniform Statutory Rule Against Perpetuities** (or some variant of it) which extends the waiting period typically to **90 years** after creation of the interest.
- Many states have **repealed** the rule in its entirety, **or extended the vesting period** of the wait and see approach for an extremely long period of time (in Florida, for example, up to 360 years for trusts). The motive behind these reforms seems at least in part the desire to take advantage of a loophole in the **1986 Tax Act** which has led to the formation of dynasty trusts. The 1986 Act allows the inheritance transfer tax to be avoided if a trust is set up that is valued over a floor minimum (US$2.5 million in 2005) for each transfer which would be allowed by the Rule Against Perpetuities. The result is that states with no Rule Against Perpetuities, or an extremely long perpetuities period, will attract more large trusts as there would never be a transfer tax on the trust.

Several famous illustrations of the bizarre outcomes possible under the rule against perpetuities include the "fertile octogenarian", the "unborn widow", and the "precocious toddler".

A common example of the rule in application would be as follows. T writes a will. T already has great-grandchildren, has met them, and likes them. T also has Blackacre. It is T's desire to leave Blackacre for her family to enjoy, and wants to ensure that her great-grandchildren, whom she knows, get to enjoy Blackacre as well without her great-grandchildren's older ancestors, such as T's children and grandchildren, selling Blackacre. After her great-grandchildren, T really has no interest in who enjoys Blackacre, as she does not know them.

T goes to her lawyer and explains her desire. T's lawyer drafts a will with the following clause:

" Blackacre to my children for their lives, then to their children for their lives, then to their children their heirs and assigns. "

What the lawyer has created is a life estate in Blackacre to T's children, a successive life estate in Blackacre to T's grandchildren followed by a Fee Simple future interest in T's great-grandchildren. However, the Rule Against Perpetuities would void the interest to T's great-grandchildren, and leave the will creating the successive life estates with a reversionary interest in T's estate.

Why? The rules states that any interest must vest, if at all, within 21 years of a life in being at the time of the instrument. The instrument here is a will, so the time of the instrument is T's death, not when the will was drafted. Next, we need to find every possible person, whether named in the instrument or not, who could, regardless how remote the possibility, affect the instrument. T's children, grandchildren etc. are our possible measuring lives because they control who will take Blackacre. For a measuring life to be valid, it must be a life in being at the time of the interest. For a class, such as children, grandchildren, to be valid measuring lives, it must be a closed class, meaning it would be impossible for another class member to come into existence after the time of the instrument.

In the above example, T's children are a valid measuring life. T's children are a class, so the class must be closed at the time of the instrument for T's children to be valid measuring lives. Here, the class that is T's children would be closed at the time of the instrument as it is impossible for T to have any children after T dies. So any interest which must vest within 21 years after T's children die is valid. The class that is T's grandchildren is NOT a valid measuring life as T's children are free to reproduce after T dies, meaning the class is not closed at the time of the instrument. Obviously, the same goes for T's great-grandchildren for the same reason.

Now that we know our valid measuring lives, we can see which interests in Blackacre are valid. Obviously, the life estate to T's children is valid as they are the measuring lives. The life estate to T's grandchildren is also valid. Why? Because all of T's grandchildren must be born within 21 years of a measuring life. T's children are our measuring lives, all of T's grandchildren must be born before the last of T's children dies (or, at least be in the womb, which counts as being alive for RAP purposes), meaning their interest would vest within 21 years of a measuring life. T's great-grandchildren's interest is invalidated by the Rule. Why? Because T's grandchildren are free to reproduce after all of T's children have died. It is possible that one of T's grandchildren could have a child more than 21 years after T's last child died, meaning the interest might not vest within 21 years of a life in being.

Charity-to-charity exception

The Rule never applies to conditions placed on a conveyance to a charity that, if violated, would convey the property to another charity. For example, a conveyance "to the Red Cross, so long as it operates an office on the property, but if it does not, then to the Roman Catholic Church" would be void under the Rule, *except* that both parties are charities. Even though the interest of the Church might not vest for hundreds of years, the conveyance would nonetheless be held valid. The exception, however, does not apply if the conveyance, upon violation of the condition, is not from one charity to another charity. Thus, a devise "to John Smith, so long as no one operates a liquor store on the premises, but if someone does operate a liquor store on the premises, then to the Roman Catholic Church" would violate the rule. The exception would not apply to the transfer from John Smith to the Roman Catholic Church because John Smith is not a charity. However, if the original conveyance was "to John Smith and his heirs for as long as John Smith does not use the premises to sell liquor, but if he does, then to the Red Cross" the rule would not be violated, because it would necessarily vest or expire within the life of John Smith (since the restriction was on him alone).

Saving clause

To avoid problems caused by incorrectly drafted legal instruments, practitioners in some jurisdictions include a "saving clause" almost universally as a form of disclaimer. This standard clause is commonly called the "Kennedy clause" or the "Rockefeller clause" because the determinable "lives in being" are designated as the descendants of Joseph P. Kennedy (the father of John F. Kennedy), or John D. Rockefeller. Both designate well-known families with many descendants, and are consequently suitable for named, identifiable lives in being.

The class of people must be limited and determinable. Thus, one cannot say in a deed "until the last of the people in the world now living dies, plus 21 years." For a time, it was popular to use a Royal lives clause, and make the term of a deed run until the last of the descendants of (for example) Queen Victoria now living dies plus 21 years. This was grudgingly upheld by the courts.

Related rules

Jurisdictions may limit usufruct periods. For example, if a corporation builds a ski slope, and gives rights of use (usufruct) as gifts to corporate partners, these cannot last in perpetuity, but must terminate after a period that must be specified, e.g. 10 years. A perpetual usufruct is thus forbidden and "perpetual" might mean a long, but finite period, such as 99 years. Here usufruct is distinct from a share, which may be held in perpetuity.

Source (edited): "http://en.wikipedia.org/wiki/Rule_against_perpetuities"

Rule in Dearle v Hall

The **rule in *Dearle v Hall*** (1828) 3 Russ 1 is an English common law rule to determine priority between competing equitable claims to the same asset. The rule broadly provides that where the equitable owner of an asset purports to dispose of his equitable interest on two or more occasions, and the equities are equal between claimants, the claimant who first notifies the trustee or legal owner of the asset shall have a first priority claim.

Although the original decisions related to interests under a trust, most modern applications of the rule relate to the factoring of receivables or multiple grants of equitable security interests.

The rule has been subject to some scathing criticism, and has been abrogated in a number of common law countries in the Commonwealth.

History

The rule in *Dearle v Hall* has been controversial almost since its inception. In 1893, Lord Macnaghten said "I am inclined to think that the rule in *Dearle v Hall* has on the whole produced at least as much injustice as it has prevented." But this has not stopped it from being extended from a rule regulating the priority of interests in trusts to the regulation of the priority of proprietary interests in debts and other similar intangibles, such as rights under contracts, which is considerably more important in terms of modern commerce.

The actual decision in *Dearle v Hall*, on its facts, is relatively uncontroversial. The beneficial owner of a trust fund assigned it first by way of security to A, and then outright to B, in each case for valuable consideration. A had not given notice of his assignment to the trustees of the fund and, accordingly, when B made enquiries of them, he did not discover the existence of the assignment to A because the trustees were not aware of it. B did give notice of the assignment to the trustees, and then A subsequently also gave notice to them. Plumer MR and, on appeal, Lord Lyndhurst LC each decided that B took priority over A.

Judgment was given in favour of B for two reasons. The first was based on the general proposition, that, as between two equitable interests, the first in time will only take priority "if the equities are equal". In this case, by failing to give notice to the trustees, A had allowed the beneficiary of the trust to be able to hold himself out as being the unencumbered owner of the beneficial interest and had therefore enabled the beneficiary to hoodwink B into thinking he had not encumbered it. This is a perfectly straightforward application of the principle that the first in time will only prevail if the equities are equal and is not considered controversial.

The second ground for the decision was that A's failure to give notice had left the beneficiary of the trust in apparent possession of the trust fund, and A could not, therefore, rely on this assignment in a dispute with B. This latter ground has been criticised as it appears to be based on the concept of reputed ownership in bankruptcy law, which had never previously been employed in determining priority between competing equitable claims. Nevertheless, on the facts of the case most commentators feel that justice was done; A had allowed the beneficiary to commit a fraud on B, and therefore A should rank behind B.

Development

However, it was in subsequent that the rule was turned from an example of the principle that the first in time rule will not apply if the equities are not equal into an absolute rule that the first to give notice will take priority unless the later assignee was a volunteer or was aware of the earlier assignment at the time he obtained his assignment. The rule applies even if the later assignee made no enquiries of the trustees and even if the first assignee was not negligent in failing to give notice, for instance because he was not aware of it or because there was no one to whom notice could be given. In *Ward v Duncombe* AC 369, the House of Lords decided that the rule that notice determines priority of dealings applied regardless of the conduct of the competing assignees.

Criticisms

In spite of the criticisms of the way in which the rule in *Dearle v Hall* has developed, there is much to be said for the concept that the priority of assignments or charges over debts should, as a general rule, depend on the date notice is given to the person who owes the debt. Not least, this is because the person who owes the debt will get a good discharge by paying the debtor unless he has been notified of the assignment or charge. Once a debt has been paid, it ceases to exist, and the priority rule recognises this fact. That is not to say that, in appropriate cases, it would not be possible for one creditor to trace the proceeds of the debt into the hands of another. But a simple rule that both priority and discharge depend on notice has much to recommend it.

Most of the academic criticism of the rule is to the effect that it has been carried too far. Whilst it is generally accepted for a subsequent assignee for value to take priority over an earlier assignee by giving notice before he becomes aware of the earlier assignment, it seems harsh for the earlier assignee to lose priority where the notice is given by the subsequent assignee after he is aware of the earlier assignment. The net result is the priority depends upon the subsequent speed of response of the parties once one or both of them becomes aware of the problem.

Reform

The Law Commission of England & Wales, as part of a wider view of priority rules relating to security interests has recommended the abolition of the rule in *Dearle v Hall* in relation to security interests and assignments of receivables only, and its replacement with a system of registration. To date, such recommendations have not been implemented.

Source (edited): "http://en.wikipedia.org/wiki/Rule_in_Dearle_v_Hall"

Satisfaction of legacies

Satisfaction of legacies is a common law doctrine that affects the disposition of property under a will. Under the doctrine, any gift that the maker of the will (the *testator*) gives during his lifetime to a named beneficiary of the will is presumptively treated as a satisfaction of that beneficiary's inheritance. After the death of the testator, the amount of the gift would then be deducted from the amount that the beneficiary would otherwise have received, even if it operates to entirely cancel out the inheritance. The presumption applies only when the gift is made after the will has already been executed.

Many jurisdictions have repealed the satisfaction of legacies doctrine by statute. Even in those jurisdictions, however, a gift may still be treated as a satisfaction of legacy if such an intention is expressed in a written document made close to the time of the gift and signed by either the testator or the beneficiary. Jurisdictions that have enacted such a statute include Virginia.

A similar common law doctrine operates regarding inheritance by intestacy (i.e., without a will); such a gift is then called an advancement. The concepts work similarly, but are independent of one another; jurisdictions that have repealed the doctrine of satisfaction of legacies may still have the traditional doctrine of advancement in place. This may be because the law presumes that a person who was possessed of enough sophistication to make a will would know how to amend that will or otherwise document their desire that the gift be deemed satisfied.

Source (edited): "http://en.wikipedia.org/wiki/Satisfaction_of_legacies"

Secret trust

A **secret trust** is a trust which arises when property is left to a person (the legatee) under a will on the understanding that they will hold the property as trustee for the benefit of beneficiaries who are not named in the will.

Secret trusts are divided into two types:
• *Fully secret trusts*, where the will is totally silent as to the existence of a trust; and
• *Semi secret trusts* or *half secret trusts*, where the will provides that the legatee is to hold the property on trusts, but does not specify the terms of the trust or the beneficiary.

Secret trusts are something of a historical anachronism. They arose because in most common law jurisdictions, wills are public documents after they have been admitted to probate, and where the testator wishes to leave a legacy to (for example) a mistress or an illegitimate child without causing pain or embarrassment to his family, he could devise the property to a trusted person to avoid the name of the mistress or illegitimate child appearing in the will. They fall outside of the Wills Act.

Despite their rarity, secret trusts still remain a staple of many law courses at University level, as they represent a rare exception to the rule that any disposition on death must be by way of a will (or a document incorporated by reference into a will) which complies with the applicable statutory requirements in the relevant jurisdiction. Historically, the courts have felt it more important to uphold the rights of the putative beneficiary and to avoid the unjust enrichment of the legatee than to uphold the general rule of public policy that property must devolve by will on death.

Source (edited): "http://en.wikipedia.org/wiki/Secret_trust"

Settlement (trust)

In the context of trusts, a **settlement** is a deed (also called a trust instrument) whereby real estate, land, or other property is given by a settlor into trust so that the beneficiary only has the limited right to the property (for example during their life), but usually has no right to transfer the land to another or leave it in their own will. Instead the property devolves as directed by the settlement.

Today, in most jurisdictions, settlements only confer beneficial rights under a trust, but formerly they were used to create legal estates for life or in tail, also to make provision for portions for younger children.

For detailed discussion, see Trust Law

Source (edited): "http://en.wikipedia.org/wiki/Settlement_(trust)"

Settlor

In law a **settlor** is a person who settles property on trust law for the benefit of beneficiaries. In some legal systems, a settlor is also referred to as a **trustor**, or occasionally, a **grantor** or **donor**. Where the trust is a testamentary trust, the settlor is usually referred to as the **testator**. The settlor may also be the trustee of the trust (where he declares that he holds his own property on trusts) or a third party may be the trustee (where he transfers the property to the trustee on trusts). In the common law it has been held, controversially, that where a trustee declares an intention to transfer trust property to a trust of which he is one of several trustees, that is a valid settlement notwithstanding the property is not vested in the other trustees.

Capacity to be a trustee is generally co-extensive with the ability to hold and dispose of a legal or beneficial interest in property. In practice, special considerations arise only with respect to minors and mentally incapacitated persons.

A settlor may create a trust by manifesting an intention to create it. In most countries no formalities are required to create an *inter vivos* trust over personal property, but there are often formalities associated with trusts over real property, or testamentary trusts. The words or acts of the settlor must be sufficient to establish an intention that either another person or the settlor himself shall be trustee of the property the beneficiary; a general intention to benefit another person on its own is sufficient. These formalities apply to express trusts only, and not to resulting, implied or constructive trusts.

For a settlor to validly create a trust, in most common law legal systems they must satisfy the three certainties, established in Knight v Knight:

- *certainty of intention* - whether the settlor (or testator) has manifested an intention to create a trust.
- *certainty of subject matter* - whether the property identified as being settled is sufficiently accurately identified.
- *certainty of objects* - the beneficiaries must be clearly ascertainable within the perpetuity period.

Where a settlement of property on a third party trustee by a settlor fails, the property is usually said to be held on resulting trusts for the settlor. However, if a settlor validly transfers property to a third party, and the words used are held not to create a trust, the usual rule is that the donee take the property absolutely.

Source (edited): "http://en.wikipedia.org/wiki/Settlor"

Simultaneous death

Simultaneous death is a problem of inheritance which occurs when two people, at least one of whom is entitled to part or all of the other's estate on their death (usually a husband and wife) die at the same time. This is usually the result of an accident, but in some cases may occur as a result of homicide (such as the families aboard the airplanes used in the September 11, 2001 terrorist attacks). Under the common law, if there was any evidence whatsoever that one party had survived the other, even by a few moments, then the estates would be distributed in that order, though the decedents could write (or have written) a clause in the will that requires their property to be distributed as though each had predeceased the other.

In order to alleviate problems of proving simultaneous death, many states in the United States have enacted the Uniform Simultaneous Death Act, which provides that each spouse will be treated as though they predeceased the other if they die within 120 hours of one another.

Some wills now include *Titanic clauses* (named for the RMS Titanic, which caused many simultaneous deaths among testators and executors). These clauses lay out explicit instructions for dealing with simultaneous death.

England and Wales

The common law of England and Wales (also Australia) does not accept the possibility of simultaneous death. Where there is no satisfactory medical evidence as to the order of death, the elder of the two is deemed to have died first. This can cause difficulties where for example the elder person had children prior to marriage. The rules can be ousted if inappropriate by an explicit provision in a will. Wills generally have a *survivorship clause*, typically of 30 days, so that both partner's estates are dealt with as though they were already widowed at the point of death; in cases of intestacy, the survivorship clause is set at 28 days.

However it is Her Majesty's Revenue and Customs's longstanding practice to apply a concessionary treatment for inheritance tax purposes in such cases which reduces the burden on surviving family members.

Russia

According to the laws of Russia, if people die the same day their deaths are considered simultaneous and they don't inherit after each other.

Source (edited): "http://en.wikipedia.org/wiki/Simultaneous_death"

Slayer rule

The **slayer rule**, in the common law of inheritance, is a doctrine that prohibits inheritance by a person who murders someone from whom he or she stands to inherit. The effect of the slaying was that the slayer would be treated as though he or she had died before the person who had been murdered.

While convicting someone of the crime of murder requires proof beyond a reasonable doubt, the slayer rule applies to civil law, not criminal law, so it is only necessary to prove the wrongful killing by a preponderance of the evidence, as in a wrongful death claim. This means that even a slayer who is acquitted of the murder in criminal court can still be divested of the inheritance by the civil court administering the estate.

In the United States, most jurisdictions have enacted a **slayer statute**, which codifies the rule and supplies additional conditions.

Maryland Slayer Rule

The Maryland Slayer Rule is harsher than most other states. In addition to prohibiting murderers from inheriting from their victims, Maryland's slayer rule prohibits anyone else from inheriting from murder victims through their murderers. Example:

A mother leaves her son $50,000, and leaves her son's child (her grandchild) $100,000. She leaves her residuary estate (i.e., whatever else is left of the estate) to her daughter. If the son kills his mother, then under Maryland law, the son's child will inherit the $100,000; however the son's $50,000 (which is also the indirect inheritance of the grandchild through his father), is not available under Maryland law to either the son, or his child. The $50,000 becomes part of the grandmother's residuary estate and goes to the daughter.

Source (edited): "http://en.wikipedia.org/wiki/Slayer_rule"

Society of Trust and Estate Practitioners

STEP (the **Society of Trust and Estate Practitioners**) was founded by George Tasker in 1991 and is the international professional body for workers in the trust industry and the (often overlapping) field of estate administration. Its members are mainly solicitors, barristers, attorneys, accountants, trust officers and trust administrators as well as banking and insurance professionals in the trust field. STEP has branches in 33 countries with a current membership in excess of 14,500.

The main focus of the organisation is to administer the examination process to ensure the quality of the membership, to provide educational and networking opportunities for STEP members at branch level and to contribute to debate and public policy in its specialist field.

The current president of STEP worldwide is Geoffrey Shindler, who was appointed in November 2006. He is a UK qualified solicitor and one of the founder members of the organisation. The current Chairman of STEP is Michael Young a Bath based practitioner elected in November 2009. Former Chairman Rosemary Marr was elected as vice-president in November 2009.

The professional staff include CEO David Harvey, and Directors Amanda Seal, Elaine Crehan and Keith Johnston.

The designation **TEP** after a member's name is the only widely recognised mark for professionals in the trust and estate administration industry.

The 19 founder members of STEP, ie those who signed its memorandum of association in 1991 were: Timothy Bennett; Richard Citron; Owen Clutton; Jonathan Cooke; Andrew East; Anthony Holmes; Simon Jennings; James Kessler QC; Thomas Mallett; Ralph Ray; Tony Sherring; Geoffrey Shindler; George Tasker; Arthur Thompson; Nigel Trumper; Timothy Vollans; David Ward; Robert Whillis; George Williams.

Source (edited): "http://en.wikipedia.org/wiki/Society_of_Trust_and_Estate_Practitioners"

Special needs trust

A **special needs trust** is created to ensure that beneficiaries who are disabled or mentally ill can enjoy the use of property which is intended to be held for their benefit. In addition to personal planning reasons for such a trust (the person may lack the mental capacity to handle their financial affairs) there may be fiscal advantages to the use of a trust. Such trusts may also avoid beneficiaries losing access to essential government benefits.

A trust for a disabled beneficiary may be set up in any of the common law countries or other countries which recognise the concept of the trust. They have particular advantages in legislation in relation to both taxation and state benefits in, for example, Ireland and the United Kingdom, and in relation to the provision of healthcare, long-term care and nursing home benefits under the state-sponsored Medicaid welfare system in the United States of America.

Special needs trusts can provide benefits to, and protect the assets of, the physically disabled or the mentally disabled. Special Needs Trusts are frequently used to receive an inheritance or personal injury settlement proceeds on behalf of a disabled person or are founded from the proceeds of compensation for criminal injuries, litigation or insurance settlements.

A common feature of trusts in all common law jurisdictions is that they may be run either by family members (a private trust) or by trustees appointed by the court. Especially where a trust is to be established for a disabled child or young person, great care is generally taken in the choice of appropriate trustees to manage the trust assets and to deal with future replacement appointments. The use of a private discretionary trust can not only be more efficient in terms of taxation and access to government benefits but can also allow for more efficient investment of funds held than where funds are held by a court official (such as the Official Receiver in England and Wales). However where no appropriate trustees can be found, e.g. on the death of existing trustees, the court will intervene.

Special Needs Trusts are often set up under the guidance of a Structured settlement planner in cooperation with a qualified legal and financial team to ensure the trust is set up correctly.

Special Needs Trusts are also known as Supplemental Needs Trusts in the USA and a more detailed article on the US specific characteristics of such trusts, including their interaction with the Medicaid system, is found at that page.

Source (edited): "http://en.wikipedia.org/wiki/Special_needs_trust"

Specific devise

A **specific devise** is a devise of a certain piece of real estate to a certain person or persons. It is like a specific legacy, but is limited (by the word "devise") to real estate.

Source (edited): "http://en.wikipedia.org/wiki/Specific_devise"

Specific legacy

A **specific legacy** (or **specific bequest**) is a testamentary gift of a precisely identifiable object, distinguished from all other things of the same kind—such as, a gift of a particular piece of jewelry.

Source (edited): "http://en.wikipedia.org/wiki/Specific_legacy"

Spendthrift trust

A **spendthrift trust** is a trust that is created for the benefit of a person (often because he or she is unable to control spending) that gives an independent trustee full authority to make decisions as to how the trust funds may be spent for the benefit of the beneficiary. Creditors of the beneficiary generally cannot reach the funds in the trust, and the funds are not actually under the control of the beneficiary.

The creator of a trust (whether or not it is a spendthrift trust) is sometimes called the "trustor", "grantor" or "settlor" of the trust. A trust often will not be treated as a spendthrift trust unless the trust agreement contains *language showing that the creator intended the trust to qualify as spendthrift*. This is what is known as a **spendthrift clause** or **spendthrift provision**.

A spendthrift provision in an irrevocable trust prevents creditors from attaching the interest of the beneficiary in the trust before that interest (cash or property) is actually distributed to him or her. Most well drafted irrevocable trusts contain spendthrift provisions even though the beneficiaries are not known to be spendthrifts. This is because such a provision protects the trust and the beneficiary in the event a beneficiary is sued and a judgment creditor attempts to attach the beneficiary's interest in the trust.

Benefits of a Nevada Spendthrift Trust NRS 166.020

For example, the Nevada Property Code

provides:

A. There is no personal or corporate income tax imposed by the state of Nevada.

B. A Irrevocable Spendthrift Trust if properly formed in the State of Nevada, is currently not subject to income taxes of other States, as long as the Nevada Spendthrift Trust is qualified to do business in the other State (s).

C. A Nevada Spend Thrift Trust is only subject to Federal Income Tax.

D. The Settlor has the right to change beneficiaries, or add other beneficiaries at anytime without notification to any beneficiary passed or present, or the state of Nevada, or the Federal Government.

E. All rights and privileges of a Spendthrift Trust formed in the State of Nevada are clearly set out in a concise set of statutes in Nevada and are not dependent on court decisions or interpretations for the validity of the Trust.

F. There are no registration fees, annual reporting fees or any other recurring fess charged by the State of Nevada or any local Government for the continued validity of the Trust. The Trusts are also not required to retain a Resident Agent in the State of Nevada.

Benefits of a Texas Spendthrift Trust TPC 112.035

For example, the Texas Property Code provides:

(a) A settlor may provide in the terms of the trust that the interest of a beneficiary in the income or in the principal or in both may not be voluntarily or involuntarily transferred before payment or delivery of the interest to the beneficiary by the trustee.

A clause in the terms of a trust agreement that complies with the above-quoted statute is an example of what the law calls an "anti-alienation provision".

To continue with the example of the Texas law, the Texas Property Code further provides:

(b) A declaration in a trust instrument that the interest of a beneficiary shall be held subject to a "spendthrift trust" is sufficient to restrain voluntary or involuntary alienation of the interest by a beneficiary to the maximum extent permitted by this subtitle.

(c) A trust containing terms authorized under Subsection (a) or (b) of this section may be referred to as a spendthrift trust.

The above quoted language essentially means that a trust instrument does not (at least, in Texas) have to contain complex legal jargon to qualify the trust as "spendthrift"; simply using the word "spendthrift" in the trust document may be sufficient.

Necessaries, child support and alimony

Some creditors may compel payment out of the trust - particularly those who supply the beneficiary with "necessaries" (usually food and shelter, but sometimes clothing and transportation, if these are not extravagant). Most jurisdictions also permit the invasion of spendthrift trust assets to satisfy awards of child support and alimony.

Trusts where the beneficiary is also the creator

A trust created by an individual for his or her own benefit is sometimes called a "self-settled trust", and may be a kind of asset-protection trust. If the creator of a self-settled trust is also a beneficiary of the trust, a particular problem in the context of protection of creditors and prevention of fraud is presented: the danger that the creator of the trust is trying to defraud creditors.

The general rule: Self-settled trusts do not protect the trust creator

To prevent individuals from creating trusts to defeat their own creditors, the laws of most states provide that a spendthrift clause in a trust document does not protect the beneficiary to the extent that the beneficiary is **also the person who created the trust**. For example, Texas law provides:

(d) If the settlor is also a beneficiary of the trust, a provision restraining the voluntary or involuntary transfer of his beneficial interest does not prevent his creditors from satisfying claims from his interest in the trust estate.

Further, laws in some states (like Texas) are worded so broadly that anyone transferring property to the trust might be deemed to be a "creator" (i.e., settlor, grantor, or trustor), not merely the person or persons who originally set up the trust.

The exceptions: DAPT states

However, several states have changed their laws to provide that a person may create a self-settled spendthrift trust (i.e., a spendthrift trust for his or her own benefit). Such trusts are also called Domestic Asset Protection Trusts ("DAPT"), and sometimes informally called "Alaska trusts", as Alaska was a pioneer in allowing this kind of spendthrift trust. However, because of the danger of the misuse of Alaska trusts to defraud creditors, the legality of such trusts (to the extent that they purport to protect the trust share of a beneficiary who is also a creator of the trust) is uncertain in the states not allowing self-settled spendthrift trusts.

Nevada has enacted a series of statutes, codified at Chapter 166 of the Nevada Revised Statutes, that specifically enable the creation of self-settled spendthrift trusts. This form of trust is commonly referred to as a "Nevada Asset Protection Trust". Under Chapter 166, an individual can serve as the settlor, trustee and beneficiary of the trust. This network of laws is specifically designed to protect trust assets from the claims of any creditor. NRS 166.170 specifically limits the circumstances under which a creditor may bring a claim. If a creditor existed at the time of the property's transfer to the trust, then the creditor must bring it's claim against the trust within 2 years after the transfer or within six months after the creditor reasonably should have known of the transfer, whichever is later. NRS 166.170(1). If the creditor's claim surfaces after the transfer is made, the creditor must bring it's claim within two years after the transfer, regardless of notice. NRS 166.170(1). Moreover, the creditor can only sustain it's claim if it can prove by clear and convincing evidence (a tough evidentiary standard) that the transfer was made as a fraudulent conveyance. NRS 166.170(3).

It is unclear the extent to which sister states will recognize the asset protections of these DAPTs, like those created under the laws of Nevada and Alaska. relevant case law is somewhat sparse. While states are generally compelled to honor and recognize the laws of sister states, pursuant to the full faith and credit clause of the United States Constitution, some of these laws may be in direct conflict with the laws of other states. Some of these DAPT laws can be quite expansive. The scope of the Nevada law is drawn quite broadly to govern Nevada's enforcement of all trusts created within or outside the state, so long as they meet certain limited criteria. See NRS 166.015(1). The law goes onto require that the statutes be applied to the enforcement by any other state of any spendthrift trust created within Nevada, so long as the law is not in direct conflict with the other adjudicating state. NRS 166.015(3). In fact, the Nevada law does not even require that the trust assets be located within Nevada, so long as one of the trustees declares his/her domicile as Nevada. NRS 166.015(1)(d).

The following other states now have a DAPT statute: Delaware, South Dakota, Wyoming, Tennessee, Utah, Oklahoma, Colorado, Missouri, Rhode Island and New Hampshire.

Source (edited): "http://en.wikipedia.org/wiki/Spendthrift_trust"

Statute of Wills

The **Statute of Wills** (32 Hen. 8, c. 1 - enacted in 1540) was an Act of the Parliament of England. It made it possible, for the first time in English history, for landholders to determine who would inherit their land upon their death by permitting bequest by will. Prior to the enactment of this statute, land could be passed by descent only if and when the landholder had competent living relatives who survived him, and it was subject to the harsh rules of primogeniture. When a landholder died without any living relatives, his land would escheat to the Crown. The statute was something of a political compromise between Henry VIII and English landowners, who were growing increasingly frustrated with primogeniture and royal control of land.

The **Statute of Wills** created a number of requirements for the form of a will, many of which, as of 2008, survive in common law jurisdictions. Specifically, most jurisdictions still require that a will must be in writing, signed by the testator, the person making the will, and witnessed by at least two other persons.

In England and Wales, the **Statute of Wills** was repealed and superseded by the Wills Act 1837.

Source (edited): "http://en.wikipedia.org/wiki/Statute_of_Wills"

Succession (conflict)

In the conflict of laws, the subject of **succession** deals with all procedural matters relevant to estates containing a "foreign element" whether that element consists of the identity of the deceased, those who may inherit or the location of property. The relevant choice of law rules often distinguish both between the administration of the estate and the succession to it, and between the succession to movable and immovable property.

Definitions

In civil law systems, there are two types of property. Out of comity, the conflict of laws has adopted the terminology of civil law:
- *Immovables* is the equivalent of "real property" in common law systems, i.e. it is land or any permanent feature or structure above or below the surface.
- All other property is considered *movables*, the equivalent of *personal property* or *personalty* in common law systems. This property is either *tangible* or *intangible*, in that it is either physical property that can be touched like a computer. Alternatively, it is an enforceable right like a patent, other types of intellectual property, or a chose in action such as shares and bank accounts.

Connecting factors

Domicile

In common law jurisdictions, every person acquires a domicile of origin which, if the individual is legitimate, is that of their father. During their minority, children have a domicile of dependency which follows the domicile of the controlling parent.

After reaching the age of majority, a young adult can choose a new domicile, but establishing a legal domicile requires long-term residence accompanied by an intention to remain in the new state indefinitely. As such, changing a domicile of origin is not easy.

Hence, the *lex domicilii* is favored as the connecting factor for all aspects of status and capacity for parties who are involved in resolving disputes over the distribution of the property in the estate.

Nationality

Civil law states use either the concept of nationality or habitual residence as the connecting factor, i.e. the principles are the same as for domicile but the way in which they are applied is less rigorous so it a nationality can be changed by naturalization and a new habitual residence established with fewer delays and technical difficulties. As above, the *lex patriae* determines status and capacity.

Lex successionis

As with a choice of law clause or forum selection clause in contract, a testator may nominate a law or laws by which both to interpret and test the validity of the will, and to govern administration and succession, but there must be a real connection between the choice(s) and the location of assets or beneficiaries, and the choices must invoke provisions of law that are consistent with any mandatory provisions either in the *lex fori* or the *lex situs*. If a choice of law is made in respect of part of an estate, it is assumed that the deceased wishes that law to apply to the whole of the estate unless there is clear evidence to the contrary or mandatory principles of law are relevant to cover the residual assets and their inheritance.

Lex situs

The general rule is that the *lex situs* applies to determine all issues relating to title to immovable property and some issues relating to movables, that is, the law of the jurisdiction where the property is applied.

Lex fori

The courts in which lawsuits are initiated will tend to prefer the application of the *lex fori*, applying the laws at the court jurisdiction, because the fact of the litigation suggests that some aspect of the administration is to be effected within the jurisdiction. There may also be some claims arising from public policy if the forum court considers the application of the *lex causae* is going to produce a significantly unjust result.

Administration

In most states, the *lex fori* regulates the administration by Personal Representatives appointed to act within the jurisdiction of forum irrespective of the deceased's *lex domicilii* but the rights of beneficiaries is a matter for the *lex successionis*.

Testamentary capacity

Laws differ in their treatment of the ability of youths to own property and to dispose of that property by a will. It is now generally agreed that it is not rational to set the age at which full capacity is achieved. Hence, if one is old enough to get married, he should be old enough to provide for spouse and children. Many states also permit writing a will by a mouth or a foot, or by a tool that enables the disabled to write down a testamentary intent.

It is still being debated whether videotape, digital, and electronic wills should be admissible to probate. Testators may not have the physical ability to write, for example, because they are hospitalised and close to death, but there is concern that digital and electronic forms may be manipulated and altered. Hence, unless there is adequate evidence to exclude forgery, the courts are reluctant to admit such wills to probate.

Succession

In some states, there is complete freedom for testators to leave their assets to whomever or whatever purpose they wish to promote. But the majority of states allow surviving spouses, children and dependents of a locally-based deceased to claim against the estate if the will fails to make adequate provision for them. Some proactively limit the testator's capacity by imposing minimum provisions for surviving dependents.

Although these rules are relatively clear in their operation during the subsistence of the marriage, determining the effect of either a divorce or nullity decree is more problematic if, by its existence or the terms of any order made, it purports to adjust the property entitlements of the other spouse. For example, suppose that a husband obtains a nullity decree in a state declaring the marriage to have been void *Ab initio*. If that decree is recognized across state boundaries, the effect would be to remove any claim that the supposed "wife" would otherwise have had.

As to the testator, all questions of status and capacity should be determined by the personal law at the time the decree is granted. Thus, if the decree is recognized, either the status will be modified so that the testator was never married and this will retrospectively validate or invalidate previous dispositions, or the testator is now single and able to dispose of his assets in any way permitted by his personal law.

But as to the putative wife, any entitlement she will have will be determined by whether the *lex situs* of any "matrimonial" assets recognizes the decree. If the decree is not recognized, she will remain a wife for the purposes of succession protected by the local system of mandatory heirship or community property laws.

Immovables

Generally, the *lex situs* governs the succession to immovables regardless of the deceased's personal law, *lex domicilii*, *lex patriae*, or habitual residence. For example, land in France belonging to an English domiciliary will pass according to the French law on forced heirship, but complications may arise because some states apply renvoi to succession cases. Hence, English law would apply the *lex situs* to immovables located outside the jurisdiction but if that foreign law (say. as in Spain) applies the deceased's *lex patriae* and rejects any renvoi, English law would be applied if, under Spanish law, the deceased had an English nationality.

Movables

Generally, the deceased's personal law will determine succession to movables no matter where they are located unless a *lex situs* provides otherwise. Thus, for example, succession to the estate of a French testator leaving movables situated in England would be governed by French law and the French rules of forced heirship would apply given that English law does not limit the application of the *lex domicilii* on this point.

Formal validity

A will is generally considered valid if properly executed according to the law of the place where:

- it was executed;
- the testator was domiciled either when the will was executed or at the time of death (since the policy in most laws is to uphold the validity of wills to respect the demonstrated intention of the testator, if validity is established under either law, it will be deemed valid);
- the testator was a national either at the time of execution or death; or
- the testator was habitually resident

either at the time of execution or death.

Essential validity

Even though a will may be formally valid, it may not be essentially valid as above, the succession to movables will be governed by the deceased's personal law, and if there is a limitation on testamentary capacity, the terms of a will breaching that law will be invalid even if validly executed.

Similarly, a will validly executed in one state cannot override mandatory provisions in the *lex situs*. The doctrine of evasion applies because otherwise a husband who wishes to evade laws imposing community property can defeat the claims of a wife by the simple expedient of executing a formally valid will in a state that does not have such law.

Intestacy

If there is no will, the appointment and duties of personal representatives will be determined by the deceased's personal law. Succession to an intestate's estate will also be governed by his or her personal law and the *lex situs* of the assets.

Harmonization

The Hague Convention of 1 August 1989 on the Law Applicable to Succession to the Estates of Deceased Persons, if it ever comes into force, would apply to: a) the form of dispositions of property upon death; b) capacity to dispose of property upon death; c) issues relating to matrimonial property; d) property rights, interests or assets created or transferred otherwise than by succession, such as in joint ownership with right of survival, pension plans, insurance contracts, or arrangements of a similar nature. It nominates as the *lex causae* for succession the law of habitual resident if that was also the deceased's nationality. If the deceased had been resident in a state for at least five years and no other state has a better claim, the law of residence applies. In all other cases, the personal law with the best claim applies. See also the "European Commission's Green Paper Consulting on Succession with an International Dimension" by David Hayton

Australia

It is noted that the rules in South Australia differ from those applying in the other federated states, but it is proposed that a uniform system should be developed. See Issues Paper 21 (2002) - "Uniform Succession Laws: Recognition of interstate and foreign grants of probate and letters of administration." Source (edited): "http://en.wikipedia.org/wiki/Succession_(conflict)"

Supplemental Needs Trust

A **Supplemental Needs Trust** is a U.S.-specific term for a type of special needs trust (an internationally recognised term). Supplemental needs trusts are compliant with provisions of U.S. state and federal law and are designed to provide benefits to, and protect the assets of, physically disabled or mentally disabled persons and still allow such persons to be qualified for and receive governmental health care benefits, especially long-term nursing care benefits, under the Medicaid welfare program. Supplemental or Special Needs Trusts are frequently used to receive an inheritance or personal injury litigation proceeds on behalf of a disabled person in order to allow the person to qualify for Medicaid benefits.

Background of Medicaid law

Medicaid is the Federal program administered by the states which provides health care for those who can't afford it. See 42 U.S.C. § 1396 et seq. Federal law establishes certain mandatory requirements which each state must adopt in its local Medicaid program, and the states are also given options to elect certain other components in the health care plan which they may decide to provide. Accordingly, Medicaid does vary from state to state in certain aspects, but there are also mandatory Federal law provisions.

One significant governmental benefit which is available only through Medicaid is long-term nursing care which includes care for the physically disabled and the mentally disabled. Long-term nursing care can be extremely expensive. To qualify for Medicaid and its long-term nursing care benefits, the applicant must be "poor" and there is a limit to the countable assets which he or she can own. To qualify for Medicaid, the applicant must meet the asset guidelines for Supplemental Security Income (SSI). SSI allows a single applicant to own no more than $2,000 in countable assets and a married applicant to own no more than $3,000 in countable assets. Certain assets are specifically exempted and are not countable.

Trusts as Medicaid countable assets

A trust is a legal arrangement in which legal title to assets is held by a trustee under certain defined restrictions of a governing instrument (usually a will or a written trust agreement) for the benefit of another party known as the beneficiary. Trusts can be used as a vehicle to make assets available to a beneficiary but still significantly restrict them. Recognizing the gray area which trusts can provide concerning the ownership of assets, Federal Medicaid law places significant restrictions on the types of trusts which can be used to preserve assets of a beneficiary and still qualify the beneficiary for governmental benefits.

Prior to the enactment of the Omnibus Budget Reconciliation Act of 1993 (O.B.R.A), P.L. 103-66, it was possible to create a self-settled, discretionary trust for the benefit of the settlor and still allow the settlor to qualify for Medicaid's long-term nursing care benefits. These trusts were called "special needs trusts" or "supplemental needs trusts" because restrictive language in the trust agreement allowed the trustee to pay only for the support needs of the settlor-beneficiary which the government did not pay. The trust was not for the unrestricted, general support of the beneficiary which is typical in normal estate plans. Special needs trusts were perceived by the United States Congress to be abusive and were effectively abolished by O.B.R.A.

In general, with limited exceptions, regardless of the purposes, provisions, or discretion contained in the trust, a self-settled trust which is created after August 11, 1993 will be treated as an available asset which can disqualify the settlor-beneficiary from Medicaid. 42 U.S.C. § 1396p(d)(2)(C). This means that generally a person cannot create his or her own trust, transfer his or her own assets into the trust, and still be qualified for Medicaid. However, spouses can leave property in a supplemental special needs trust at their death to care for their surviving spouses and not have the trust property considered as assets available for Medicaid. 42 U.S.C. § 1396p(d)(2)(A)(ii).

Medicaid exempt trusts

Since the effective date of O.B.R.A., only limited types of trusts can now be used and still preserve an applicant's Medicaid eligibility. One major distinction should be made when analyzing Medicaid trusts. Trusts created by the disabled beneficiary (or a third party with legal authority over the disabled beneficiary) with the disabled person's own assets for the disabled person's own benefit are classified as first-party, self-settled trusts. These types of trusts must be distinguished from trusts created by a third party for the benefit of a disabled individual with the third party's own assets (such as a grandparent creating a trust for a grandchild). Legal restrictions generally exist for first-party, self-settled trusts which do not exist for third-party trusts. These trusts are a good thing to have if someone is expecting a windfall, such as an inheritance.

First-party, self-settled trusts

Most self-settled trusts holding the disabled beneficiary's own assets created after August 11, 1993 are countable resources for Medicaid. The Medicaid statute, however, provides for three specific types of trusts which can be funded with the applicant's own assets and which will not disqualify the applicant from Medicaid. These trusts are called "D-4A Trusts" after the subsection of the law which authorizes them. They are also called "Federalized Special Needs Trusts" because the Federal Medicaid statute makes them available in every state.

Because of the requirement that the State be reimbursed for medical assistance, D-4A Special Needs Trusts may have limited utility when the goal is to pass assets of the disabled individual to family members. The main benefit of the D-4A Trusts is to provide a quality of life for the Medicaid beneficiary. Assets can be held in the trust and used to pay for the beneficiary's special or supplemental needs which the government does not provide, while Medicaid pays the significant medical bills. If the medical assistance provided during life does not turn out to be costly, then upon the death of the beneficiary, there is a chance that assets may be preserved in the trust and pass to loved ones.

Disabled Individual's Special Needs Trust

Under the provisions of 42 U.S.C. § 1396p(d)(4)(A), a Disabled Individual's Trust will not be counted as a Medicaid asset even when it is funded with the applicant's own assets. The requirements for the trust are that the individual must be under age 65 at the time the trust is created (and funded), and disabled under the Social Security definition. Further, the trust must be for the "sole benefit" of the disabled individual. The trust must be created by a parent, grandparent, guardian, or court. Upon the death of the individual, the State Medicaid agency must be reimbursed for the costs of the medical assistance which was provided by Medicaid during the disabled individual's lifetime. This is often called the "payback" provision.

It is important to note that the Disabled Individual's Trust must be created by a parent, grandparent, guardian, or court. The statute does not allow the disabled individual to create his or her own trust, even if he or she is otherwise legally competent. Action by a third party is required in creating the trust. In this regard, these types of special needs trusts are often established by a court on behalf of a disabled person as a part of or ancillary to a serious personal injury lawsuit.

"Miller" Trust

A "Miller" Trust can be used to qualify a Medicaid applicant with income in excess of the eligibility limit (not imposed in all states) for long-term care assistance from Medicaid. Such a trust is not really a "special needs" trust at all; it is not funded with the beneficiary's assets. The Miller trust can be named as recipient of the individual's income, from a pension plan, Social Security, or other source. The Miller trust takes its name from the Colorado case of Miller v. Ibarra, 746 F. Supp. 19 (D. Colo. 1990), and is specifically sanctioned by 42 U.S.C. § 1396p(d)(4)(B). As with a self-settled special needs trust (referred to above as a "Disabled Individual's Trust"), upon the death of the beneficiary, the State Medicaid agency must be paid back for its medical assistance from any remaining assets in the Miller trust. An older name for the Miller trust, still occasionally used, is "Utah Gap" trusts, reportedly coined by a Colorado advocate describing the gap between the income cap for eligibility and the actual cost of nursing home care as similar to the yawning chasm between mesas dotting the Southern Utah landscape. The Miller trust is significant only in those states which impose an income cap on Medicaid long-term care eligibility; ironically, Utah is not one of those states. Income caps are in place in about half of the states.

Also referred to as a qualified income trust.

Nonprofit Pooled Income Special Needs Trust

A Nonprofit Pooled Income Special Needs Trust is authorized by 42 U.S.C. § 1396p(d)(4)(C). Again, the individual must be disabled under the Social Security definition. Unlike the other exempt trusts which can be administered by a private trustee who is an individual (such as a family member), the Pooled Income Trust is run by a nonprofit association, and a separate account is maintained for each individual beneficiary. All accounts are pooled for investment and management purposes. The trust (or more accurately, an account in the pooled trust) may be created by a parent, grandparent, guardian, or court, and it can also be created by the disabled individual himself. Upon the death of the disabled individual, the balance is either retained in the trust for the nonprofit association or paid back to the State Medicaid agency for its medical assistance.

In some states, a disabled individual over age 65 is entitled to transfer assets to a pooled trust and then be immediately eligible for Medicaid. In other states, the transfer must be made before the disabled individual attains the age of 66.

Third-party trusts

Medicaid law governing trusts is designed to prevent disabled individuals qualifying for benefits while still retaining full control over their assets. A third party, however, is still free to plan with his or her own assets and either give them outright to a disabled individual or tie them up and restrict them in trust as they see fit. Accordingly, trusts which are created by a third party with the third party's own assets to benefit a beneficiary who is on Medicaid have their own separate rules and treatment.

Generally, a properly drafted third-party, discretionary trust is not countable as an asset available to the beneficiary receiving Supplemental Security Income (SSI) and/or Medicaid benefits. Such a trust must be created by a party other than the SSI/Medicaid beneficiary, must not receive any assets belonging to the beneficiary, and must be restricted (not accessible or available) to the beneficiary. The operative principle is whether the trust assets or income are available to the beneficiary. If appropriate trust language is used (and the appropriate language varies from state to state), Medicaid will not treat the resources in the trust as a countable resource. Typically, a third-party trust provides that the trustee is given unfettered discretion to distribute (or not to distribute) principal or income for the benefit of the disabled beneficiary. Often, the trustee is directed only to make distributions for the "supplemental" or "special" needs of the beneficiary or as long as the distributions do not disqualify the beneficiary from governmental benefits. Frequently the trustee will be specifically prohibited from making distributions which provide the beneficiary with food or shelter (the two disqualifying categories under SSI and Medicaid regulations). There is no requirement that the trustee be so restricted, however; it may be preferable in most cases to permit the trustee to make the decision to make distributions which reduce or even eliminate public benefits in cases where the availability of trust resources is more important than continued eligibility for SSI and Medicaid.

A third-party special needs trust should not be drafted as a general support trust or mandate distribution of current income to the beneficiary. In such a case, the trust can be deemed to be "available" and can disqualify the beneficiary from Medicaid. The Medicaid beneficiary should not be given any power to revoke the trust or direct the trustee to make distributions to the beneficiary. The trust can be revocable by the third-party settlor. This means that a parent can fund a trust for a disabled child with the parent's assets and give it a test run, revoking it later and re-acquiring the assets if the parent decides that it is not serving its purpose. Finally, the third-party trust does not need to include a D-4 "payback" provision reimbursing the State for the medical assistance of the beneficiary upon the beneficiary's death.

Source (edited): "http://en.wikipedia.org/wiki/Supplemental_Needs_Trust"

Swynfen will case

The **Swynfen** (or **Swinfen**) **will case** was a series of English trials over the will of Samuel Swynfen that ran from 1856 to 1864 and raised important questions of ethics in the legal profession.

The case

Samuel Swynfen of Swinfen Hall, Staffordshire, died in 1854 and, in his will, left £60,000 (£4.1 million in present-day terms) to his widowed daughter-in-law Patience Swynfen. However, Samuel possessed another large estate that was not mentioned in his will. Patience claimed that too.

However, Frederick Hay Swynfen, Samuel's nephew, also claimed the estate. Litigation followed with eminent barristers Sir Frederick Thesiger representing Patience, and Sir Alexander Cockburn, the nephew. However, contrary to Patience's instructions, Thesiger negotiated a settlement with Cockburn and put it to the judge. Patience was furious and succeeded in having the agreement set aside and a new trial listed. Dismissing Thesiger, Patience instructed a young and little known barrister named Charles Rann Kennedy, promising to pay him £20,000 (£1.4 million in present-day terms) if he succeeded in her cause.

No doubt spurred by the incentive, and the fact that he was engaged in a sexual relationship with Patience, Kennedy won the estate. However, she went on to marry a Charles Broun and then to declare that she had no intention of paying Kennedy. Kennedy sued and won, but his claim was overturned on appeal on the grounds that, what was effectively a contingency fee agreement, offended ancient prohibitions on champerty and maintenance. In the case of *Kennedy v. Broun*, Sir William Erle CJ held that the relationship between client and barrister was not a contract. Patience now sued Thesiger over his original professional misconduct. Further, she alleged that Sir Cresswell Cresswell, the judge in the original trial, had induced Thesiger's agreement to a settlement by suggesting that he had formed an unfavourable opinion of Patience's case. Her claim was unsuccessful.

Source (edited): "http://en.wikipedia.org/wiki/Swynfen_will_case"

Taxation of trusts (United Kingdom)

The **taxation of trusts in the United Kingdom** is governed by a different set of principles to those tax laws which apply to individuals or companies.

Inheritance tax

See main article Inheritance tax (United Kingdom).

The inheritance tax ("IHT") treatment of trusts was substantially revised by the Finance Act 2006, with effect from 22 March 2006. The possible types of trust which can now exist for inheritance tax purposes are set out in the table below:
NOTES:
- An "interest-in-possession" means that a specific beneficiary has a right to the current income of the trust.
- The spouse exemption exempts from tax any assets passing between spouses and civil partners.

Relevant property trusts are taxed:
- On creation:
  - If the trust is created inter vivos (i.e. during the settlor's lifetime):
    - It is taxed at half of the current death rate for IHT. The death rate is 40%, and the 2007/8 IHT "nil-band" is £300,000. Therefore if the settlor has made no gifts and settled no trusts in the seven years prior to settling a trust in 2007/8, it would be taxed at nil rate (0%) on the first £300,000 and 20% on the balance.
  - If the settlor dies within seven years of the settlement, the initial 20% charge will be recalculated as if it were a PET, and if that is more than the tax already paid, the balance will be due (but there is no repayment if the recalculation produces a lower result).
  - If the trust is created on death (i.e. a testamentary trust) it will usually suffer IHT at creation under the normal rules, because of the death. There is therefore no need for the trust to be taxed separately on creation.
- To "ten-year charges", on each tenth anniversary of the settlement (or of the date of death, in the case of a testamentary trust). The rate is 6% on the value of the trust's assets exceeding the nil-band at that time.
- To "exit charges" when money leaves the trust: most usually by appointment to a beneficiary. Simplifying a little, the rate of IHT is that proportion of what the next ten-year charge would have been, that the time which has elapsed since creation or the last ten year charge bears to ten years.

The **Interest-in possession** treatment, since 2006, applies only to some trusts with an interest-in-possession (as defined above). Where it applies, such trusts are taxed by attributing the trust's value to the beneficiary who is currently entitled to the income. Accordingly:
- On creation:
  - In the rare cases where they can be created in lifetime they are taxed as PETs.
  - They are taxed as part of the death estate, when created by will. A spouse exemption is available where the interest-in-possession beneficiary is a spouse or civil partner of the deceased.
- On termination *(i.e. termination of the interest-in-possession, which may, or may not, be the termination of the trust)*:
  - The value of the trust's assets is taxed at death rates upon the death of the interest-in-possession beneficiary. It aggregates with that beneficiary's estate, and the trust and the estate share the nil-band between them, in proportion to their values.
  - The value of the trust's assets is taxed as if it were a "PET" where the beneficiary's right to receive income ceases in his or her lifetime.

Source: Schedule 20 Finance Act 2006.
Source (edited). "http://en.wikipedia.org/wiki/Taxation_of_trusts_(United_Kingdom)"

Testamentary capacity

In the common law tradition, **testamentary capacity** is the legal term of art used to describe a person's legal and mental ability to make or alter a valid will. This concept has also been called **sound mind and memory** or **disposing mind and memory**.

Presumption of capacity

Adults are presumed to have the ability to make a will. Litigation about testamentary capacity typically revolves around charges that the testator, by virtue of senility, dementia, insanity, or other unsoundness of mind, lacked the mental capacity to make a will. In essence, the doctrine requires those who would challenge a validly executed will to demonstrate that the testator did not know the consequence of his conduct when he executed the will.

Certain people, such as minors, are usually deemed to be conclusively incapable of making a will by the common law; however, minors who serve in the military are conceded the right to make a will by statute in many jurisdictions. In South Africa, however, one acquires testamentary capacity at the age of 16 years.

Requirements

The requirements for testamentary capacity are minimal. Some courts have held that a person who lacked the capacity to make a contract can nevertheless make a valid will. While the wording of statutes or judicial rulings will vary from one jurisdiction to another, the test generally requires that the testator was aware of:
- The extent and value of their property
- The persons who are the natural beneficiaries
- The disposition he is making
- How these elements relate to form an orderly plan of distribution of property.

The legal test implies that a typical claimant in a will contest is a disgruntled heir who believes he or she should have received a larger share than they did under the will. Once the challenging party meets the burden of proof that the testator did not possess the capacity, the burden subsequently shifts to the party propounding the will to show by clear and convincing evidence that the testator did have the requisite capacity.

Those who contest a will for lack of testamentary capacity must typically show that the decedent suffered from mental unsoundness that left them unable to remember family members or caused them to hold insane delusions about them. Dead Man's Statutes sometimes restrict evidence which can be admitted concerning transactions with the decedent.

Lawyers for people whose testamentary capacity might be called into question often arrange for a will execution to be video taped. On video, they ask the testator about his property and about his family, and go over the contents of the testator's will.

Along with resolving an examinee's testamentary capacity, a forensic specialist observes for signs of undue influence by a concerned party that exploits an emotionally vulnerable individual who might otherwise be cognitively intact. The testamentary capacity matter is most frequently raised posthumously, when an aggrieved heir contests the will entered into probate. For this reason, the forensic psychiatrist or forensic psychologist studies the testatrix' cognition through videotape record of the drafting of the will, or by reviewing email, letters and other records.

Even when a testator are found to have lacked testamentary capacity due to senility, loss of memory due to the aging process, infirmity or insanity, courts will sometimes rule that the testator had a "temporary period of lucidity" or a "lucid moment" at the time of the execution of the testamentary instrument. Such finding will validate a will that would otherwise be denied probate.

A way to forestall a will contest would be to have a self-proving will, in which an affidavit of the witnesses to the will specifically swear or affirm that the will was prepared under the supervision of an attorney.

Source (edited): "http://en.wikipedia.org/wiki/Testamentary_capacity"

Testamentary disposition

A **testamentary disposition** is any gift of any property by a testator under the terms of a will.

Types

Types of testamentary dispositions include.
- Gift (law), assets that have been legally transferred from one person to another
- Legacy, testamentary gift of personal property, traditionally of money but may be real or personal property
- Life estate, a concept used in common and statutory law to designate the ownership of land for the duration of a person's life
- Demonstrative legacy, a gift of a specific sum of money with a direction that is to be paid out of a particular fund

Source (edited): "http://en.wikipedia.org/wiki/Testamentary_disposition"

Testamentary trust

A **testamentary trust** (sometimes referred to as a **will trust**) is a trust which arises upon the death of the testator, and which is specified in his or her will (testamentary trust literally means *a trust in a will*). A will may contain more than one testamentary trust, and may address all or any portion of the estate.

Testamentary trusts are distinguished from *inter vivos* trusts, which are created during the settlor's lifetime.

There are four parties involved in a testamentary trust:
- the person who specifies that the trust be created, usually as a part of his or her will, but it may be set up in abeyance during the person's lifetime. This person may be called the *grantor* or *trustor*, but is usually referred to as the *settlor*;
- the *trustee*, whose duty is to carry out the terms of the will. He or she may be named in the will, or may be appointed by the probate court which handles the will;
- the *beneficiary(s)*, who will receive the benefits of the trust;
- Although not a party to the trust itself, the *probate court* is a necessary component of the trust's activity. It oversees the trustee's handling of the trust.

A testamentary trust is a legal entity created as specified in a person's will, and is occasioned by the death of that person. It is created to address any estate accumulated during that person's lifetime or generated as a result of the death itself, such as a settlement in a wrongful-death suit, or the proceeds from a life insurance policy held on the settlor. A trust can be created to oversee such assets. A trustee is appointed to direct the trust until a set time when the trust expires, such as when minor beneficiaries reach a specified age or accomplish a deed such as completing a set educational goal or achieving a specified matrimonial status.

For a testamentary trust, as the settlor is deceased, he or she will generally not have any influence over the trustee's exercise of discretion, although in some jurisdictions it is common for the testator to leave a letter of wishes for the trustee.

In practical terms, testamentary trusts tend to be driven more by the needs of the beneficiaries (particularly infant beneficiaries) than by tax considerations, which are the usual considerations in *inter vivos* trusts.

If a testamentary trust fails, the property will usually be held on resulting trusts for the testator's residuary estate. Many famous English trust law cases were on behalf of the residuary legatees under a will seeking to have testamentary trusts declared void so as to inherit the trust property (the most famous, or infamous, example of which is probably *Re Diplock* Ch 253, which resulted in the suicide of one of the trustees who was personally liable to account for trust funds that had been disbursed for what he thought were perfectly valid charitable trusts).

Advantages of a testamentary trust

- A testamentary trust provides a way for assets devolving to minor children to be protected until the children are capable of fending for themselves;
- A testamentary trust has low upfront costs, usually only the cost of preparing the will in such a way as to address the trust, and the fees involved in dealing with the judicial system during probate.

Disadvantages of a testamentary trust

- The trustee is required to meet with the probate court regularly (at least annually in many jurisdictions) and prove that the trust is being handled in a responsible manner and in strict accordance with provisions of the will which created the trust. This may involve considerable legal fees, especially if the trust endures for several years or involves a sophisticated financial or investment structure, and always involves the fees imposed by the judicial system. Such fees and expenses are deducted from the principal of the estate;
- The trustee must be prepared to oversee the trust for its duration, which involves a considerable commitment in time, possible emotional attachment, and legal liability;
- A candidate for trustee may be named in the will, but that person has no legal obligation to accept the appointment. If no trustee is named in the will (or is unavailable, even if named), the probate court will appoint a trustee;
- It can be difficult for beneficiaries to bring a dishonest trustee to account. They may sue at law, or the malfeasance may be pointed out at the annual probate court review, but such remedies are slow, time-consuming and expensive, and are not guaranteed to succeed.

Summary

Due to the potential problems, lawyers often advise that a *revocable living will* or *inter vivos trust* be created instead of a testamentary trust. However, a testamentary trust may be a better solution if the expected estate is small compared to potential life-insurance settlement amounts.

Source (edited): "http://en.wikipedia.org/wiki/Testamentary_trust"

Testator

A testator is a person who has written and executed a last will and testament that is in effect at the time of his/her death. It is any "person who makes a will."

Related terms

- A female testator is sometimes referred to as a **testatrix**, particularly in older cases.
- The adjectival form of the word is **testamentary**, as in:
- Testamentary capacity, or mental capacity or ability to execute a will and
- Testamentary disposition, or gift made in a will (see that article for types).
- A will is also known as a **last will and testament**.
- **Testacy** means the status of being **testate**, that is, having executed a will. The property of such a person goes through the probate process.
- **Intestacy** means the status of *not* having made a will, or to have died *without* a valid will. The estate of a person who dies **intestate**, undergoes administration, rather than probate.
- The attestation clause of a will is where the witnesses to a will attest to certain facts concerning the making of the will by the testator, and where they sign their names as witnesses.

Source (edited): "http://en.wikipedia.org/wiki/Testator"

Trust instrument

A **trust instrument** (also sometimes called a **deed of trust**, where executed by way of deed) is an instrument in writing executed by a settlor used to constitute a trust. Trust instruments are generally only used in relation to an *inter vivos* trust; testamentary trusts are usually created under a will.

Formalities

Although in most legal systems there are certain formalities associated with settling a trust, most legal systems impose few, if any, strictures on the trust instrument itself. Historically, the concept of a trust is the intervention of the courts of equity to prevent a legal owner treating the property as beneficially his own; provided that state of affairs exists, a trust arises notwithstanding any lack of formality in relation to the form of the trust instrument.

However, notwithstanding the flexible approach taken by the law, characteristically the legal profession has taken an extremely formalised approach to trust instruments. Not only are they invariably always executed under seal as a deed, but frequently the initial trust fund (usually a nominal amount), will actually be physically affixed to the trust instrument itself to prove that the initial trust property was transferred.

Some slightly unusual practices have arisen in relation to the drafting of trust instruments, which again, are rigidly adhered to by professionals in many common-law countries (although not the U.S.A.). For example, trust deeds will generally avoid all punctuation (including full stops) - to avoid confusion, all new sentences commence with a new, numbered, paragraph. Dates, including years, are conventionally spelled out in words rather than using figures.

Part of the over-formalisation which attends the creation of trusts is justified by the significant tax implications which may follow if a trust were to be subsequently held to be void, as most professionally drafted trust instruments are prepared as a part of tax mitigation schemes.

Most jurisdictions do not require trust instruments to be publicly filed (in contrast to wills). But in many jurisdictions they are subject to stamp duty.

Provisions

The provisions of a trust instrument will vary according to the type of trust, and the nature of the trust property.

- A bare trust over a single asset will characteristically have very few provisions.
- A discretionary trust over a mixed bag of investments will usually have far greater provisions regulation the exercise and management of the trust fund.
- A trust which is set up as a unit trust will have additional specific provisions specific to the calculation of the NAV and acquisition and redemption of units.
- Settled land act settlements have specific provisions relating to the underlying subject matter.
- Trusts which are set up to protect vulnerable beneficiaries, such as blind trusts or spendthrift trusts will have specific provisions relating to the nature of the beneficiaries.

However, in general, most trust instruments will have provisions which address the following aspects of the administration of the trust:

- The name of the settlement and definitions and interpretation provisions
- The legal nature of the trust (ie. a trust for sale)
- Powers to add and exclude beneficiaries
- Trusts over property added to the trust fund
- Power of appointment (ie. distribution)
- Trusts in default of appointment, and, sometimes, ultimate default trusts
- General administrative powers of the trustees
- Extended power of maintenance
- Extended power of advancement
- Usually, a trustee charging clause
- Regulation of the appointment of new trustees
- The proper law and forum and place of administration for the settlement
- Often, an exclusion of settlor (and spouse) from benefiting from the trust (where required for tax reasons)
- Usually, an indemnity for the trustees out of the trust fund

Most trust instruments will then also have two schedules:

- a schedule setting out the powers of the trustees (often in addition to any powers granted or implied by operation of law)
- a summary of the initial trust fund (usually a nominal amount of money)

Source (edited): "http://en.wikipedia.org/wiki/Trust_instrument"

Trust law

In common law legal systems, a **trust** is a relationship whereby property (including real, tangible and intangible) is managed by one person (or persons, or organizations) for the benefit of another. A trust is created by a settlor (also known as grantor, or archaically *feoffor to uses*), who entrusts some or all of their property to people of their choice (the trustees or *feoffee to uses*). The trustees hold legal title to the trust property (or *trust corpus*), but they are obliged to hold the property for the benefit of one or more individuals or organizations (the beneficiary, *cestui que use*, or *cestui que trust*), usually specified by the settlor, who hold equitable title. The trustees owe a fiduciary duty to the beneficiaries, who are the "beneficial" owners of the trust property.

The trust is governed by the terms of the trust document, which is usually written and occasionally set out in deed form. It is also governed by local law. The trustee is obliged to administer the trust in accordance with both the terms of the trust document and the governing law.

In the United States, the settlor is also called the trustor, grantor, donor or creator. In some other jurisdictions, the settlor may also be known as the founder.

History

Roman law had a well-developed concept of the trust (*fideicommissum*) in terms of "testamentary trusts" created by wills but never developed the concept of the "inter vivos trust" that applied while the creator was still alive. This was created by later common law jurisdictions.

Personal trust law developed in England at the time of the Crusades, during the 12th and 13th centuries.

At the time, land ownership in England was based on the feudal system. When a landowner left England to fight in the Crusades, he needed someone to run his estate in his absence, often to pay and receive feudal dues. To achieve this, he would convey ownership of his lands to an acquaintance, on the understanding that the ownership would be conveyed back on his return. However, Crusaders would often return to find the legal owners' refusal to hand over the property.

Unfortunately for the Crusader, English law did not recognize his claim. As far as the courts were concerned, the land belonged to the trustee, who was under no obligation to return it. The Crusader had no legal claim. The disgruntled Crusader would then petition the king, who would refer the matter to his Lord Chancellor. The Lord Chancellor could do what was "just" and "equitable", and had the power to decide a case according to his conscience. At this time, the principle of equity was born.

The Lord Chancellor would consider it unjust that the legal owner could deny the claims of the Crusader (the "true" owner). Therefore, he would find in favor of the returning Crusader. Over time, it became known that the Lord Chancellor's court (the Court of Chancery) would continually recognize the claim of a returning Crusader. The legal owner would hold the land for the benefit of the original owner, and would be compelled to convey it back to him when requested. The Crusader was the "beneficiary" and the friend the "trustee". The term *use of land* was coined, and in time developed into what we now know as a *trust*.

Also, the Primogeniture system could be considered as a form of trust. In Primogeniture system, the first born male inherited all the property and "usually assumes the responsibility of trusteeship of the property and of adjudicating attendant disputes."

The waqf is an equivalent institution in Islamic law, restricted to charitable trusts.

"Antitrust law" emerged in the 19th century when industries created monopolistic trusts by entrusting their shares to a board of trustees in exchange for shares of equal value with dividend rights; these boards could then enforce a monopoly. However, trusts were used in this case because a corporation could not own other companies' stock and thereby become a holding company without a "special act of the legislature". Holding companies were used after the restriction on owning other companies' shares was lifted.

Significance

The trust is widely considered to be the most innovative contribution to the English legal system. Today, trusts play a significant role in all common law systems, and their success has led some civil law jurisdictions to incorporate trusts into their civil codes. France, for example, recently added a similar though-not-quite-comparable notion to its own law with *la fiducie*, which was modified in 2009; *la fiducie*, unlike the trust, is a contract. Trusts are recognized internationally under the Hague Convention on the Law Applicable to Trusts and on their Recognition which also regulates conflict of trusts.

Although trusts are often associated with intrafamily wealth transfers, they have become very important in American capital markets, particularly through pension funds (essentially always trusts) and mutual funds (often trusts).

Basic principles

Property of any sort may be held on trust, but growth assets are more commonly placed into trust (for tax and estate planning benefits). The uses of trusts are many and varied. Trusts may be created during a person's life (usually by a trust instrument) or after death in a will.

In a relevant sense, a trust can be viewed as a generic form of a corporation where the settlors (investors) are also the beneficiaries. This is particularly evident in the Delaware business trust, which could theoretically, with the language in the "governing instrument", be organized as a cooperative corporation, limited liability corporation, or perhaps even a nonprofit corporation. One of the most significant aspects of trusts is the ability to partition and shield assets from the trustee, multiple beneficiaries, and their respective creditors (particularly the trustee's creditors), making it "bankruptcy remote", and leading to its use in pensions, mutual funds, and asset securitization.

Creation

Trusts may be created by the expressed intentions of the settlor (express trusts) or they may be created by operation of law (resulting trusts).

Typically a trust is created by one of the following:

- a written trust document created by the settlor and signed by both the settlor and the trustees (often referred to as an *inter vivos* or "living trust");
- an oral declaration;
- the will of a decedent, usually called a testamentary trust; or
- a court order (for example in family proceedings).

In some jurisdictions certain types of assets may not be the subject of a trust without a written document.

Formalities

Generally, a trust requires three certainties, as determined in *Knight v Knight*:

- **Intention**. There must be a clear intention to create a trust (*Re Adams and the Kensington Vestry*)
- **Subject Matter**. The property subject to the trust must be clearly identified (*Palmer v Simmonds*). One may not, for example, settle "the majority of my estate", as the precise extent cannot be ascertained. Trust property may be any form of specific property, be it real or personal, tangible or intangible. It is often, for example, real estate, shares or cash.
- **Objects**. The beneficiaries of the trust must be clearly identified, or at least be ascertainable (*Re Hain's Settlement*). In the case of discretionary trusts, where the trustees have power to decide who the beneficiaries will be, the settlor must have described a clear **class** of beneficiaries (*McPhail v Doulton*). Beneficiaries may include people not born at the date of the trust (for example, "my future grandchildren"). Alternatively, the object of a trust could be a charitable purpose rather than specific beneficiaries.

Trustees

The trustee may be either a person or a legal entity such as a company. A trust may have one or multiple trustees. A trustee has many rights and responsibilities; these vary from trust to trust depending on the type of the trust. A trust generally will not fail solely for want of a trustee. A court may appoint a trustee, or in Ireland the trustee may be any administrator of a charity to which the trust is related. Trustees are usually appointed in the document (instrument) which creates the trust.

A trustee may be held personally liable for certain problems which arise with the trust. For example, if a trustee does not properly invest trust monies to expand the trust fund, he or she may be liable for the difference. There are two main types of trustees, professional and non-professional. Liability is different for the two types.

The trustees are the legal owners of the trust's property. The trustees administer the affairs attendant to the trust. The trust's affairs may include investing the assets of the trust, ensuring trust property is preserved and productive for the beneficiaries, accounting for and reporting periodically to the beneficiaries concerning all transactions associated with trust property, filing any required tax returns on behalf of the trust, and other duties. In some cases, the trustees must make decisions as to whether beneficiaries should receive trust assets for their benefit. The circumstances in which this discretionary authority is exercised by trustees is usually provided for under the terms of the trust instrument. The trustee's duty is to determine in the specific instance of a beneficiary request whether to provide any funds and in what manner.

By default, being a trustee is an unpaid job. In modern times trustees are often lawyers, bankers or other professionals who will not work for free. Therefore, often a trust document will state specifically that trustees are entitled to reasonable payment for their work.

Beneficiaries

The beneficiaries are beneficial (or **equitable**) owners of the trust property. Either immediately or eventually, the beneficiaries will receive income from the trust property, or they will receive the property itself. The extent of a beneficiary's interest depends on the wording of the trust document. One beneficiary may be entitled to income (for example, interest from a bank account), whereas another may be entitled to the entirety of the trust property when he attains the age of twenty-five years. The settlor has much discretion when creating the trust, subject to some limitations imposed by law.

Purposes

Common purposes for trusts include:

- **Privacy.** Trusts may be created purely for privacy. The terms of a will are public and the terms of a trust are not. In some families this alone makes use of trusts ideal.
- **Spendthrift Protection.** Trusts may be used to protect beneficiaries (for example, one's children) against their own inability to handle money. It is not unusual for an individual to create an inter vivos trust with a corporate trustee who may then disburse funds only for causes articulated in the trust document. These are especially attractive for spendthrifts. In many cases a family member or friend has prevailed upon the spendthrift/settlor to enter into such a relationship. However, over time, courts were asked to determine the efficacy of spendthrift clauses as against the trust beneficiaries seeking to engage in such assignments, and the creditors of those beneficiaries seeking to reach trust assets. A case law doctrine developed whereby courts may generally recognize the efficacy of spendthrift clauses as against trust beneficiaries and their creditors, but not against creditors of a settlor.
- **Wills and Estate Planning.** Trusts frequently appear in wills (indeed, technically, the administration of every deceased's estate is a form of trust). A fairly conventional will, even for a comparatively poor person, often leaves assets to the deceased's spouse (if any), and then to the children equally. If the children are under 18, or under some other age mentioned in the will (21 and 25 are common), a trust must come into existence until the **contingency age** is reached. The executor of the will is (usually) the trustee, and the children are the beneficiaries. The trustee will have powers to assist the beneficiaries during their minority.
- **Charities.** In some common law jurisdictions all charities must take the form of trusts. In others, corporations may be charities also, but even there a trust is the most usual form for a charity to take. In most jurisdictions, charities are tightly

regulated for the public benefit (in England, for example, by the Charity Commission).
- **Unit Trusts.** The trust has proved to be such a flexible concept that it has proved capable of working as an investment vehicle: the unit trust.
- **Pension Plans.** Pension plans are typically set up as a trust, with the employer as settlor, and the employees and their dependents as beneficiaries.
- **Remuneration Trusts.** Trusts for the benefit of directors and employees or companies or their families or dependents. This form of trust was developed by Paul Baxendale-Walker and has since gained widespread use.
- **Corporate Structures.** Complex business arrangements, most often in the finance and insurance sectors, sometimes use trusts among various other entities (e.g. corporations) in their structure.
- **Asset Protection.** The principle of "asset protection" is for a person to divorce himself or herself personally from the assets he or she would otherwise own, with the intention that future creditors will not be able to attack that money, even though they may be able to bankrupt him or her personally. One method of asset protection is the creation of a discretionary trust, of which the settlor may be the protector and a beneficiary, but not the trustee and not the sole beneficiary. In such an arrangement the settlor may be in a position to benefit from the trust assets, without owning them, and therefore without them being available to his creditors. Such a trust will usually preserve anonymity with a completely unconnected name (e.g. "The Teddy Bear Trust"). The above is a considerable simplification of the scope of asset protection. It is a subject which straddles ethical boundaries. Some asset protection is legal and (arguably) moral, while some asset protection is illegal and/or (arguably) immoral.
- **Tax Planning.** The tax consequences of doing anything using a trust are usually different from the tax consequences of achieving the same effect by another route (if, indeed, it would be possible to do so). In many cases the tax consequences of using the trust are better than the alternative, and trusts are therefore frequently used for legal tax avoidance. *For an example see the "nil-band discretionary trust", explained at Inheritance Tax (United Kingdom).*
- **Co-ownership.** Ownership of property by more than one person is facilitated by a trust. In particular, ownership of a matrimonial home is commonly effected by a trust with both partners as beneficiaries and one, or both, owning the legal title as trustee.

Types

Trusts go by many different names, depending on the characteristics or the purpose of the trust. Because trusts often have multiple characteristics or purposes, a single trust might accurately be described in several ways. For example, a living trust is often an express trust, which is also a revocable trust, and might include an incentive trust, and so forth.

- **Constructive trust.** Unlike an express or implied trust, a constructive trust is not created by an agreement between a settlor and the trustee. A constructive trust is imposed by the law as an "equitable remedy." This generally occurs due to some wrongdoing, where the wrongdoer has acquired legal title to some property and cannot in good conscience be allowed to benefit from it. A constructive trust is, essentially, a legal fiction. For example, a court of equity recognizing a plaintiff's request for the equitable remedy of a constructive trust may decide that a constructive trust has been "raised" and simply order the person holding the assets to the person who rightfully should have them. The constructive trustee is not necessarily the person who is guilty of the wrongdoing, and in practice it is often a bank or similar organization.
- **Dynasty Trust** also known as a **Generation-skipping trust.** A type of trust in which assets are passed down to the grantor's grandchildren, not the grantor's children. The children of the grantor never take title to the assets. This allows the grantor to avoid the estate taxes that would apply if the assets were transferred to his or her children first. Generation-skipping trusts can still be used to provide financial benefits to a grantor's children, however, because any income generated by the trust's assets can be made accessible to the grantor's children while still leaving the assets in trust for the grandchildren.
- **Express trust.** An express trust arises where a settlor deliberately and consciously decides to create a trust, over their assets, either now, or upon his or her later death. In these cases this will be achieved by signing a trust instrument, which will either be a will or a trust deed. Almost all trusts dealt with in the trust industry are of this type. They contrast with resulting and constructive trusts. The intention of the parties to create the trust must be shown clearly by their language or conduct. For an express trust to exist, there must be certainty to the objects of the trust and the trust property. In the USA Statute of Frauds provisions require express trusts to be evidenced in writing if the trust property is above a certain value, or is real estate.
- **Fixed trust.** In a *fixed trust*, the entitlement of the beneficiaries is fixed by the settlor. The trustee has little or no discretion. Common examples are:
  - a trust for a minor ("to x if she attains 21");
  - a **life interest** ("to pay the income to x for her lifetime"); and
  - a **remainder** ("to pay the capital

to y after the death of x")
- **Hybrid trust.** A *hybrid trust* combines elements of both fixed and discretionary trusts. In a hybrid trust, the trustee must pay a certain amount of the trust property to each beneficiary fixed by the settlor. But the trustee has discretion as to how any remaining trust property, once these fixed amounts have been paid out, is to be paid to the beneficiaries.
- **Implied trust.** An implied trust, as distinct from an express trust, is created where some of the legal requirements for an express trust are not met, but an intention on behalf of the parties to create a trust can be presumed to exist. A resulting trust may be deemed to be present where a trust instrument is not properly drafted and a portion of the equitable title has not been provided for. In such a case, the law may raise a resulting trust for the benefit of the grantor (the creator of the trust). In other words, the grantor may be deemed to be a beneficiary of the portion of the equitable title that was not properly provided for in the trust document.
- **Incentive trust.** A trust that uses distributions from income or principal as an incentive to encourage or discourage certain behaviors on the part of the beneficiary. The term "incentive trust" is sometimes used to distinguish trusts that provide fixed conditions for access to trust funds from discretionary trusts that leave such decisions up to the trustee.
- **Inter vivos trust** (or **living trust**). A settlor who is living at the time the trust is established creates an *inter vivos* trust.
- **Irrevocable trust.** In contrast to a revocable trust, an irrevocable trust is one in which the terms of the trust cannot be amended or revised until the terms or purposes of the trust have been completed. Although in rare cases, a court may change the terms of the trust due to unexpected changes in circumstances that make the trust uneconomical or unwieldy to administer, under normal circumstances an irrevocable trust may not be changed by the trustee or the beneficiaries of the trust.
- **Offshore trust.** Strictly speaking, an offshore trust is a trust which is resident in any jurisdiction other than that in which the settlor is resident. However, the term is more commonly used to describe a trust in one of the jurisdictions known as offshore financial centers or, colloquially, as tax havens. Offshore trusts are usually conceptually similar to onshore trusts in common law countries, but usually with legislative modifications to make them more commercially attractive by abolishing or modifying certain common law restrictions. By extension, "onshore trust" has come to mean any trust resident in a high-tax jurisdiction.
- **Personal injury trust.** A personal injury trust is any form of trust where funds are held by trustees for the benefit of a person who has suffered an injury and funded exclusively by funds derived from payments made in consequence of that injury.
- **Private and public trusts.** A *private trust* has one or more particular individuals as its beneficiary. By contrast, a *public trust* (also called a *charitable trust*) has some charitable end as its beneficiary. In order to qualify as a charitable trust, the trust must have as its object certain purposes such as alleviating poverty, providing education, carrying out some religious purpose, etc. The permissible objects are generally set out in legislation, but objects not explicitly set out may also be an object of a charitable trust, by analogy. Charitable trusts are entitled to special treatment under the law of trusts and also the law of taxation.
- **Protective trust.** Here the terminology is different between the UK and the USA:
  - In the UK, a protective trust is a life interest which terminates on the happening of a specified event such as the bankruptcy of the beneficiary or any attempt by him to dispose of his interest. They have become comparatively rare.
  - In the USA, a *protective trust* is a type of trust that was devised for use in estate planning. (In another jurisdiction this might be thought of as one type of asset protection trust.) Often a person, *A*, wishes to leave property to another person *B*. *A* however fears that the property might be claimed by creditors before *A* dies, and that therefore *B* would receive none of it. *A* could establish a trust with *B* as the beneficiary, but then *A* would not be entitled to use of the property before they died. Protective trusts were developed as a solution to this situation. *A* would establish a trust with both *A* and *B* as beneficiaries, with the trustee instructed to allow *A* use of the property until they died, and thereafter to allow its use to *B*. The property is then safe from being claimed by *A*'s creditors, at least so long as the debt was entered into after the trust's establishment. This use of trusts is similar to life estates and remainders, and are frequently used as alternatives to them.
- **Purpose trust.** Or, more accurately, non-charitable purpose trust (all charitable trusts are purpose trusts). Generally, the law does not permit non-charitable purpose trusts outside of certain anomalous exceptions which arose under the eighteenth century common law (and, arguable, *Quistclose* trusts). Certain jurisdictions (principally, offshore jurisdictions) have enacted legislation validating non-charitable purpose trusts generally.
- **Resulting trust.** A resulting trust is a form of implied trust which occurs where (1) a trust fails, wholly or in part, as a result of which the settlor becomes entitled to the assets; or (2)

a voluntary payment is made by A to B in circumstances which do not suggest gifting. B becomes the resulting trustee of A's payment.
- **Revocable trust.** A trust of this kind may be amended, altered or revoked by its settlor at any time, provided the settlor is not mentally incapacitated. Revocable trusts are becoming increasingly common in the US as a substitute for a will to minimize administrative costs associated with probate and to provide centralized administration of a person's final affairs after death.
- **Secret trust.** A *post mortem* trust constituted externally from a will but imposing obligations as a trustee on one, or more, legatees of a will.
- **Simple trust.** This term is only used in the US, but in that jurisdiction has two distinct meanings:
  - In a *simple trust* the trustee has no active duty beyond conveying the property to the beneficiary at some future time determined by the trust. This is also called a *bare trust*. All other trusts are *special trusts* where the trustee has active duties beyond this.
  - A simple trust in Federal income tax law is one in which, under the terms of the trust document, all net income must be distributed on an annual basis.
- **Special trust.** In the US, a special trust contrasts with a simple trust (see above).
- A **Spendthrift trust** is a trust put into place for the benefit of a person who is unable to control their spending. It gives the trustee the power to decide how the trust funds may be spent for the benefit of the beneficiary.
- **Standby Trust** or **Pourover Trust**. The trust is empty at creation during life and the will transfers the property into the trust at death. This is a statutory trust.
- **Testamentary trust** or **Will Trust**. A trust created in an individual's will is called a testamentary trust. Because a will can become effective only upon death, a testamentary trust is generally created at or following the date of the settlor's death.
- **Unit trust.** A unit trust is a trust where the beneficiaries (called *unitholders*) each possess a certain share (called *units*) and can direct the trustee to pay money to them out of the trust property according to the number of units they possess. A unit trust is a vehicle for collective investment, rather than disposition, as the person who gives the property to the trustee is also the beneficiary.

While the preceding list is a great starting point in trust education, this is an ever-expanding field of law. New types of trusts continue to be created, as the IRS continues to expand tax law, and individuals seek to find new ways to properly transfer their wealth to individuals, charities, etc.

Terms

- **Appointment.** In trust law, "appointment" often has its everyday meaning. It is common to talk of "the appointment of a trustee", for example. However, "appointment" also has a technical trust law meaning, either:
  - the act of *appointing* (i.e. giving) an asset from the trust to a beneficiary (usually where there is some choice in the matter—such as in a discretionary trust); or
  - the name of the document which gives effect to the appointment.

  The trustee's right to do this, where it exists, is called a power of appointment. Sometimes, a power of appointment is given to someone other than the trustee, such as the settlor, the protector, or a beneficiary.
- **Protector.** A protector may be appointed in an express, inter vivos trust, as a person who has some control over the trustee—usually including a power to dismiss the trustee and appoint another. The legal status of a protector is the subject of some debate. No-one doubts that a *trustee* has fiduciary responsibilities. If a *protector* also has fiduciary responsibilities then the courts—if asked by beneficiaries—could order him or her to act in the way the court decrees. However, a protector is unnecessary to the nature of a trust—many trusts can and do operate without one. Also, protectors are comparatively new, while the nature of trusts has been established over hundreds of years. It is therefore thought by some that protectors have fiduciary duties, and by others that they do not. The case law has not yet established this point.
- **Trustee.** A person (either an individual, a corporation or more than one of either) who administers a trust. A trustee is considered a fiduciary and owes the highest duty under the law to protect trust assets from unreasonable loss for the trust's beneficiaries.

Tax and regulation

Trusts can be used to avoid taxes and regulation, although in the United States the IRS allows trusts to be taxed as corporations, partnerships, or not at all depending on the circumstances. Tax avoidance concerns have historically been one of the reasons that European countries have been reluctant to adopt trusts.

The trust-preferred security is a hybrid (debt and equity) security with favorable tax treatment which is treated as regulatory capital on banks' balance sheets. The Dodd-Frank Wall Street Reform and Consumer Protection Act changed this somewhat by not allowing these assets to be a part of (large) banks' regulatory capital.

Inter vivos trusts in the United States

In the United States, a living trust refers to a trust that may be revocable by the trust creator or settlor (known by the IRS as the Grantor). Living trusts are often used because they may allow assets to be passed to heirs without going through the process of probate. Avoiding probate will normally save substantial costs (the probate courts, in some states, charge a fee based on a percentage net worth of the deceased), time, and maintain privacy (the probate records are available to the public, while distribution through a trust is private). Both living trusts and wills can also be used to plan for unforeseen circumstances such as incapacity or disability, by giving discretionary powers to the trustee or executor of the will.

The grantor/settlor may also serve as a trustee or co-trustee. In the case where two or more co-trustees serve, the trust instrument may provide that either trustee may act alone on behalf of the trust or require both co-trustees to act/sign. The trust instrument may also provide that the other co-trustee shall act as sole trustee if the grantor becomes incompetent and is unable to continue administering the trust.

There are also some negative aspects to a living trust in the United States. Beneficiaries do not save on federal estate or state inheritance taxes. Setting up a trust may be expensive, and the expense is immediate, not delayed till after the grantor's death. The legal drafting of the trust instrument, which creates the trust, usually costs much more than the legal drafting of a will. Trust administration can be more expensive than the administration of a will in the long run, as most state laws allow a fee of 1% of the estate's gross assets to be paid to the trustee for every year the trust is in existence. The fees for probate estate administration under a will are usually from 1% of the gross estate (for very large estates) to 4% of the gross estate (for very small estates), but this is a one-time fee, not yearly. The same one-time fees apply when a person dies without a will or a trust (dies Intestate): State laws require that an intestate probate be opened at the local courthouse, that the decedent's closest relatives be identified, located and notified, and that the decedent's real and personal property be collected, accounted, and distributed to said relatives.

Important safeguards contained in the probate laws of most U.S. jurisdictions do not apply to trust administration. If the decedent leaves a will, his/her probate proceedings must be conducted under the auspices of the probate court. Unlike trusts, wills must be signed by two to three witnesses, the number depending on state law. Several safety provisions of probate law in the U.S. protect the decedent's assets from mismanagement, loss, and embezzlement, such as the requirement that the executor of the will be bonded, the real property insured, the executor's sale of real estate monitored, and itemized accountings filed with the court during and at the end of probate administration. These procedures do not occur when a decedent's estate passes by trust. Trusts are conducted in private, unless a conflict develops and one of the parties seeks resolution by a court order.

Living trusts generally do not shelter assets from the U.S. Federal estate tax. A married couple having a trust can, however, effectively double the estate tax exemption amount (the amount of net worth above which an estate tax is levied) by setting up the trust with a formula clause. A formula clause takes advantage of the unlimited spousal deduction allowed under the internal revenue code. When the first married individual dies, the trust pays out to the beneficiaries an amount up to the total unified credit. The amount is set by the formula clause, not strict dollar amounts, because the unified credit increases over time. Without a formula clause, the unified credit could be wasted. The remaining amount of the estate (after the unified credit is exhausted) is paid to the spouse. Thus, when the first spouse dies, no estate tax is owed (just as if the individual died intestate). However, when the second spouse dies, the distribution to the trust beneficiaries is subject to that decedent's unified credit. The rest is subject to estate tax. If the married couple had died intestate, the first decedent's unified credit is lost because everything is transferred to the spouse upon his/her death. A formula clause is necessary only if the value of the estate is larger than the amount of the unified credit. Due to changes in Federal Estate Tax Laws that affect the year 2010 and later, using the Unified Credit formula may have some unintended consequences for persons who die during 2010 and later.

For a living trust, the grantor/settlor will often retain some level of relevance to the trust, usually by appointing him- or herself as the trustee and/or as the protector under the trust instrument (in jurisdictions where protectors are recognised). Living trusts also, in practical terms, tend to be driven to large extent by tax considerations. If a living trust fails, the property will usually be held for the grantor/settlor on resulting trusts, which in some notable cases, has had catastrophic tax consequences. A living trust is not under the control and supervision of the probate court, and property held by such a trust is not part of a decedent's probated estate.

Inter vivos trusts in South Africa

In South Africa, there are basically three types of trusts. These are living trusts (in South Africa called *inter vivos trusts*), testamentary trusts and bewind trusts.

Testamentary trusts are created at the winding up of a deceased estate following a specific stipulation in the deceased person's will that a trust must be set up. Testamentary trusts are usually created to hold assets on behalf of minor children, since minor children can not in terms of South African law inherit anything (in the absence of a trust, assets from the deceased estate left to minor children are sold, and the money is paid to them when they reach adulthood). Bewind trusts are created as trading vehicles providing trustees with limited liability and certain tax advantages.

There are two types of living trusts in South Africa, namely vested trusts and discretionary trusts. In vested trusts, the benefits of the beneficiaries are set out in the trust deed, whereas in discretionary trusts the trustees have full discretion at all times as to how much and when each beneficiary is to benefit.

Parties to the trust

There are three parties in a living trust, namely the founder, the trustees and the beneficiaries. The trust is managed by the trustees for the benefit of the beneficiaries. The beneficiaries can be any legal persons, including living people, other trusts, and registered businesses. Trustees may also be beneficiaries.

Establishing a living trust

The trust is created by drafting a trust deed (usually in co-operation with an attorney specialising in trust law) and registering the trust with the local High Court. The trust becomes effective as soon as it is registered.

Asset protection

Until recently, there were tax advantages to living trusts in South Africa, although most of these advantages have fallen away with new legislation. The remaining advantage of a living trust is the protection of assets from creditors. In an ideal situation, since assets held by the trust aren't owned by the trustees or the beneficiaries, the creditors of trustees or beneficiaries can have no claim against the trust (there are exceptions). A common scenario of using living trusts for asset protection is a husband and wife acting as trustees along with a third unrelated trustee. The trust is granted a loan equal to the value of their assets, then the trust buys their assets using the loan, and finally the trust pays off the loan over time. When any of trustees die, the trust and any assets owned by it, remain unaffected.

Assets transferred into a living trust remain at risk from external creditors for 6 months if the previous owner of the assets is solvent at the time of transfer, or 24 months if he/she is insolvent at the time of transfer. After 24 months, creditors have no claim against assets in the trust, although they can attempt to attach the loan account, thereby forcing the trust to sell its assets.

Assets can be transferred into the living trust by selling it to the trust (through a loan granted to the trust) or donating cash to it (any person can donate R30 000 per year tax free; 20% donations tax applies to further donations within the year).

Tax considerations

In terms of South African tax law, living trusts are considered tax payers. Two types of tax apply to living trusts, namely income tax and capital gains tax (CGT). A trust pays income tax at a flat rate of 40% (individuals pay according to income scales, usually less than 20%). The trust's income can, however, be taxed in the hands of either the trust or the beneficiary. A trust pays CGT at the rate of 20% (individuals pay 10%). Trusts do not pay deceased estate tax (although trusts may be required to pay back outstanding loans to a deceased estate, in which the loan amounts are taxable with deceased estate tax).

The taxpayer whose residence has been "locked" in to a trust has now been given another opportunity to take advantage of these CGT exemptions. The Taxation Law Amendment Act was promulgated on 30 September 2009 and takes effect on 1 January 2010 allowing a window period of 2 (two) years from 1 January 2010 to 31 December 2011 for the opportunity of a natural person to take transfer of the residence with advantage of no transfer duty being payable or CGT consequences. Whilst taxpayers can take advantage of this opening of a window of opportunity is not likely that it will ever become available thereafter.

Source (edited): "http://en.wikipedia.org/wiki/Trust_law"

Trust law in Civil law jurisdictions

Trust law in civil law jurisdictions

Most jurisdictions that have the **trust** concept do so because their legal systems are based on the English legal system, (a common law system), where the trust was developed. As such, trusts tend to be most prevalent in Commonwealth jurisdictions.

However, at least two jurisdictions, Switzerland and Liechtenstein, are civil law jurisdictions which have "imported" the trust concept into their laws by means of statute. The basic principles of trust law in those jurisdictions are very much as set out in this article, with some variations, but the legal and intellectual underpinning of that law is entirely different.

The private foundation, if founded in a civil law jurisdiction, may be seen as a civil law equivalent of the common law trust.

Source (edited): "http://en.wikipedia.org/wiki/Trust_law_in_Civil_law_jurisdictions"

Trustee de son tort

A **trustee de son tort** is a person who may be regarded as owing fiduciary duties by a course of conduct that amounts to a wrong, or a tort. Accordingly, a trustee de son tort is not a person who is formally appointed as a trustee, but one who assumes such a role, and then cannot be heard to argue that she did not owe fiduciary duties.

Overview

Instead of prosecuting this person, the courts may hold him or her to be a constructive trustee and, thereby, impose the liabilities of an actual trustee in accounting for his or her acts.

Lewin on Trusts says at 42-74:

" If a person by mistake or otherwise assumes the character of trustee when it does not really belong to him, he becomes a trustee de son tort and he may be called to account by the beneficiaries for the money he has received " under the colour of the trust. A trustee de son tort closely resembles an express trustee. The principle is that a person who assumes an office ought not to be in a better position than if he were what he pretends; he is accountable as if he had the authority which he has assumed. While it is essential, if a person is to become a trustee de son tort, that he consciously takes the office of trustee, it does not matter whether he knows all the trusts or the extent of his powers.

Thomas and Hudson's *The Law on Trusts* says at para 30.03:

" ... trustees de son tort are not expressly declared by the settlor to be trustees but rather are deemed to be constructive trustees by operation of law,"

due to their meddling with trust affairs, they are therefore constructive trustees.

A "trustee de son tort" is to be contrasted with a delegate who is appointed by a trustee to undertake certain functions: such a person derives his authority from the trustee and is entitled to act in accordance with the delegated authority without himself becoming a trustee. A delegate, in such circumstance, has done no "wrong" and is not intermeddling in the trust and so does not become a "trustee de son tort".

The court also considered the concept of a trustee de son tort and whether an agent, appointed by a duly constituted trustee, could itself be a trustee de son tort in circumstances where the agent's actions caused loss to the trust fund.

It was argued that it was commonplace in the trust industry for the administration of a trust to be carried out largely by another company (other than the trustee) within the same group of companies as the corporate trustee. It would cause considerable surprise in the industry if such a company was to find itself designated a trustee de son tort. Because it was common practice it was important that an authoritative decision be given as to whether such an administrative company should be treated as a trustee de son tort.

Cases

- *Dubai Aluminium Company Ltd v. Salaam* UKHL 48 (5 December 2002), House of Lords (UK)
- *Barnes v Addy* (1874) LR 9 Ch App 244
- *Mara v Browne* 1 Ch 199
- *Re Barney* 2 Ch 265
- *Williams-Ashman v Price and Williams* Ch 219

Source (edited): "http://en.wikipedia.org/wiki/Trustee_de_son_tort"

Trusts & Estates (journal)

Trusts & Estates is a wealth management journal published by Penton Media. It was first published in 1904 (as a periodical called *Trust Companies*) under the direction of Christian A. Luhnow, who was the editor, publisher and owner of the magazine at the time.

Today, *Trusts & Estates* publishes articles contributed by practitioners in the fields of estate planning and taxation, fiduciary professionals, family offices, insurance, investments, philanthropy, retirement benefits and valuations. According to trustsandestates.com, articles are generally peer-reviewed by an editorial advisory board. The journal is published 12 times a year with a Wealth Management Resource Guide bonus issue in December.

History

Christian A. Luhnow founded Trust Companies in March 1904 in response to the rise of the trust banking industry in the United States. Most of the 1,300 United States trust companies then in existence had been formed in the previous 25 years. Yet, according to the magazine back then, "no other financial institutions of comparatively recent growth have made such giant strides and at the same time are so little understood outside of those immediately interested."trusts in the 1800 were used as business techniques during the industrial growth these ways were often used by large companies

Source (edited): "http://en.wikipedia.org/wiki/Trusts_%26_Estates_(journal)"

Trusts and estates

The **law of trusts and estates** is generally considered the body of law which governs the management of personal affairs and the disposition of property of an individual in anticipation of the event of such person's incapacity or death, also known as the law of successions in civil law. Its techniques are also used to fulfil the wishes of philanthropic bequests or gifts through the creation, maintenance and supervision of charitable trusts.

In some jurisdictions, such as the United States, it can overlap with the area that has come to be known as elder law that deals not only with estate planning but other issues that face the elderly, such as home care, long term care insurance or social security or disability benefits. There may also be overlap with areas of the law touching on End-of-life issues, not solely for the elderly, but also persons with terminal conditions.

Estates

In common law, an estate consisted of

the tangible assets of real and personal property which belong to a natural person. More recently, the concept of an estate has been expanded to encompass any thing of value to which the deceased person was or might have been entitled to claim during his or her lifetime. The property of the estate must either be bequeathed through a will or transferred through the laws of intestacy if there is no will. A will is the most commonly used legal instrument for the distribution of the property of a deceased person. Before property can be disposed of pursuant to the terms of a will, the will must be submitted to a probate court having jurisdiction of the estate of the deceased. Probate is often considered a relatively lengthy and expensive process, albeit one which may provide greater safeguards with regard to the rights of a deceased person's beneficiaries, though probate often is contested by creditors or disgruntled members of the family of the deceased who feel they have not received their fair share of the deceased's property.

Uses of trusts

In order to expedite the process of transferring assets to intended beneficiaries, some people choose to arrange their property so that it can bypass the probate process upon their deaths. For example, placing property into a trust before death (as opposed to a testamentary trust) will often allow the accomplishment of the objectives of property distribution without coming under the jurisdiction of a court and the possible redistribution after a lengthy contested probate process and trial. Similarly, jointly held property (in common law systems), life insurance, annuities, US Tax Code section 401(k) Retirement Plans or Individual Retirement Accounts (also known as Registered Retirement Savings Plans in Canada) will also avoid probate as these devices allow property to transfer to beneficiaries outside the probate process.

Special needs trusts are created to ensure that beneficiaries who are developmentally disabled or mentally ill can receive inheritances without losing access to essential government benefits.

Use of estates and trusts

Another major factor in trusts and estates law may be to minimize one's tax exposure. After an applicable exempt amount, the United States federal estate tax very quickly approaches 50% of one's taxable estate. The proper use of trusts may reduce one's tax burden. The applicable exempt amount is currently two million dollars in 2006. The exempt amount is scheduled to increase to three and a half million in 2009, after which the estate tax is temporarily repealed for one year in 2010. The year after, the estate tax is scheduled to be reinstated, with the previous exemption of one million dollars.

Trusts may also allow people a certain limited amount of control of how the amount held by the trust is handled. For example, one could leave money for somebody who may not be mature enough to handle money, and state that the money can only be used for health, education, support and maintenance of that person until the age of 35, upon which time the remaining income and principal will be distributed. One can also distribute one's assets to charitable purposes by creating an irrevocable charitable trust that may distribute the principal or the income of the trust much in the same manner as a private foundation.

Source (edited): "http://en.wikipedia.org/wiki/Trusts_and_estates"

Trusts of Land and Appointment of Trustees Act 1996

The **Trusts of Land and Appointment of Trustees Act 1996** (abbreviated as 'TOLATA') is an Act of Parliament of the United Kingdom, which altered the law in relation to trusts of land in England, Wales, Scotland and Northern Ireland.

Background

TOLATA 1996 came into force on 1 January 1997 and was a result of a recognised need for reform in the part of the Law of Property Act 1925 which dealt with trusts. Some problems included the fact that it was hard to establish a trust without it coming under the auspices of the Settled Land Act 1925, which brought with it a range of problems. In particular, the co-owners of property were regarded as having beneficial interests in money and not in the land. Problems arose where partners disagreed over when they wanted to sell a property - usually in the case of separation, and this led to situations where spouses and children might find themselves homeless.

One of the key features of TOLATA was to try and redress the problem above by the imposition of statutory considerations which had to be taken into account when dealing with the disposition of trusts and ordering a sale of the family home.

Requirements

Particularly notable requirements come from two parts of the legislation, firstly section 14 and more importantly 15, where the requirements for consideration in determining applications are dealt with. Secondly, the imposition of section 335a in the Insolvency Act 1986.

Section 15

- The matters to which the court is to have regard in determining an application for an order under section 14 include -
  - the intentions of the person or persons (if any) who created the trust.
  - the purposes for which the property subject to the trust is held,
  - the welfare of any minor who occupies or might reasonably be expected to occupy any land subject to the trust as his home, and
  - the interest of any secured creditor of any beneficiary.

Insolvency Act 1986, S. 335a

(3) Where such an application is made after the end of the period of one year beginning with the first vesting under chapter IV of this part of the bankrupt's estate in a trustee, the court shall assume, unless the circumstances of the case are exceptional, that the interests of the bankrupt's creditors outweigh all other considerations.

Case Law
In 2001, in the Case of *Re Shaire*, Neuberger J assessed the requirements of TOLATA in the light of the case before him and stated that the statute had intended "to tip the balance somewhat more in favour of families and against banks and other charges", when assessing a claim.

Source (edited): "http://en.wikipedia.org/wiki/Trusts_of_Land_and_Appointment_of_Trustees_Act_1996"

Undue influence

Undue influence (as a term in jurisprudence) is an equitable doctrine that involves one person taking advantage of a position of power over another person. It is where free will to bargain is not possible.

Undue influence in contract law
If undue influence is proved in a contract, in U.S. law, the contract is voidable by the innocent party, and the remedy is rescission. There are two categories to consider:
- Presumed undue influence
- Actual undue influence

Presumed undue influence

First subgroup
In the first subgroup, the relationship falls in a class of relationships that as a matter of law will raise a presumption of undue influence. Such classes include:
- Government/People
- Parent/child
- Guardian/ward
- Priest/member of parish
- Solicitor (attorney)/client
- Doctor/patient

In such cases, the onus of proof lies on a doctor, say, to disprove undue influence on a patient.

Second subgroup
The second subgroup covers relationships that do not fall into the first subgroup, but on the facts of case, there was an antecedent relationship between the parties that led to undue influence. The test is one of whether there was a relationship of such trust and confidence that it should give rise to such a presumption (see *Johnson v. Buttress* (1936) 56 CLR 113).

In *Garcia v National Australia Bank* (1998) 194 CLR 395, the High Court of Australia distinguished between cases of actual undue influence and situations where the transaction is set aside because the guarantor does not understand the nature of the transaction. Although there is no presumption of undue influence, a "lender is to be taken to have understood that, as a wife, the surety may repose trust and confidence in her husband in matters of business and therefore to have understood that the husband may not fully and accurately explain the purport and effect of the transaction to his wife; and yet... did not itself take steps to explain the transaction to the wife or find out that a stranger had explained it to her."

Actual undue influence

An innocent party may also seek to have a contract set aside for actual undue influence, where there is no presumption of undue influence, but there is evidence that the power was unbalanced at the time of the signing of the contract.

Undue influence in probate law
"Undue influence" is the most common ground for will contests and are often accompanied by a capacity challenge. In probate law, it is generally defined as a testator's loss of free agency regarding property disposition through contemporaneous psychological domination by an advisor which results in an excessive benefit to the advisor. It is important to note that "undue influence" is only an issue when the advisor is benefiting, not when advisor is getting a benefit for someone else; in that case it would be considered fraud. In litigation most jurisdictions place the burden of proving undue influence on the party challenging the will.

Source (edited): "http://en.wikipedia.org/wiki/Undue_influence"

Uniform Probate Code

The **Uniform Probate Code** (commonly abbreviated **UPC**) is a uniform act drafted by National Conference of Commissioners on Uniform State Laws (NCCUSL) governing inheritance and the decedents' estates in the United States. The primary purposes of the act were to streamline the probate process and to standardize and modernize the various state laws governing wills, trusts, and intestacy.

History of the Uniform Probate Code
Drafting of the Uniform Probate Code began in 1964. The final version of the original UPC was promulgated in 1969 as a joint project between NCCUSL and the Real Property, Probate and Trust Law Section of the American Bar Association. Richard V. Wellman served as Chief Reporter on the project. The UPC has been revised several times, most recently in 2006.

Adoption by the states
Although the UPC was intended for

adoption by all 50 states, the original 1969 version of the code was adopted in its entirety by only sixteen states: Alaska, Arizona, Colorado, Florida, Hawaii, Idaho, Maine, Michigan, Minnesota, Montana, Nebraska, New Mexico, North Dakota, South Carolina, South Dakota, and Utah. The remaining states have adopted various portions of the code in a piecemeal fashion. In any case, even among the adopting jurisdictions, there are variations from state to state, some of which are significant. A person attempting to determine the law in a particular state should check the code *as actually adopted* in that jurisdiction and not rely on the text of the UPC as promulgated by NCCUSL. In general, the UPC has not been as successful a standardization of the law as the Uniform Commercial Code has been.

In *Payne v. Stalley*, 672 So. 2d 822 (Fla. 2d DCA 1995), a lawyer relied on the official text of the Uniform Probate Code and failed to check the statute as it had been adopted in Florida. As a result, the lawyer missed a filing deadline on a $3,760,909.49 claim. As the Florida appellate court pointed out, "[w]e cannot rewrite Florida probate law to accommodate a Michigan attorney more familiar with the Uniform Probate Code." Id. at 823.

Basic outline of the Uniform Probate Code

The UPC has seven articles, each covering a different set of rules for this area of the law:

Source (edited): "http://en.wikipedia.org/wiki/Uniform_Probate_Code"

Uniform Simultaneous Death Act

The **Uniform Simultaneous Death Act** is a uniform act enacted in some U.S. states to alleviate the problem of simultaneous death in determining inheritance. The Act specifies that, if two or more people die within 120 hours of one another, each is considered to have predeceased the others. When a will or other document provides for this situation explicitly, the Act does not apply.

The Act was promulgated in 1940, when it was adopted by 49 states. It was last amended in 1993. As of 2010, 19 states (Alaska, Arizona, Arkansas, Colorado, Hawaii, Kansas, Kentucky, Massachusetts, Montana, New Hampshire, New Mexico, North Carolina, North Dakota, Ohio, Oregon, South Dakota, Utah, Virginia, and Wisconsin) and the District of Columbia have explicitly adopted the Act in its current version. A number of other states have indirectly adopted the Act as part of the Uniform Probate Code. The Virgin Islands adopted the Act in 2010.

Inheritance

The Act primarily helps to determine the heirs of a person who has died intestate. For example, Alice and Bob are a married, retired couple with no offspring. They die in a plane crash, and it cannot be determined which person died first. Neither had executed a will, so both Alice's and Bob's families claim inheritance of the couple's estate. The court uses the Uniform Simultaneous Death Act to resolve the dispute. In accordance with the Act, Alice is considered to have predeceased Bob, but Bob is also considered to have predeceased Alice. The inheritance is divided equally among their closest living relatives, according to degree of kinship.

The 120-hour period is intended to simplify estate administration by preventing an inheritance from being transferred more times than necessary. For example, assume that the Act does not exist. Alice dies immediately, but Bob dies in the hospital the next day. Because Bob outlives Alice, he would inherit her estate, and Bob's heirs would inherit the combined estate the next day. This would increase the legal costs involved, and cause Alice's estate to be subject to tax twice: once alone, and once as part of Bob's. However, if tax was paid in Alice's estate, Bob's would receive a Federal Estate Tax credit for the same property transferred by Alice (state death and inheritance tax provisions may differ). Under the Act, neither inherits the other's estate, each is taxed separately, and their heirs inherit both estates once.

Insurance

The Act may also help to resolve a life insurance case where the insured and beneficiary die in a common disaster. Different rules apply for insurance. For example, Carol has a life insurance policy through her employer. Her husband Dave is its beneficiary. They are both killed in a car crash, dying at or near the same time. If Carol has named a secondary beneficiary in her policy, that person will receive the life insurance benefit. If Carol has not named a secondary beneficiary, then it is assumed that she outlived Dave, and the benefit is inherited through Carol's estate.

Source (edited): "http://en.wikipedia.org/wiki/Uniform_Simultaneous_Death_Act"

Unit Valuation System

The **Unit Valuation System** (UVS) was developed by Mutual Funds and Unit Trusts, as a means of determining fund performance in an environment where there are frequent cash contributions and withdrawals. The UVS is commonly used by Investment Clubs to apportion ownership between Investment Club members, however it can also be used by individual investors as a time weighted return metric. UVS is now commonly used by Investment Clubs as it enables club members to make flexible monthly contributions (subscriptions) and withdrawals through the process of purchasing and cancelling units.

Purpose

UVS is a time weighted performance metric that is used by Investment Clubs to apportion ownership between Investment Club members. It enables club members to make flexible monthly contributions (subscriptions) and withdrawals through the process of purchasing and cancelling units. As a performance metric the Unit Valuation System strength lies in the ability to apportion ownership at any point in time, as club members buy and sell units through making subscriptions and withdrawals. It is an effective means of reflecting changes between day to day investment performance, however it should not be used as a metric for comparing investment performance between for example two Investment Clubs.

When comparing performance Money Weighted metrics, it is recommended that you use Internal Rate of Return calculations.

Implementation

The equation for calculating Unit Value is based on net assets (which are included in the UVS calculations) divided by the number of allocated units:

$$\text{Unit Value} = \frac{\text{Market value of Investments} + \text{Other Assets} + \text{Income} - \text{Liabilities} - \text{Expenses}}{\text{Number of allocated units}}$$

Investment Club member subscriptions (or from an individual perspective, 'deposits') are used to 'buy units' based on the current unit value and if a club member wants to make a withdrawal, they then 'sell units' typically through a process referred to as 'unit cancellation' based on the current unit value. Unit Cancellation can also be applied to trading expenses such as subscriptions to real time data or charting packages, in order for the Unit Value to only reflect trading performance.

Consider an Investment Club with 10 member, who normally contribute £100 in monthly subscriptions to their Investment Club fund. We are going to focus on one member of the club called 'Joe Bloggs'. If you take a look at the following table it provides an overview of the club's performance over time:

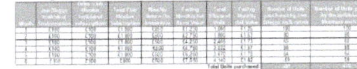

For the first 5 months, each club member contributes and equal amount of money and as the club performance increases and decrease, the unit value changes accordingly.

At the start of the first month, each member contributed £100, which is a total subscription of £1,000. The starting unit value was set to £1 by the club members, therefore the number of units allocated to each member was 100 (i.e. each club members monthly subscription divided by the unit value). The club then invested the £1,000 and the end of the first month made a return on investment of £250, therefore increasing the club Net Asset Value to £1,250. At the end of the first month the unit value has now increased because the Net Asset Value has increased. The resulting Unit Value is increased from £1 to £1.25 (i.e. the end of month Net Asset Value divided by the number of allocated units = £1,250 / 1,000 = £1.25).

At the start of the second month, each of the club members contribute a further £100 each, which increases the Net Asset Value by £1,000. This time they receive less unit for their £100 contribution as the unit value has increased from £1 to £1.25. The number of units that they get for their monthly subscription of £100 is 80 units, which is determined by dividing the subscription contribution by the unit value i.e. £100 / £1.25 = 80 units.

In the third, fourth and fifth month each club member continues to contribute £100 per month and the number of units that get is based on the previous ending monthly Unit Value.

At the start of the sixth month, Joe Bloggs decides to withdraw £100 from the investment club when the unit value is £1.70. To do so he 'sells' units back to the club, who in turn cancel the units. To withdraw £100 Joe Bloggs must sell approximately 59 units at a price of £1.70 per unit. As the Net Asset Value is reduced by £100 and the number of allocated units is reduced by 59 units due to the process of unit cancellation, with the result being that the unit value remains consistent at £1.70 (i.e. the ending Net Asset Value in month 5 is reduced £100 from £6,250 to £6,150 and the number of units are reduced by 59 due to member withdrawal of £100 therefore reducing the total number of units from 3,670 to 3,611; the resulting unit value is then unchanged because £6,250/3,670 units = £6,150/3,611 units = £1.70)

Unit Cancellation

Unit Cancellation is typically used for withdrawals and when you want to exclude none tax deductible expenses from Unit Value calculations.

The exclusion of none tax deductible expenses ensure that the Unit Value calculations are only based on investment performance. Unit Value is determined by the total assets divided by the number of units allocated. If you deduct a none trading expense from the total assets, without changing the number of allocated units, then the unit value will be reduced. This would have the side effect of making the investment performance appear to have decreased - whereas you may have simply elected to use funds for some common purpose, such as an annual meal.

To ensure that unit value remains consistent after a withdrawal or after the payment of an expenses, a commonly used solution to this problem is to cancel a number of allocated units, such that the number of allocated units is reduced in line with the reduced value of the club assets. The net effect being that the Unit Value remains constant.

If you do not want to include income or expenditures transactions in the calculation of the unit value you can either:

- set up a separate Ledger that is not included in the UVS calculations, such as a Petty Cash Ledger
- or you can exclude specific income or expenditure transactions from a Ledger that is included in the Unit Value calculations

Given the complexity of these calcuations most investment clubs use investment club accounting software.

When using unit cancellation on a transaction, the transaction is ignored for the purposes of calculating the Unit Value, but still considered when calculating the club's total assets. As the assets and Unit Value remain unchanged after a transaction is exclude through the process of unit cancellation, the number of units can therefore be derived. This has the effect of removing (or cancelling) a number of units from the club's accounts. Each member's units are therefore decreased by an equal amount during unit cancellation. Source (edited): "http://en.wikipedia.org/wiki/Unit_Valuation_System"

United States trust law

United States trust law is the body of law regulating the legal instrument for holding wealth known as a trust.

Most law regulating the creation and administration of trusts in the United States is now statutory at the state level. In August 2004, the National Conference of Commissioners on Uniform State Laws created the first attempt to codify generally accepted common law principles in Anglo-American law regarding trusts into a uniform statutory code for the fifty states, called the Uniform Trust Code (UTC). As of October 2009, 24 states have adopted some substantive form of the UTC with three others having introduced it into the legislature for adoption. The goal of the uniform law is to standardize the law of trusts to a greater extent, given their increased use as a substitute for the "last will and testament" as the primary estate planning mechanism for the affluent.

Despite the uniform law, however, differences remain, as states still harbor rich differences in fiduciary law. It has been a common practice of American lawyers for the past 150 years or so to choose the law of Massachusetts to govern the disposition of property conveyed in trust. In the absence of a nationally uniform law, their justification was that the courts of Massachusetts ruled on trust questions with far greater experience and authority than any other State (much like choosing corporate law in Delaware for a new company). Each state adopting the UTC has incorporated changes to their version of the Code, reflecting certain peculiar or long-standing exceptions in their own state's law that legislators intend to preserve.

Overview

Trusts are essentially creatures of contract. Virtually all trusts are made in written form, either through an *inter vivos* or "living trust" instrument (created while the settlor is living) or in a will (which creates a testamentary trust). Therefore, in understanding certain terms in a trust, general rules of construction regarding interpretation of wills or other testamentary documents will apply. Subject to certain fundamental requirements of trusts, the UTC generally states that the terms of a trust instrument as written by the settlor will control over the "default rules" of the UTC. Where a document does **not** contain a provision that is otherwise covered by the UTC's default rules, the UTC will control.

Where a document contains obnoxious, unworkable, impractical, or outdated language, the beneficiaries and trustees have recourse to local courts having general jurisdiction in equity – most commonly for a declaratory judgment, judicial construction or reformation of the trust to bring it into compliance with the original intent of the settlor. Also, the court may be called upon to deal with circumstances not imaginable by the settlor at the time the trust was created to make the trust *cy pres* or as close as possible to the original intent.

Trusts are a special breed of contract in that they often govern the disposition of property in the same way a "last will and testament" does via a probate proceeding. Many states differ as to their procedures concerning the interpretation and administration of trusts created during life (i.e., the *inter vivos* trust) versus those created in a will which are typically subject to jurisdiction in probate proceedings (the testamentary trust). The UTC attempts to standardize the general *composition* of both trust forms and their requirements, but does not generally attempt to address the *procedural* questions as to overall subject-matter jurisdiction and other aspects of proceedings involving trusts. Instead, the vagaries of various state and local procedural rules will generally apply.

When titling property or otherwise referring to an existing trust, practitioners persist in referring to trusts as "Tr. u/a" (trusts under agreement, i.e. inter vivos trusts) or "Tr. u/w" (trusts under will, i.e. testamentary trusts. Industry convention is for the settlor's name to appear in the title. In the USA, the name follows a shorthand for the type of instrument. Hence: "Tr. u/a John Smith FBO Alma Smith" or, if appropriate, "Tr. u/a John Smith FBO Alma Smith irrevocable" (FBO means for benefit of). Titles also frequently include more information such as the existence of more than one trustee ("Co-tr. u/a John Smith": "co-tr" means co-trustee) or that one or more of the trustees are not the original trustee (Successor Co-Tr. u/a John Smith).

In understanding American trust law, it is helpful to understanding the terminology and definitions of various terms as they relate to trusts. The following section contains a discussion of some of these terms.

The "three characters" in the play

A trust generally involves three "persons" in its creation and administration: (A) a settlor or grantor who creates the trust; (B) a trustee who administers and manages the trust and its assets; and (C) a beneficiary who receives the benefit of the administered property in the trust. In many instances where a revocable living trust is involved, one person can serve as grantor, trustee and beneficiary simultaneously until they die. In many other instances, especially after the death of the initial grantor, there will be different persons named to be trustee(s) or beneficiary(ies). There can be more than one of any of these "persons" in a trust at any one time.

The settlor/grantor
Strictly speaking, the Grantor of a trust is merely the person creating the trust, usually by executing a trust agreement which details the terms and conditions of the trust. Such a trust can be ***revocable*** or ***irrevocable***. A revocable trust is one in which the settlor retains the ability to alter, change or even revoke the trust at any time and remove funds from it at any time. It is sometimes also referred to as a grantor trust. *See below.* Unlike under older common law rules, the Uniform Trust Code presumes that all trusts are revocable unless the terms of the trust specifically state otherwise. Generally, the Grantor is also the one charged with funding the initial assets into the trust, either through an instrument (i.e., deed, security certificates, accounts retitled into the trust's name) or by a declaration (i.e., for tangible personal property without a formal title).

From both a historical and practical perspective, trusts have generally been designed to have only one Settlor or Grantor. This is due to the complications that can arise, particularly in non-community property jurisdictions, in determining the nature of property deposited into the trust and the proportionality of the multiple grantors' contributions within it. However, a growing trend for husbands and wives is to create "joint trusts" where both are "grantors" of the trust, thus mirroring the familiar concept of joint tenancy ownership.

For a revocable trust, the grantor retains the power to direct transactions for the trust, even if a third party serves as the trustee. This may even include situations where there may be a conflict in the grantor's direction and the actual terms of the trust. In an irrevocable trust, there has developed a growing use of a so-called **trust protector**. This is generally an unaffiliated, third party (often a lawyer or an accountant) who is granted the power to amend or change the terms of the trust in order to accommodate unexpected changes in tax or fiduciary law, unexpected changes in the trust's circumstances or other contingencies. The Code permits the use of such third parties to amend or alter even an irrevocable trust. The trustee is to act in accordance with such powers unless "the attempted exercise is manifestly contrary to the terms of the trust or the trustee knows the attempted exercise would constitute a serious breach of a fiduciary duty that the person holding the power owes to the beneficiaries of the trust." Furthermore, the Code assumes such trust protectors act in a fiduciary capacity and must act in good faith with respect to the trust's purposes and the best interests of the beneficiaries.

The term "grantor trust" also has a special meaning in tax law. A grantor trust is defined under the Internal Revenue Code as one in which the federal income tax consequences of the trust's investment activities are entirely the responsibility of the grantor or another individual who has unfettered power to take out all the assets. Unlike other trusts, the grantor trust completely passes through **all** income tax consequences of transactions inside the trust and the trust itself is a virtual shell. This is generally favorable in the current tax climate since in most cases less income will be taxed when a trust is treated as a "grantor trust."

The trustee
Trustees are the persons appointed to manage all duties required for the trust to function. In most cases, the acting trustee (and the successor to that trustee in the event the trustee can no longer serve) is named specifically in the trust instrument. A person nominated as a trustee can decline to serve as a trustee or if serving may choose to resign as a trustee upon notice to the trust's beneficiaries. Also, in some instances, the trust instrument can specify that trustees can be removed. Any Grantor of a revocable trust would implicitly hold this power with a third-party trustee, given their power to amend or revoke the trust. In an irrevocable trust, the trust instrument may, in some instances, grant the beneficiaries a power to remove a trustee by a majority vote. Absent this provision, in most UTC jurisdictions, other co-trustees or beneficiaries can remove a trustee only by court action. However, the threshold for removal under the UTC is not substantial. In most cases, all the court must find is that there has been a "substantial change in circumstances" in which removal would "best [serve] the interests of all of the beneficiaries and is not inconsistent with a material purpose of the trust, and a suitable cotrustee or successor trustee is available."

A trust can have one trustee or many. In the event of multiple trustees, the older common law rules required that all trustees act unanimously. The modern rule reflected in the UTC permits co-trustees to act by majority vote. Where a co-trustee is unable to be actively involved in the management of the trust due to age or illness, the remaining co-trustees can generally act on behalf of the trust "to achieve the purposes of the trust or to avoid injury to the trust property." However, it is generally better practice for the co-trustee either to resign or to otherwise delegate his decision-making functions while incapacitated to one or all of the remaining co-trustees. A trustee who dissents from acting in a certain way with his fellow co-trustees is protected under the Code from liability provided the trustee has indicated his dissent and only acts based on the direction of the majority co-trustees. In practical terms, the use of co-trustees can often become unwieldy. The Code generally notes this and advises great care for attorneys who draft documents that use multiple co-trustees.

Trustees may be competent individuals or state or federally chartered corporations with trust powers (usually banks or trust companies). Typically corporate trustees will have integrated their fiduciary organization into their investment management or private banking groups. It is not unusual for an individual to serve as trustee alongside a bank trustee. Both individual and corporate trustees may charge fees for their services, although individual trustees typically serve *gratis* when they are part of the settlor's family or the settlor him/herself. The term "co-trustee" may fool either the bank trust officer or the individual co-trustee into thinking their roles are identical. If the roles are not further defined in the document, then their roles are legally the same. As a practical matter however, the corporate trustee will nearly always do the custody work and keep the books. But many documents will give the individual co-trustee powers that differ from the corporate trustees. For example, the individual co-trustee's rights and duties may be limited to dealing with discretionary distributions of principal and income, sale of a personal residence held in the trust, or sale of a "heartstring asset."

All trustees have several fundamental duties and responsibilities imposed by the Code and general principles of longstanding common law. The following is a brief description of these duties as enunciated in the Uniform Trust Code and how they generally apply in the actual administration of a trust by the trustees.

Duty of prudent administration

It goes without saying that the trustees essentially "run" the trust. They are responsible to collect trust assets, collect receipts from trust investments, pay required expenses of the trust, enforce and defend claims on its behalf, determine what amount (if any) to distribute to beneficiaries as provided under the trust agreement, properly make a record of such receipts and disbursements, and many other tasks. The UTC generally states that trustees must conduct these activities in "good faith, in accordance with its terms and purposes and the interests of the beneficiaries, and in accordance with this [Code]." Trustees cannot act (or omit to act) if the trust's purposes are illegal, impossible to achieve or else against public policy. The standard for a trustee actions under the UTC is that a trustee must act "as a prudent person would, by considering the purposes, terms, distributional requirements, and other circumstances of the trust." In satisfying this standard, the trustee must exercise reasonable care, skill, and caution.

One of the most important responsibilities for a trustee is to prudently manage the trust's assets. The Uniform Trust Code presumes that trustees will be held to the same standard as that adopted by the Uniform Law Commissioners in the Prudent Investor Act [UPIA]. A trustee must invest and manage trust assets as a "prudent investor" would, by considering the purposes, terms, distribution requirements, and other circumstances of the trust. In satisfying this standard, the trustee shall exercise reasonable care, skill, and caution. The UPIA adopts a very holistic approach to the standards of what constitutes "prudent investing." The trustee's conduct is not to be reviewed on the basis of any one decision or one investment holding, but on the portfolio and its management as a whole. No particular investment is considered "off limits" due to some intrinsic risk inherent in it – the key is whether such individual investments are part of a trust portfolio that fits an overarching strategy "having risk and return objectives reasonably suited to the trust." Also, the trustee is not expected to have a "crystal ball" to predict outcomes with respects to specific decisions. As the UPIA states, "Compliance with the prudent investor rule is determined in light of the facts and circumstances existing at the time of a trustee's decision or action and not by hindsight." Among the factors a trustee may consider in formulating the investment strategy and the asset portfolio are (1) general economic conditions; (2) the possible effect of inflation or deflation; (3) the expected tax consequences of investment decisions or strategies;(4) the role that each investment or course of action plays within the overall trust portfolio, which may include financial assets, interests in closely held enterprises, tangible and intangible personal property, and real property; (5) the expected total return from income and the appreciation of capital;(6) other resources of the beneficiaries; (7) needs for liquidity, regularity of income, and preservation or appreciation of capital; and (8) an asset's special relationship or special value, if any, to the purposes of the trust or to one or more of the beneficiaries."

One of the primary guiding forces in the UPIA is the emergence of modern portfolio theory and the concept of correlations in the performance of various asset classes. For example, in most cases, it is established that stocks and bonds have low correlations in terms of performance in a given timeframe. This means that when stocks are better than average in performance, bonds perform lower than average. The converse is also true. This concept of correlation allows for diversification of a portfolio so that a portfolio can perform more consistently in various economic climate by having a variety of asset classes, in specific proportions, in the trust portfolio. The UPIA's default rule mandates to a trustee that he or she diversify a trust portfolio "unless the trustee reasonably determines that, because of special circumstances, the purposes of the trust are better served without diversifying." The UPIA also states that trustees should invest impartially without favoritism to one class of beneficiaries over another (i.e., beneficiaries receiving current income versus beneficiaries receiving principal from the trust at its termination.)."

If a trustee has special skills or expertise, or is named trustee in reliance upon the trustee's representation that the trustee has special skills or expertise, he or she must use them. In many cases, a trustee, particularly an individual, who may not have certain expertise in various areas (i.e., investing, real estate management, ongoing business management, etc.) may wish to use an agent who is an expert and delegate authority to that expert as to certain incidentals of trust administration. The Code permits this, provided that: (a) the task is one a prudent trustee of comparable skills could properly delegate under the circumstances; (b) the trustee prudently selects the agent, setting the proper scope and function of the agent's task; and (c) periodically monitors the agent's performance and compliance with his or her duties. Once appropriately delegated under Section 807(a), the duty to exercise reasonable care in performing that function then shifts from the trustee to the agent, and the trustee is no longer liable for any act or omission undertaken by the agent.

Many trusts provide for trustees to use discretion in the distribution of trust assets to beneficiaries. Often, if the grantor is particularly wary of the spendthrift nature of the beneficiaries, he or she may give the trustee extremely broad powers to distribute or not distribute funds. Notwithstanding such broad terms, however, the UTC generally requires trustees to exercise such discretionary powers in "good faith and in accordance with the terms and purposes of the trust and the interests of the beneficiaries."

Duty of loyalty

One of the oldest and most venerated duties of trustees has been to avoid "conflicts of interest." Centuries of English and American common law have detailed the rules for trustees to avoid both direct conflicts and to avoid "appearances of impropriety" that might compromise the fiduciary's standing as an impartial decision-maker for the beneficiaries. The trustees should administer the trust for the sole benefit of the beneficiaries, against all others who might seek to benefit or profit from trust assets.

The first cardinal principle is that the trustee should not personally profit form any transactions that occur with respect to trust property. This is generally been referred to in the common law as the "no further inquiry" rule, meaning that transactions entered into by a trustee for a trustee's own account are presumed suspect with "no further inquiry" and are considered voidable upon an action by the beneficiaries.

Furthermore, if trustee exercises "significant influence over the beneficiary and from which the trustee obtains an advantage" in a transaction, even if it does not concern trust property, the trustee can be held liable for violating his or her prime duty of loyalty to act solely for the trust and its beneficiaries. This usually involves business transactions outside of the trust relationship but again may have the "appearance of impropriety" due to the trustee's power over assets to which the beneficiary may have a right. The trustee can generally overcome the appearance by fully disclosing the transaction, take no advantage of his trustee position, and show that the objective facts of the transaction appear fair and reasonable to all parties. Trustees also cannot take advantage of their superior knowledge or an opportunity discovered during their tenure as a trustee to profit themselves on their own account in most situations.

This prime rule has been gradually moderated over time, based on the law's recognition that in many cases, corporate trustees engage in transactions **necessarily** because they are in a for-profit business. Thus exceptions have crept increasingly into the general rule. Thus, a trustee can be exonerated from the "self-dealing" rules on property in situations where: (1) the transaction was authorized by the terms of the trust; (2) the transaction was approved by the court;(3) the beneficiary did not commence a judicial proceeding within the time allowed under statutes of limitation; (4) the beneficiary somehow consented to the trustee's conduct, ratified the transaction, or released the trustee; or (5) the transaction involves a contract entered into or claim acquired by the trustee before the person became or contemplated becoming trustee. In addition, for corporate trustees, if the trustee utilizes mutual funds or common trust funds in which they are compensated for managing the fund (as well as a customary trustees fee), such arrangements are **not** considered conflicts of interest provided there is full disclosure to the beneficiaries of the relationship. Finally, the Code does not consider certain transactions precluded under the Code solely because they involve "others" to the possible detriment of the beneficiaries. These can include a corporate trustee that conducts transactions with other trusts in which the entity may also be a trustee, the executor of an estate or other fiduciary. All that would be required is that the transactions appear fair and reasonable to all parties.

As part of the duty of loyalty, trustees also have a duty to act impartially with respect to trust beneficiaries. If a trust has two or more beneficiaries, the trustee shall act impartially in investing, managing, and distributing the trust property, giving due regard to the beneficiaries' respective interests.

Duty to keep records and report

Trustees are required to keep beneficiaries reasonably informed about the administration of the trust and of the material facts necessary for them to protect their interests. If a beneficiary asks for information, the trustee is charged to give it (unless the request is somehow unreasonable under the circumstances). This includes providing the beneficiary a copy of the trust agreement, notice of the acceptance or change of trustee and the contact information for the trustee, notice that a trust has become irrevocable due to the grantor's death, and any changes in the trustee's rate of compensation.

The trustee must also keep adequate records of the administration of the trust generally. All trust property must stay separate from the trustee's own personal property and must not be "commingled." A trustee **can** hold certain securities, usually publicly traded ones, in a "street name" or nominee registration for ease of management. However, they are still subject to the rule that such securities must be "earmarked" specifically in records to a specific trust account.

The beneficiaries

The generic term "beneficiary" under the Uniform Trust Code is defined as a person that (A) has a present or future beneficial interest in a trust, vested or contingent; or (B) in a capacity other than that of trustee, holds a power of appointment over trust property. Beneficiaries are the holders of "equitable title" of trust assets and receive the benefits of trust property, subject to the trustee's "legal title" ownership and control under the terms of the trust agreement as established by the grantor.

The Code makes a distinction between certain classes of beneficiaries with respect to the traditional reporting requirements for trustees with respect to the assets and transactions actually held in the trust. Under the older common law, only **current** beneficiaries (sometimes termed "income beneficiaries") were entitled to receive reports or accountings of trust transactions and that such reports were sufficient to protect the interest of those current beneficiaries. However, the Code has now permitted "**qualified beneficiaries**" to at least be informed of their right to receive a trustee's periodic report of trust transactions and assets and are entitled to receive it if they do in fact request it. "Qualified beneficiaries" are defined as a beneficiary who, on the date the beneficiary's qualification is determined: (A) is a distributee or permissible distributee of trust income or principal; (B) would **become** a distributee or permissible distributee of trust income or principal if a present distributees' interest ended on that date without causing the trust to terminate; or (C) would become a distributee or permissible distributee of trust income or principal if the trust **did** terminate on that date. Essentially, this means that **future** beneficiaries (i.e., children or grandchildren) might be exposed to information that the grantor only intended to pass to the **current** beneficiaries. Although the UTC limited the reporting requirements to trustees accepting duties after the Code's enactment, a number of states have changed the standard UTC language, often in response to concerns from corporate trustees of the unwieldiness of such requirements and the danger that future trust beneficiaries may interfere and create contention concerning the operation of the trust.

Purposes of a trust

The purposes and uses of trusts historically had to do with management of property in absence of owner, mostly during medieval times when a lord left to fight in battle. Gradually, the device also found usefulness to control property "beyond the grave", although the so-called Rule Against Perpetuities limited this power. *See* trust law#History. In modern times in the United States, trusts have several principal purposes.

Asset management

Trusts are generally unique in that they can provide comprehensive asset management for multiple family generations over great spans of time, something which other estate planning devices cannot completely replicate. Trusts can hold title to a virtually inifinite number and type of disparate assets, from publicly traded securities, to illiquid closely-held business interests, to real estate, to even collectibles and tangible personal property. Unlike other methods of transferring title, the trust allows continued management of the assets, despite the infirmity or even death of the owner – allowing them to specify to successor trustees exactly how to manage the property and use it for the future beneficiaries. This can extend for multiple generations or even, in some jurisdictions, in perpetuity (as some states have permitted in some instances the creation of trusts that can last beyond the Rule Against Perpetuities).

The third-party management of property for the benefit of another is especially valuable for persons who have some form of incapacity, infirmity or are simply unwise with the use of money. Many create trusts to protect family members from themselves. It is not unusual to see a will in which four children get funds free of trust or any other encumbrances from their father but a fifth child's funds are all or mostly placed in trust. This is usually for good cause – drug abuse, demonstrated inability to hold onto money, fear of divorce, criminal activity, a wish to see the funds go to grandchildren rather than one's own children, etc. Such trusts help to conserve assets for the longer term needs of such individuals and help to slow or eliminate the "wasting" of assets through unwise purchases or losses.

In addition, the trustees' powers over the assets can be incredibly broad and flexible and do not require the supervisory eye of a court (and the attendant additional cost such oversight can create). Particularly in cases where a corporate trustee is used, the grantor and subsequent beneficiaries receive the benefits of a vast array of financial services – portfolio management, real estate and business management, bill paying, insurance claim processing, tax and legal assistance, and financial planning just to name a few.

Revocable living trusts were often touted and marketed as valuable **solely** because of their ability to "avoid probate" and the costs and complications that surrounded it. Although probate avoidance is certainly a consideration in the use of a "living trust", there are many other estate planning techniques which also "avoid" probate. Typically however, such alternatives do not provide the kind of consolidated asset management that a trust can. Although trusts are certainly not for everyone in the context of estate planning, even persons with modest net worths often find the living trust an ideal planning tool.

Estate tax avoidance

Trusts are often created pursuant to an estate plan for wealthy individuals to avoid the onerous effects of the federal estate tax. Under current federal estate tax law, in 2008, individuals that own interests in **any** property (individually owned, jointly held, or otherwise) which exceeds a fair market value of $2 million is subject to the estate tax at death; in 2009, the amount is $3.5 million. In 2010 there is no federal estate tax unless Congress acts. An estate that exceeds that value will pay tax on that excess at a rate of **45%** under current law. Naturally, this rate is a huge inducement among many with substantial wealth to use various estate planning devices to reduce or eliminate the effect of the tax for their family. Below is a brief summary of certain specific techniques that employ trusts as the vehicle for achieving such savings.

The credit shelter trust

The credit shelter trust is by far the most common device used to extend the $2 million applicable credit ($3.5 million in 2009) for married couples. In this technique, each spouse creates a trust and divides their assets (usually evenly) between the two trusts. The terms of the credit shelter trust provide that upon the first spouse's death, the other is left an amount in trust for the benefit of the surviving spouse up to the current federal exemption equivalent to the federal estate tax. Thus an individual would leave, say, $2 million in trust for his wife (keep the $2 million out of her estate), give his widow the net income from his trust, and leave the remaining corpus to his children at her death. The Internal Revenue Code does not consider the assets in the first spouse's trust includible in the surviving spouse's estate at death for estate tax purposes, because the spouse's rights to the principal of the "credit shelter" trust do not constitute full ownership of the trust assets. In essence, this allows the couple to now shelter $4 million in assets rather than just $2 million (at the death of the second spouse).

The "Credit Shelter Trust" can permit the surviving spouse to also access principal from the trust. However, the IRS generally limits this power to distribute principal only for the "health, education, maintenance or support" of the surviving spouse. This language is relatively broad in its practical application; however, the IRS has agreed it is a sufficient limitation to allow the "credit shelter" trust not to be counted in the estate of the second spouse when she dies.

An additional benefit of the "credit shelter" is that future appreciation of trust assets passes on to the future beneficiaries (i.e., children or grandchildren) free of the estate tax. So, for example, if the surviving spouse lived another 10 years and the assets inside the first spouse's "credit shelter" grew to $4 million, the appreciation would pass to the children **without** estate tax on the increased value, since the estate tax value was "locked in" at the first spouse's death.

Unfortunately, the "credit shelter trust" generally only works for married couples since (a) the tax code provides the opportunity to shift assets between married persons for an unlimited amount by means of the unlimited marital deduction; and (b) unmarried persons attempting to do the same would be impacted by the "gift tax" during life. However, the mechanism is often useful in *multiple* marriage situations to allow for the use of income by the spouse while also conserving principal for the children later after the "stepparent" passes away.

Charitable remainder / Lead trusts

Trusts are often created as a way to contribute to a charity and retain certain benefits for oneself or another family member. A common technique is to create a charitable remainder unitrust ("CRUT"). Typically, this irrevocable trusts are funded with assets which often are highly appreciated, meaning their cost basis for capital gains tax purposes is very low relative to their current fair market value. This can be real estate, highly appreciated stock or a business interest with a low (or zero) tax basis.

Once the trust is funded, typically the asset is sold and invested in a more diversified investment portfolio that can provide income or liquid securities to provide an "annuity" to one or two individual persons, based on a set percentage provided for under the trust instrument and under IRS regulations. The annuity can be set for a certain term of years or can last for the lifetime of individual beneficiary(ies). Then, after the annuity term expires, the principal of the trust goes outright to a charity or charities the grantor named in the trust document.

If the trust meets the requirements of the IRS regulations, the grantor of the trust will receive a charitable **income tax** deduction for the calculated future value of the gift. Moreover, when he transfers the property into the CRUT irrevocably, the value of that property is out of his estate for **estate tax** purposes as well, even if he himself receive the individual annuity interest in the trust. In many cases, when properly structured, the CRUT can provide enough tax benefits to beneficiaries through the use of the annuity interest to justify the "giving away" of the asset to charity. However, this "giving away" of assets often causes many to forgo this technique, preferring to leave the assets directly to children regardless of the potential tax consequences it may create.

Grantor retained annuity trusts

Trusts may be created to get funds to the next generation where there is significant wealth and federal exclusionary gifts have already been used up. A common such vehicle is called the grantor retained annuity trust (GRAT). Federal tax law specifically allows for this vehicle. Here the grantor places an asset in the trust – one he expects will grow rapidly during the term of the trust. The document then requires the trustee to pay to the settlor a specific sum of money (the annuity) at certain intervals during the life of the trust. If there are assets in the trust at the end of the term, those assets go without estate or gift tax to the remaindermen. Here's a typical case: settlor owns large block of low cost basis stock in a publicly traded company. He does not wish to sell the stock and pay capital gains tax. He also has estate tax problems since his net worth when he dies is likely to be $10 million or more. His attorney drafts a GRAT in which he places $2 million of the single company's stock. The document calls for the smallest legal interest rate (published monthly by the Federal Government), which is then paid through the term of the trust. Upon the termination of the trust, the annuity has been paid back to the grantor and the remaining corpus is delivered to the remaindermen (typically children) without tax. Money has now passed from the grantor to his/her children without gift or estate tax. There has been no capital gains tax.

Irrevocable life insurance trust

view section in Wiki http://en.wikipedia.org/wiki/ILIT

Government benefit protection

Trusts may be created to protect an individual's welfare or other state benefits. These are typically called "special needs trusts." Typically, an individual has Medicaid and Social Security Supplemental Security Income (SSI) coming in. For such individual to then be given access to funds in excess of, usually, $2,000 ("countable" assets), risks immediate termination of his government benefits. To assure the individual a life of some ease beyond what he can afford from Social Security checks, a family member will place several hundred thousand dollars into a special needs trust for the little extras in life: dinner out, a birthday party, some new clothes, et alia. Such trusts require the expertise of a member of the "elder law" bar and must be administered with great care. It is best to have a family member as a co- or sole trustee. Given the small size of these trusts, they are typically not profitable for a corporate trustee.

Creation of a trust

A trust may be created by: (1) transfer of property to another person as trustee during the settlor's lifetime or by will or other disposition taking effect upon the settlor's death; (2) declaration by the owner of property that the owner holds identifiable property as trustee; or (3) exercise of a power of appointment in favor of a trustee. The ancient rule from English common law is that a trust is not established until it has property or a *res*. However, the actual property interest required to fund and create the trust is nothing substantial. Furthermore, the property interest need not be transferred contemporaneously with the signing of the trust instrument. Many trusts allow for additional deposits (cash, securities, real estate, etc.) at the direction of the settlor or others, provided the trustee is willing to accept those assets. It can even be funded after death by a "pour-over" provision in the grantor's last will, specifying his or her intent to transfer property from the estate to a trust. It can also be created by a court order or statute, imposing certain rights, duties and responsibilities as to particular property.

Intent

Trusts have certain requirements for creation. First, the grantor must show an intent to create a trust. Concordantly, the grantor must have the mental capacity to form such an intent and to create the trust. Also, if the grantor was "forced" to create the trust due to fraud, duress or undue influence, it is deemed void.

Nearly all trusts created by individuals are the subject of some type of writing (either a trust agreement or a will), which provides evidence of not only the **intent** to create the trust, but the intended operative terms of it. However, abiding by the old common law rules, the Uniform Trust Code does recognize that a trust can be created *orally*. However, to prove the **terms** of such a trust can only be established by "clear and convincing evidence." Such oral trusts are extremely rare in modern practice.

Occasionally, the intent to create a trust is manifested not by a writing *per se* but by the circumstances in which the "grantor" has entrusted the care of property to another party. This is often referred to as a constructive trust or a resulting trust. Again, such devices are generally rare and are created as the result of a court-imposed equitable remedy due to litigation between parties as to the "ownership" of certain property.

Definite beneficiary

Second, the trust must have some "definite beneficiary" – a person or class of persons whose identity can be determined in some fashion. The persons' specific identities need **not** be "known" at the time the grantor creates the trust; it will be sufficient if the persons can be "readily ascertainable" within a certain time period. That time period, historically, was determined under the old English "Rule Against Perpetuities", which defined this identification period as a person could be ascertained by a "life in being" (i.e., a child *in utero*) plus 21 years. So typically, if a person can be specifically identified at the time of a grantor's death as a "life in being", the trust is valid and can run up to the Perpetuity Rule of 21 years after the birth of that "person."

There are a few exceptions to this provision concerning a "definite beneficiary." The most obvious is in the case of a "charitable trust" that is for the benefit of an organization that is usually not-for-profit and is intended "for the relief of poverty, the advancement of education or religion, the promotion of health, governmental or municipal purposes, or other purposes the achievement of which is beneficial to the community." Another exception is the much-publicized (and often ridiculed) trust for the benefit of an animal, usually owned by the grantor prior to death. Finally, a trust may be created for a certain non-charitable purpose without an ascertainable beneficiary for a certain period (21 years, under the default rules of the UTC.) The most common example of a trust for a specific non-charitable purpose is a trust for the care of a cemetery plot.

Active trustee

The third requirement under the UTC is that the trustee must have duties he or she must perform. Otherwise, if the beneficiaries are able to manage the property as they wish, there is no "trust" *per se*.

No merger of property interests

Finally, the UTC requires that a trust must not have the same person as the sole trustee **and** sole beneficiary. Under ancient common law principles, a trust could not exist unless there was at least some "title split" – that is, the same person cannot generally hold all legal **and** all equitable title at the same time. If the legal and equitable title merge in the same person, the trust is considered nonexistent under the so-called merger doctrine.

Validity of trust in other

jurisdictions

The UTC states that a trust is valid if, under the law of the jurisdiction in which it was created, it was properly created. In most cases, this would be the law of the jurisdiction of the grantor's domicile. Trusts must also, under the Code, have a lawful purpose which is possible to achieve. For example, a trust must not violate public policy by encouraging criminal or tortious conduct, interfering with freedom to marry or encouraging divorce, limiting religious freedom, or is otherwise frivolous or capricious.

"Oddball" trusts

The UTC also covers a trust created for the purpose of caring for an animal that was alive at the time of a grantor's death or a trust for a non-charitable purpose but does not have an ascertainable beneficiary (such as a cemetery trust.) The Code imposes several limits on such trusts. First, the trust can only last as long as the lifetime of the animal (or the last surviving animal in a group) or in the case of a cemetery trust, no more than 21 years. Also, the trust's corpus can only be applied to the intended use of caring for the animal or the cemetery plot. In essence, then, a court can determine that if the trust has property that exceeds the amount required for the animal's care, the court may intervene and distribute the funds to the grantor's successors in interest.

Termination / reformation of a trust

With the exception of certain charitable trusts that can run perpetually, virtually all trusts with individual beneficiaries must end at a date certain. Of course, if a grantor has the power to do so, a trust terminates when it is revoked. Grantors also may amend the trust as they see fit during their lifetime, so long as they continue to retain the capacity to do so. For irrevocable trusts, the trust terminates when a trust "expires pursuant to its terms, no purpose of the trust remains to be achieved, or the purposes of the trust have become unlawful, contrary to public policy, or impossible to achieve." Most typically, such events occur when a certain class of beneficiaries receive all trust property outright, free of the restriction of the trust agreement, and trust administration is then "wrapped" up and the trust closed.

In some instances, however, it may be desirable to change the trust's terms or even terminate the trust by a method that the original grantor did not contemplate. For example, the trust may be depleted to such an extent that the management of the trust by a professional may be uneconomical. Changes in the law or circumstances surrounding the formation of the trust after the death of the grantor may dictate changes in the terms of the trust (or the termination of the trust itself.) The most infamous example would be beneficiaries who clamor against the trustee to "bust the trust" based on the strict limits the trust (or the trustee) may impose on the trust assets. In many of these cases, the UTC provides beneficiaries (and trustees) relief to provide the flexibility needed to dispose of trust property under certain rules.

Reformation / Termination by consent

The Code permits the modification or termination of a non-charitable irrevocable trust if: (a) the grantor and **all** beneficiaries consent and (b) a court of proper jurisdiction approves it. The court can approve such change or termination even if such may be inconsistent with the original purposes of the trust. Also, if the grantor does **not** consent (or is deceased) but if all beneficiaries of a non-charitable irrevocable trust consent, upon a petition to a court, the trust can be terminated "if the court concludes that continuance of the trust is not necessary to achieve any material purpose of the trust." The court may also reform the trust with all beneficiaries' consent as long as the change is not inconsistent with a material purpose of the trust.

The rationale for this difference lies with the grantor. If the grantor is living and consents to a change that radically changes the trust or eliminates it altogether, the UTC permits parties to essentially undo what originally was intended not to be undone. If the grantor is dead or does not consent, the UTC presumes the grantor would not want a "material purpose" of the trust compromised, regardless of the beneficiaries' wishes.

The consent of "all" beneficiaries might seem virtually impossible to obtain. Certainly, some such "representatives" for beneficiaries are obvious (i.e., guardians for incapacitated persons, parents for minors, etc.) However, the UTC provides rules to allow certain persons as beneficiaries to represent other far-removed, potential beneficiaries and their interests. The key is whether the beneficiaries that may "stand in" and bind the **distant** beneficiaries is whether they have a "substantially identical interest with respect to the question...."

Reformation to "fix the trust"

The Code permits a court to reform (or terminate) non-charitable irrevocable trusts to essentially make them work better, to fix a problem that has developed due to changes in the law or surrounding circumstances, or simply correct mistakes in the trust. If the change is due to "unanticipated consequences", the court's goal under the code is to fix the problem "in accordance with the settlor's probable intention." The terms of the trust can be changed if continuing the trust under its terms would be "impracticable or wasteful, perhaps unneeded" if the settlor's intent and trust terms were the result of a mistake in fact or law, or to achieve the imperfectly completed tax consequences of the settlor.

Termination to close uneconomical trusts

The Code also contains a provision to allow a trustee with a trust that has a marginal sum of assets to terminate it. After notice to the qualified beneficiaries, the trustee of a trust consisting of trust property having a total value less than $50,000 may terminate the trust if the trustee concludes that the value of the trust property is insufficient to justify the cost of administration. A court can also (regardless of the dollar amount) modify or terminate a trust or remove the trustee and appoint a different trustee if it determines that the value of the trust property is insufficient to justify the cost of administration. Upon termination under these provisions, the trustee is to distribute the funds "in a manner consistent with the purposes of the trust." Typically, this would mean outright distribution to the qualified beneficiaries of the trust in proportion to the actuarial value of their interests.

Income tax implications

Fiduciary tax law is both federal (see the Internal Revenue Code) and state. For Federal income tax purposes in the United States, there are several kinds of trusts: **grantor trusts** whose tax consequences flow directly to the settlor's Form 1040 (U.S. Individual Income Tax Return) and state return, **simple trusts** in which all the income created must be distributed to one or more beneficiaries and is therefore taxed to the non-settlor beneficiary (e.g. the widow of a trust created by the late husband), whether or not the income is actually distributed (it happens), and **complex trusts**, which are, in general, all trusts that aren't grantor trusts or simple trusts. Some trusts may alternate between simple and complex under certain conditions. Many but not all trust organizations do their own tax work. This can be highly specialized work.

All simple and complex trusts are irrevocable and in both cases any capital gains realized in the portfolios are taxed to the trust corpus or principal.

Source (edited): "http://en.wikipedia.org/wiki/United_States_trust_law"

Vesting

In law, **vesting** is to give an immediately secured right of present or future enjoyment. One has a **vested right** to an asset that cannot be taken away by any third party, even though one may not yet possess the asset. When the right, interest or title to the present or future possession of a legal estate can be transferred to any other party, it is termed a **vested interest**. The concept can arise in any number of contexts, but the most common are inheritance law and retirement plan law. In real estate to **vest** is to create an entitlement to a privilege or a right. For example, one may cross someone else's property regularly and unrestrictedly for several years, and one's right to an easement becomes vested. The original owner still retains the possession, but can no longer prevent the other party from crossing.

Inheritance law

Some bequests do not vest immediately upon death of the testator. For example, many wills specify that an heir who dies within a set period (such as 60 days) is not to inherit, and further specify how the corresponding share is to be distributed. This is generally done to obviate disputes over the precise time of death, and to avoid paying taxes twice in rapid succession should multiple members of a family die in the wake of a disaster. Such a bequest does not vest until the expiration of the specified period, because the actual heir cannot be determined with certainty.

It is also possible to give a person, A, a life interest in a property, with the remainder to go to another person or persons, B. If the beneficiary of the remainder cannot yet be known, then the remainder is said not to have vested, and the remainder is said to be contingent. This may happen with entailed estates, or when property is left in trust to care for a child or relative without heirs. (See trust law for details.)

Employee rights

Retirement plans

Vesting is an issue in conjunction with employer contributions to an employee stock option plan, or to a retirement plan such as a 401(k), annuity or pension plan.

A **vested right** is "an absolute right; when a retirement plan is fully vested, the employee has an absolute right to the entire amount of money in the account." It is a "basic right that has been granted, or has accrued, and cannot be taken away. Example: one's right to a vested pension."

The portion *vested* cannot be reclaimed by the employer, nor can it be used to satisfy the employer's debts. Any portion not vested may be forfeited under certain conditions, such as termination of employment. The portion invested is often determined pro-rata.

For retirement plans in the United States, employees are fully vested in their own salary deferral contributions upon inception. For employer contributions, the employer has limited options under the Employee Retirement Income Security Act (ERISA) to delay the vesting of their contributions to the employee. For example, the employer can say that the employee must work with the company for three years or they lose any employer contributed money, which is known as *cliff vesting*. Or it can choose to have the 20 percent of the contributions vest each year over five years, known as *graduated vesting*.

Choosing a vesting plan allows an employer to selectively reward employees who remain employed for a period of time. In theory, this allows the employer to make greater contributions than would otherwise be prudent, because the money they contribute on behalf of employees goes to the ones they most want to reward.

Ownership in startup companies

Small entrepreneurial companies usually offer grants of common stock or positions in an employee stock option plan to employees and other key participants such as contractors, board members, and major vendors. To make the reward commensurate with the extent of contribution, encourage loyalty, and avoid spreading ownership widely among former participants, these grants are usually subject to vesting arrangements.

Vesting of options is straightforward. The grantee receives an option to purchase a block of common stock, typically on commencement of employment, which vests over time. The option may be exercised at any time but only with respect to the vested portion. The entire option is lost if not exercised within a short period after the end of the employer relationship. The vesting operates simply by changing the status of the option over time from fully unexercisable to fully exercisable according to the vesting schedule.

Common stock grants are similar in function but the mechanism is different. An employee, typically a company founder, purchases stock in the company at nominal price shortly after the company is formed. The company retains a repurchase right to buy the stock back at the same price should the employee leave. The repurchase right diminishes over time so that the company eventually has no right to repurchase the stock, i.e. the stock becomes fully vested.

Vesting periods are usually 3–5 years for employees, but shorter for Board members and others whose expected tenure at a company is shorter. The vesting schedule is most often a pro-rata monthly vesting over the period with a six or twelve month cliff.

In the case of both stock and options, large initial grants that vest over time are preferable to periodic smaller grants because they are easier to account for and administer, they establish the arrangement up-front and are thus more predictable, and (subject to some complexities and limitations) the value of the grants and holding period requirements for tax purposes are set upon the initial grant date, giving a considerable tax advantage to the employee.

Profit-sharing

Profit-sharing plans are usually vested in 10 years, although in some cases a plan may essentially serve as a pension by allowing a limited amount of vesting should the employee retire or leave on good terms after an extended period of employment.

Vesting arrangements and terminology

A **vesting period** is a period of time an investor or other person holding a right to something must wait until they are capable of fully exercising their rights and until those rights may not be taken away.

In many cases vesting does not occur all at once. Specific portions of the rights grant vest on different dates over the duration of the period of the vesting. When part of a right is vested and part remains unvested, it is considered **partly vested**.

In the case of partial vesting, a **vesting schedule** is a table or chart showing the portion of a right that is vested over time. Most typically the schedule provides for equal portions to vest on periodic **vesting dates**, usually once per day, month, quarter, or year, in stair-step fashion over the course of the vesting period. There is often a **cliff** by which the first few steps in the graph are missing, so that there is no vesting at all for a period (usually six or twelve months in the case of employee equity), after which there is a **cliff date** upon which a large amount of vesting occurs all at once. Some arrangements provide for **accelerated vesting**, by which all or a major portion of the unvested right vests all at once upon the occurrence of a specified event such as a termination of employment by the company or acquisition of the company by another. Less commonly, the vesting schedule may call for variable grands or subject to conditions such as reaching milestones or employee performance.

Vested rights doctrine in zoning law

The **vested rights doctrine** is the rule of zoning law by which an owner/developer is entitled to proceed in accordance with the prior zoning provision where there has been a substantial change of position, expenditures or incurrence of obligations made in good faith by an innocent party under a building permit or in reliance upon the probability of its issuance.

Source (edited): "http://en.wikipedia.org/wiki/Vesting"

Voting trust

A **voting trust** is a trust whereby the shares in a company of one or more shareholders and the voting rights attached thereto are legally transferred to a trustee, usually for a specified period of time (the "trust period"). In some voting trusts, the trustee may also be granted additional powers (such as to sell or redeem the shares). At the end of the trust period, the shares would ordinarily be re-transferred to the beneficiary(ies), although in practice many voting trusts contain provisions for them to re-vested on the voting trusts with identical terms.

Voting trusts were made popular in Delaware corporate law, but they have since been adopted widely by other states in the U.S.A. They have also been extensively adopted in offshore jurisdictions.

Purposes

There are several reasons why shareholders may wish to put a voting trust arrangement in place.

- Several shareholders may wish to create a unified block of votes, which together gives them more power than the collective sum of their fragmented interests.
- In many countries, in order to call general meetings, shareholders need to hold a certain percentage of the issued shares of the company. By aggregating their shares, the shareholders can confer this power on themselves collectively where they might not have it individually.
- Locking shares up in voting trusts can in some countries help deter a hostile takeover.
- Voting trusts are also sometimes

used to resolve conflicts of interest. By putting the shares in a trustee who can vote them at arm's-length from the beneficiary(ies) of the trust, this can in some circumstances mitigate or absolve the original shareholder from what might otherwise constitute a conflict of interest (although in practice, to resolve conflicts of interest the trust will ordinarily be "blind trust"; while all blind trusts are necessarily voting trusts, not all voting trusts are blind trusts).

- Shares are sometimes aggregated into a voting trust to facilitate a corporate reorganisation.
- Promoters of companies sometimes aggregate their shares in a voting trust to safeguard control of the company.

Sample

Sample Voting trust agreement
Source (edited): "http://en.wikipedia.org/wiki/Voting_trust"

Will (law)

A **will** or **testament** is a legal declaration by which a person, the testator, names one or more persons to manage his/her estate and provides for the transfer of his/her property at death. For the devolution of property not disposed of by will, see inheritance and intestacy.

In the strictest sense, a "will" has historically been limited to real property while "testament" applies only to dispositions of personal property (thus giving rise to the popular title of the document as "Last Will and Testament"), though this distinction is seldom observed today. A will may also create a testamentary trust that is effective only after the death of the testator.

Requirements for creation

Any person over the age of majority and of sound mind (having appropriate mental capacity) can draft his or her own will with or without the aid of an attorney. Additional requirements may vary, depending on the jurisdiction, but generally include the following requirements:

- The testator must clearly identify himself or herself as the maker of the will, and that a will is being made; this is commonly called "publication" of the will, and is typically satisfied by the words "last will and testament" on the face of the document.
- The testator should declare that he or she revokes all previous wills and codicils. Otherwise, a subsequent will revokes earlier wills and codicils only to the extent to which they are inconsistent. However, if a subsequent will is completely inconsistent with an earlier one, the earlier will is considered completely revoked by implication.
- The testator may demonstrate that he or she has the capacity to dispose of his or her property ("sound mind"), and does so freely and willingly.
- The testator must sign and date the will, usually in the presence of at least two disinterested witnesses (persons who are not beneficiaries). There may be extra witnesses, these are called "supernumerary" witnesses, if there is a question as to an interested-party conflict. Some jurisdictions, notably Pennsylvania, have long abolished any requirement for witnesses. In the United States, Louisiana requires both attestation by two witnesses as well as notarization by a notary public. "Holographic" or handwritten wills generally require no witnesses to be valid.
- If witnesses are designated to receive property under the will they are witnesses to, this has the effect, in many jurisdictions, of either (i) disallowing them to receive under the will, or (ii) invalidating their status as a witness. In a growing number of states in the United States, however, an interested party is only an improper witness as to the clauses that benefit him or her (for instance, in Illinois).
- The testator's signature must be placed at the end of the will. If this is not observed, any text following the signature will be ignored, or the entire will may be invalidated if what comes after the signature is so material that ignoring it would defeat the testator's intentions.
- One or more beneficiaries (devisees, legatees) must generally be clearly stated in the text, but some jurisdictions allow a valid will that merely revokes a previous will, revokes a disposition in a previous will, or names an executor.

There is no legal requirement that a will be drawn up by a lawyer, although there are pitfalls into which home-made wills can fall. The person who makes a will is not available to explain him or herself, or to correct any technical deficiency or error in expression, when it comes into effect on that person's death, and so there is little room for mistake. A common error (for example) in the execution of home-made wills in England is to use a beneficiary (typically a spouse or other close family members) as a witness – although this has the effect in law of disinheriting the witness regardless of the provisions of the will.

Some jurisdictions recognize a holographic will, made out entirely in the testator's own hand, or in some modern formulations, with material provisions in the testator's hand. The distinctive feature of a holographic will is less that it is handwritten by the testator and often that it need not be witnessed. In England, the formalities of wills are relaxed for soldiers who express their wishes on active service; any such will is known as a serviceman's will. A minority of jurisdictions even recognize the validity of nuncupative wills (oral wills), particularly for military personnel or merchant sailors. However, there are often constraints on the disposition of property if such an oral will is used.

A will may not include a requirement that an heir commit an illegal, immoral, or other act against public policy as a condition of receipt. In community property jurisdictions, a will cannot be used to disinherit a surviving spouse, who is entitled to at least a portion of the testator's estate. In the United States, children may be disinherited by a parent's will, except in Louisiana, where a minimum share is guaranteed to surviving children. Many civil law countries follow a similar rule. In England, a will may disinherit a spouse, but close relations, including spouses, excluded from a will may apply to the court for provision to be made for them at the court's discretion.

Types of wills generally include:
- nuncupative (non-culpatory) will - oral or dictated; often limited to sailors or military personnel
- holographic will - written in the hand of the testator; in many jurisdictions, the signature and the material terms of the holographic will must be in the handwriting of the testator.
- self-proved will - in solemn form with affidavits of subscribing witnesses to avoid probate
- notarial will - will in public form and prepared by a civil-law notary (civil-law jurisdictions and Louisiana, United States)
- mystic will - sealed until death
- serviceman's will - will of person in active-duty military service and usually lacking certain formalities, particularly under English law
- reciprocal/mirror/mutual/husband and wife wills - wills made by two or more parties (typically spouses) that make similar or identical provisions in favor of each other
- unsolemn will - will in which the executor is unnamed
- will in solemn form - signed by testator and witnesses

Probate

After the testator has died, a probate proceeding may be initiated in court to determine the validity of the will or wills that the testator may have created, i.e., which will satisfy the legal requirements, and to appoint an executor. In most cases, during probate, at least one witness is called upon to testify or sign a "proof of witness" affidavit. In some jurisdictions, however, statutes may provide requirements for a "self-proving" will (must be met during the execution of the will), in which case witness testimony may be forgone during probate. If the will is ruled invalid in probate, then inheritance will occur under the laws of intestacy as if a will were never drafted. Often there is a time limit, usually 30 days, within which a will must be admitted to probate. Only an original will can be admitted to probate in the vast majority of jurisdictions – even the most accurate photocopy will not suffice.

It is a good idea that the testator give his executor the power to pay debts, taxes, and administration expenses (probate, etc.). Warren Burger's will did not contain this, which wound up costing his estate thousands. This is not a consideration under English law, which provides that all such expenses will fall on the estate in any case.

Revocation

Methods and effect

Intentional physical destruction of a will by the testator will revoke it, through deliberately burning or tearing the physical document itself, or by striking out the signature. In most jurisdictions, partial revocation is allowed if only part of the text or a particular provision is crossed out. Other jurisdictions will either ignore the attempt or hold that the entire will was actually revoked. A testator may also be able to revoke by the physical act of another (as would be necessary if he is physically incapacitated), if this is done in his presence and in the presence of witnesses. Some jurisdictions may presume that a will has been destroyed if it had been last seen in the possession of the testator but is found mutilated or cannot be found after his or her death.

A will may also be revoked by the execution of a new will. Most wills contain stock language that expressly revokes any wills that came before them, however, because normally a court will still attempt to read the wills together to the extent they are consistent.

In some jurisdictions, the complete revocation of a will automatically revives the next most recent will, while others hold that revocation leaves the testator with no will so that his or her heirs will instead inherit by intestate succession.

In England and Wales, marriage will automatically revoke a will as it is presumed that upon marriage, a testator will want to review the will. A statement in a will that it is made in contemplation of forthcoming marriage to a named person will override this.

Divorce, conversely, will not revoke a will, but in many jurisdictions, will have the effect that the former spouse is treated as if they had died before the testator and so will not benefit.

Where a will has been accidentally destroyed, on evidence that this is the case, a copy will or draft will may be admitted to probate.

Dependent relative revocation

Many jurisdictions exercise an equitable doctrine known as *dependent relative revocation* ("DRR"). Under this doctrine, courts may disregard a revocation that was based on a mistake of law on the part of the testator as to the effect of the revocation. For example, if a testator mistakenly believes that an earlier will can be revived by the revocation of a later will, the court will ignore the later revocation if the later will comes closer to fulfilling the testator's intent than not having a will at all. The doctrine also applies when a testator executes a second, or new will and revokes his old will under the (mistaken) belief that the new will would be valid. However, for some reason the new will is not valid and a court may apply the doctrine to reinstate and probate the old will, as the court holds that the testator would prefer the old will to intestate succession.

Before applying the doctrine, courts may require (with rare exceptions) that there have been an alternative plan of disposition of the property. That is, after revoking the prior will, the testator could have made an alternative plan of disposition. Such a plan would show that the testator intended the revocation to result in the property going elsewhere, rather than just being a revoked disposition. Secondly, courts require either that the testator have recited his mistake in the terms of the revoking instrument, or that the mistake be established by clear and convincing evidence. For example, when the testator made the original revocation, he must have erroneously noted that he was revoking the gift "because the intended recipient has died" or "because I will enact a new will tomorrow."

DRR may be applied to restore a gift erroneously struck from a will if the intent of the testator was to enlarge that gift, but will not apply to restore such a gift if the intent of the testator was to revoke the gift in favor of another person. For example, suppose Tom has a will that bequeaths $5,000 to his secretary, Alice Johnson. If Tom crosses out that clause and writes "$7,000 to Alice Johnson" in the margin, but does not sign or date the writing in the margin, most states would find that Tom had revoked the earlier provision, but had not effectively amended his will to add the second; however, under DRR the revocation would be undone because Tom was acting under the mistaken belief that he could increase the gift to $7,000 by writing that in the margin. Therefore, Alice will get 5,000 dollars. However, the doctrine of relative revocation will not apply if the interlineation decreases the amount of the gift from the original provision (e.g., "$5,000 to Alice Johnson" is crossed out and replaced with "$3,000 to Alice Johnson" without Testator's signature or the date in the margin; DRR does not apply and Alice Johnson will take nothing).

Similarly, if Tom crosses out that clause and writes in the margin "$5,000 to Betty Smith" without signing or dating the writing, the gift to Alice will be effectively revoked. In this case, it will not be restored under the doctrine of DRR because even though Tom was mistaken about the effectiveness of the gift to Betty, that mistake does not affect Tom's intent to revoke the gift to Alice. Because the gift to Betty will be invalid for lack of proper execution, that $5,000 will go to Tom's residuary estate.

Election under the will

Also referred to as "electing to take against the will." In the United States, many states have probate statutes which permit the surviving spouse of the decedent to choose to receive a particular share of deceased spouse's estate in lieu of receiving the specified share left to him or her under the deceased spouse's will. As a simple example, under Iowa law (see Code of Iowa Section 633.238 (2005)), the deceased spouse leaves a will which expressly gifts the marital home to someone other than the surviving spouse. The surviving spouse may elect, contrary to the intent of the will, to live in the home for the remainder of his/her lifetime. This is called a "life estate" and terminates immediately upon the surviving spouse's death.

The historical and social policy purposes of such statutes are to assure that the surviving spouse receives a statutorily set minimum amount of property from the decedent. Historically, these statutes were enacted to prevent the deceased spouse from leaving the survivor destitute, thereby shifting the burden of care to the social welfare system.

In history

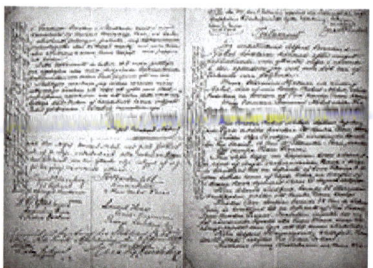

Alfred Nobel's will, in which he endows the Nobel prize.

Charles Vance Millar's will was notorious for offering the bulk of his estate to the Toronto woman who had the greatest number of children in the ten years after his death (the Great Stork Derby). Attempts to invalidate it by his would-be heirs were unsuccessful, and the bulk of Millar's fortune eventually went to four women.

The Thellusson Will Case was fictionalized by Charles Dickens as *Jarndyce and Jarndyce* in *Bleak House*, and led to Parliament legislating against such accumulation of money for later distribution.

According to *Consumer Reports*, as many as 56% of Americans don't have a will. Among the notables who died either without a valid will or no will at all are Ross Alexander, Fatty Arbuckle, Anura Bandaranaike, Madhav Prasad Birla, Sonny Bono, George Brent, Lenny Bruce, Jacob A. Cantor, Kurt Cobain, Russ Columbo, Sam Cooke, James Dean, Sandy Dennis, John Denver, Divine, Duke Ellington, Cass Elliot, Chris Farley, Bobby Fischer, Redd Foxx, Mary Frann, James A. Garfield, Marvin Gaye, Ulysses S. Grant, Billie Holiday, Buddy Holly, Shemp Howard, Howard Hughes, Andrew Johnson, Florence Griffith-Joyner, Martin Luther King, Jr., Ernie Kovacs, Harry Langdon, Bruce Lee, Abraham Lincoln, Peter Lorre, Jayne Mansfield, Rocky Marciano, Karl Marx, Steve McNair, Sal Mineo, Carmen Miranda, Keith Moon, Rosa Parks, Pablo Picasso, Mihajlo Idvorski Pupin, Tupac Shakur, Don Simpson, Anna Nicole Smith, William Desmond Taylor, Sharon Tate, Tiny Tim, Ritchie Valens, Hervé Villechaize, Barry White, and Jimmy Witherspoon.

The longest known legal will is that of Englishwoman Frederica Evelyn Stilwell Cook. Probated in 1925, it was 1,066 pages, and had to be bound in 4 volumes; her estate was worth $100,000. The shortest known legal wills are those of Bimla Rishi of Delhi, India and Karl Tausch of Hesse, Germany, both containing only three words.

Freedom of disposition

The conception of the freedom of disposition by will, familiar as it is in modern England and the United States, both generally considered common law systems, is by no means universal. In fact, complete freedom is the exception rather than the rule. Civil law systems often put some restrictions on the possibilities of disposal; see for example "Forced heirship".

Advocates for gays and lesbians have pointed to the inheritance rights of spouses as desirable for same-sex couples as well, through same-sex marriage or civil unions. Opponents of such advocacy rebut this claim by pointing to the ability of same-sex couples to disperse their assets by will. Historically, courts have been more willing to strike down wills leaving property to a same-sex partner for reasons such as incapacity or undue influence. *See*, for example, *In Re Kaufmann*s **Will**, *20 A.D.2d 464, 247 N.Y.S.2d 664 (1964)*, aff*d*, 15 N.Y.2d 825, 257 N.Y.S.2d 941, 205 N.E.2d 864 (1965)

Terminology

- **Administrator** - person appointed or who petitions to administer an estate in an intestate succession. The antiquated English term of **administratrix** was used to refer to a female but is generally no longer in standard legal usage.
- **beneficiary** - anyone receiving a gift or benefitting from a trust
- **bequest** - testamentary gift of personal property, traditionally other than money.
- **codicil** - (1) amendment to a will; (2) a will that modifies or partially revokes an existing or earlier will.
- **Decedent** - the deceased (U.S. term)
- **demonstrative legacy** - a gift of a specific sum of money with a direction that is to be paid out of a particular fund.
- **Descent** - succession to real property.
- **devise** - testamentary gift of real property.
- **devisee** - beneficiary of real property under a will.
- **distribution** - succession to personal property.
- **executor/executrix** or **personal representative** [PR] - person named to administer the estate, generally subject to the supervision of the probate court, in accordance with the testator's wishes in the will. In most cases, the testator will nominate an executor/PR in the will unless that person is unable or unwilling to serve.
- **Inheritor** - a beneficiary in a succession, testate or intestate.
- **Intestate** - person who has not created a will, or who does not have a valid will at the time of death.
- **Legacy** - testamentary gift of personal property, traditionally of money. Note: historically, a legacy has referred to either a gift of real property or personal property.
- **Legatee** - beneficiary of personal property under a will, i.e., a person receiving a legacy.
- **Probate** - legal process of settling the estate of a deceased person.
- **Specific legacy** (or specific bequest) - a testamentary gift of a precisely identifiable object.
- **Testate** - person who dies having created a will before death.
- **Testator** - person who executes or signs a will; that is, the person whose will it is. The antiquated English term of **Testatrix** was used to refer to a female and is still in use in the US.

Source (edited): "http://en.wikipedia.org/wiki/Will_(law)"

Will Aid

Will Aid is a charity will-writing scheme designed to reinforce the need for everyone to have a professionally drawn-up will and to raise funds for the participating charities.

Will Aid was originally founded in 1988 following the example set by Band Aid and Live Aid and continues to run each November.

Scheme Operation

Will Aid recruits solicitors all over the UK who agree to waive their usual fee for writing basic Wills during 'Make a Will Month' (November). In return, the client is invited to donate to the Will Aid group of charities the fee that the solicitor would usually charge.

The suggested minimum donations are £75 for a single will, or £110 for a pair of mirror wills.

Supported Charities

Will Aid is a partnership of nine charities: ActionAid, Age UK , the British Red Cross , Christian Aid , NSPCC, Save the Children , SCIAF , Sightsavers and Trócaire.

All the funds raised by Will Aid are shared between these charities and used to support their projects helping vulnerable people in the UK around the world.

Fundraising

Will Aid has raised over £8m since its launch and many tens of million more has been pledged as legacies by people making their Will through the scheme. The 2009 campaign raised £1.3m in donations and Gift Aid.

Will Aid and the legal profession

Will Aid is the largest scheme of its kind in the UK and is a major charitable contribution from legal profession. Over 1,100 solicitors firms take part each year. Since the scheme was launched, participating solicitors have drawn up wills for over 130,000 people.

Will Aid is endorsed by the Probate Section of the Law Society who encourage their members to participate. The scheme is run entirely through solicitors firms.

Publicity

Will Aid has received extensive press coverage in the UK.

Source (edited): "http://en.wikipedia.org/wiki/Will_Aid"

Will contest

A **will contest**, in the law of property, is a formal objection raised against the validity of a will, based on the contention that the will does not reflect the actual intent of the testator (the party who made the will). Will contests generally focus on the assertion that the testator lacked testamentary capacity, was operating under an insane delusion, or was subject to undue influence or fraud. A will may be challenged in its entirety, or only in part.

In many states, a legal presumption of undue influence arises where a beneficiary under the will stands in a confidential relationship with the testator. For example, where a testator leaves property to the attorney who drew up the will. However, this is dependent of the circumstances of such a relationship and the burden is initially on the person contesting to show undue influence.

A will may include an *in terrorem* clause, with language along the lines of "any person who contests this will shall forfeit his legacy", which operates to disinherit any person who challenges the validity of the will. However, since this clause is within the will itself, a successful challenge to the will renders the clause meaningless. Many states consider such clauses void as a matter of public policy.

Standing to contest a will

Typically, standing to contest the validity of a will is limited to two classes of persons:
- Those who are named on the face of the will (i.e. any beneficiary);
- Those who would inherit from the testator if the will was invalid

The following example is instructive: Monica makes a will leaving $5,000 each to her husband, Chandler, her brother, Ross, her neighbor, Joey, and her best friend, Rachel. Chandler tells Monica that he will divorce her if she does not disown Ross, which would humiliate her; later, Ross tells Monica (untruthfully) that Chandler is having an affair with Phoebe, which Monica believes. Distraught, Monica rewrites her will, disowning *both* Chandler and Ross. The attorney who drafts the will accidentally writes the gift to Rachel as $500 instead of $5,000; and also accidentally leaves Joey out entirely.

Under these facts, Chandler can contest the will as the product of fraud in the inducement, because if the will is invalid, he will inherit Monica's property, as the surviving spouse. Ross can contest the will as the product of Chandler's undue influence, because Ross will inherit Monica's property if Chandler's behavior disqualifies Chandler from inheriting (note, however, that many jurisdictions do not consider a threat of divorce to be undue influence). Rachel has *standing* to contest the will, because she is named in the document – but she will not be permitted to submit any evidence as to the mistake because it is not an ambiguous term. Instead, she will have to sue Monica's lawyer for legal malpractice to recover the difference. Finally, Joey is neither someone who stands to inherit from Monica, nor named in the will, and therefore is barred from contesting the will altogether.

The most common grounds, or reasons, for contesting a Will are:
- Lack of disposing mind and memory or Testamentary capacity
- Insane delusion
- Duress
- Fraud
- Undue Influence. Undue influence typically involves a trusted friend, relative or caregiver who actively procures a new will. For example, Florida law gives a list of the types of active procurement that will be considered in invalidating a will: (a) presence of the beneficiary at the execution of the will; (b) presence of the beneficiary on those occasions when the testator expressed a desire to make a will; (c) recommendation by the beneficiary of an attorney to draw the will; (d) knowledge of the contents of the will by the beneficiary prior to execution; (e) giving of instructions on preparation of the will by the beneficiary to the attorney drawing the will; (f) securing of witnesses to the will by the beneficiary; and (g) safekeeping of the will by the beneficiary subsequent to execution. In most states, including Florida, if the challenger of a will is able to establish that it was actively procured, the burden of proof shifts to the person seeking to uphold the will to establish that the will is not the product of undue influence.

Some jurisdictions permit an election against the will by a widowed spouse or orphaned children. This is not a contest against the will itself (the validity of the will is irrelevant), but an alternate procedure established by statute to contest the disposition of property.

Practicability of contests

Courts will not necessarily look to "fairness" during will contests. In other words, just because the provisions of a will may seem "unfair" does not mean that the will is invalid. Therefore, wills cannot be challenged simply because they seem unfair. The decedent has a legal right to dispose of his or her property in any way that is legal. Due to a large number of will contests, judges are often wary of contests especially when involving the willing of property to charitable organizations.

Depending on the grounds, the result may be
- Invalidity of the entire Last Will and Testament, resulting in an intestasy.
- Invalidity of a clause or gift, requiring the court to decide which charity receives the charitable bequest, using the equitable doctrine of cy pres.
- Diminution of certain gifts, and increase of other gifts to the widowed spouse or orphaned children, who would now get their elective share.

Source (edited): "http://en.wikipedia.org/wiki/Will_contest"

Will contract

A **will contract** is a term used in the law of wills describing a contract to exchange a current performance for a future bequest. In such an agreement, one party (the promisee) will provide some performance in exchange for a promise by the other party (the testator, because they must draft a will) to make a specific bequest to the promisee party in the testator's will. Most jurisdictions recognize such contracts as valid, although a few hold them as void against public policy. Some jurisdictions will not recognize an oral contract for such a purpose, requiring instead that the contract be executed in writing and signed by both parties.

The general rule, where such contracts are recognized, is that the promisee can not specifically enforce the contract if the testator later revokes or supersedes the will making the promised bequest, but can only sue the testator's estate for breach of contract. This protects the testator's very strong freedom to dispose of his property however he sees fit. For example, suppose Joey agrees to execute a will bequeathing his house to Rachel in exchange for services provided by Rachel. If Joey later revokes that will, Rachel can not force Joey's estate to convey the house to her, but can only sue for the value of the house.

Typically, will contracts are made between people who have different heirs to whom they wish to leave their property at death, but they may wish for the other person to have the use of until all of their combined assets until the death of the second to die. A married couple with children from an earlier marriage is a good example. The husband may leave his separate estate to his wife at his death, instead of directly to his children from his earlier marriage and in exchange, she may agree to combine his separate estate with her separate estate at her death and split the combined estate up between all of their children. It would work the same if she died first. A will contract only becomes irrevocable only at the first party's death. Because of differences in state laws regarding will contracts, an estate planning attorney should be consulted before use of this planning device.

The law behind wills becomes tedious when many parties are not present, typically in cases with limited family members. This mainly occurred after World War Two where many wills had no possible recipients so the assets went to the government. Wills are often confused with trust funds, but wills are only present at death where as trust funds can be accessed during the time that the creator of the fund is still alive.

Source (edited): "http://en.wikipedia.org/wiki/Will_contract"

Wills Act 1837

The **Wills Act 1837** (1 Vict. c.26) is an Act of the Parliament of the United Kingdom that confirms the power of every adult to dispose of their real and personal property, whether they are the outright owner or a beneficiary under a trust, by will on their death (s.3). The act extends to all testamentary dispositions or gifts, where "a person makes a disposition of his property to take effect after his decease, and which is in its own nature ambulatory and revocable during his life." As of 2010, much of it remains in force in England and Wales.

Background

Under ecclesiastical law, common law and equity, various customary rules had long existed for disposing of personal property by will. However, the power to gift real property by will had been first granted by the Statute of Wills (1540). Various rules grew up around the formalities necessary to create a valid will and the Statute of Frauds (1677) created the requirement that a will of real property must be in writing. By the early nineteenth century, the rules had become complex, with different rules for formalising wills of real and personal property. The 4th report of the Commissioners for Inquiring into the Law of Real Property recommended a simplified and unified scheme. As the Commissioners observed "Any scrap of paper, or *memorandum* in ink or in pencil, mentioning an intended disposition of his property, is admitted as a will and will be valid, although written by another person, and not read over to the testator, or even seen by him, if proved to be made in his lifetime according to his instructions." A bill was introduced by the Attorney General Sir John Campbell, one of the Commissioners, in 1834 though it was much delayed for want of parliamentary time. The bill was introduced in the House of Lords by Lord Langdale.

Though the requirement that a will be in writing stems from an attempt to frustrate fraud, an apparent exception to the requirements for the formal execution of the Act under section 9 is a secret trust.

Provisions of the Act currently in force

Capacity

A minor, as of 2008 a person under the age of 18, cannot make a valid will (s.7), unless they are a member of the armed forces on active service or a mariner at sea (s.11). These provisions were clarified by the **Wills (Soldiers and Sailors) Act 1918** (see below).

Requirements of a valid will

A will is only valid if (s.9):
- It is made in writing;
- It is signed by the testator, or at his direction and in his presence;
- The testator intends that the signature give effect to the will;

- The will is made or acknowledged in the presence of two or more witnesses, present at the same time; and
- Each witness attests and signs, or acknowledges, his signature in the presence of the testator.

There is no requirement to publish a will (s.13). If any of the witnesses was, or subsequently becomes, incapable of proving the will, that alone will not make it invalid (s.14). Alterations must be executed in the same manner as a will (s.21).

Revocation of a will

Section 18 revokes the will in the event of the marriage of the testator. However, this section was amended in 1982 so that where the testator makes the will in the expectation of marriage to a particular person, the will is not revoked by such a marriage. Section 18A was added in 1982 to the effect that divorce and annulment have the same effect as the death of a spouse.

A will or codicil cannot be revoked by any presumption of the intention of the testator or on the grounds of any alteration in his circumstances (s.19). A will can only be revoked by (s.20):

- Another properly executed will or codicil;
- A document executed under the same formalities as a will, declaring an intention to revoke the will; or
- Destruction of the will by the testator, or some person in his presence, with the intention of revoking the will.

A revoked will or codicil cannot be revived other than by its re-execution or by a formally executed codicil (s.22).

Gifts to witnesses

Gifts under the will to an attesting witness, or their spouse, are null and void. However, such a witness can still prove the will (s.15). There is no bar on a creditor of the testator or the executor of the will being a witness (ss.16-17).

Gifts to children

Where the testator makes a gift to one of his children or a remoter descendant, and that child dies before the testator, the gift will not lapse so long as the deceased descendant himself leaves children surviving at the death of the testator. The surviving descendants receive the gift (s.33). The rule also applies to illegitimate children (s.33(4)(a)) and a person conceived before the death of the testator is deemed to have been living at the testator's death (s.33(4)(b)).

Interpretation

The will is interpreted in respect of the testator's property immediately before his death (s.24). Where the testator makes a gift of all his real property, it is deemed to include property over which he has a power of appointment (s.27).

Ireland and Northern Ireland

The Act was in force in Ireland until partition. It consequently became the law of the Irish Free State on 6 December 1922, and then of its successor states. When the autonomous region of Northern Ireland seceded from the Irish Free State and rejoined the United Kingdom on 7 December 1922, the Act became the law of Northern Ireland. However, all save sections 1 and 11 were repealed and re-enacted, with amendments, in Northern Ireland in 1995 following the recommendations of the Land Law Working Group.

Provisions repealed by the Act

- Statute of Wills
- ...

Provisions of the Act, since repealed

Sections 4 to 6 addressed various technicalities of land law since rendered obsolete. The Act did not extend to estates *pur autre vie* and various manorial rights were preserved over the land devised. Where land was held subject to a Lord of the Manor, for example under a copyhold, the Act required that the will was recorded in the Court Roll of the manor and that various fees and duties were paid. These provisions became irrelevant following the demise of the manorial system with the Law of Property Act 1925.

Section 8 maintained the earlier incapacity of a *feme covert* to make a will.

The **Wills (Soldiers and Sailors) Act 1918** clarifies and extends the Wills Act 1837. Section 1 makes if clear that a soldier on active service or sailor at sea, can make, and always could have made, a valid will, even though under 18 years of age. Section 2 extends the provision to sailors not at sea but who are employed in similar service to a soldier on active service. "Soldier" include a member of the Air Force (s.5). This Act is in force in Scotland, but this may be to no effect as it acts only by reference to the Wills Act 1837, which is not in effect there but is in effect, in modified form, in Northern Ireland.

Source (edited): "http://en.wikipedia.org/wiki/Wills_Act_1837"